AWAITING
armageddon

AWAITING
armageddon

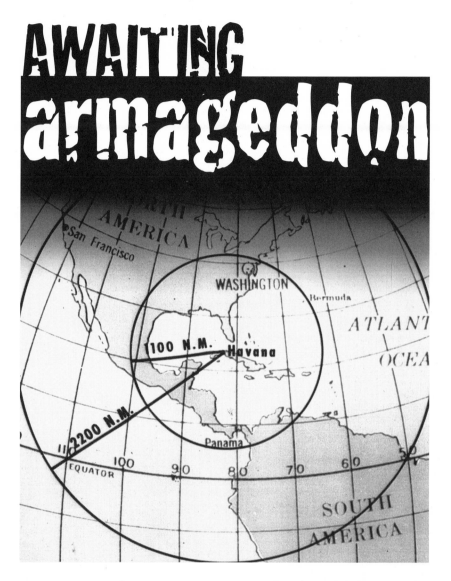

HOW AMERICANS FACED THE CUBAN MISSILE CRISIS

ALICE L. GEORGE

THE UNIVERSITY OF NORTH CAROLINA PRESS CHAPEL HILL AND LONDON

Manufactured in the United States of America
Set in Charter, Meta, and Crackhouse types
by Tseng Information Systems, Inc.
The paper in this book meets the guidelines for
permanence and durability of the Committee on
Production Guidelines for Book Longevity of the
Council on Library Resources.

Library of Congress Cataloging-in-Publication Data
George, Alice L., 1952–
Awaiting Armageddon : how Americans faced the Cuban
Missile Crisis / Alice L. George.
    p. cm.
Includes bibliographical references and index.
ISBN 0-8078-2828-9 (cloth : alk. paper)
1. Cuban Missile Crisis, 1962. 2. Cuban Missile Crisis, 1962—
Social aspects. 3. Cuban Missile Crisis, 1962—Public opinion.
4. Civil defense—United States—History—20th century.
5. Nuclear warfare—Social aspects—United States—History—
20th century. 6. Cold War—Social aspects—United States.
7. United States—Social conditions—1960–1980. 8. United
States—Politics and government—1961–1963. 9. Public
opinion—United States—History—20th century. I. Title.
E841 .G39 2003
973.922—dc21

                2003002760

07 06 05 04 03   5 4 3 2 1

To my strong and

commonsensical mother

and my late father,

whose tender-hearted

and playful spirit

lives on

contents

illustrations

acknowledgments

This work would not have been possible without the assistance of many people. I am indebted to Lou Oschmann for his patience and his proofreading prowess. I also thank Todd Davis and the members of my dissertation committee—Allen F. Davis, James W. Hilty, Murray Murphey, Herb Ershkowitz, and Jay Lockenour—for their assistance and input.

I want to express my deep gratitude to the librarians at the John F. Kennedy Library and to all of those who assisted me at the Dwight D. Eisenhower Library, the Lyndon B. Johnson Library, the National Archives, the Library of Congress, the National Security Archive, the Naval Institute, the Army War College, the State Historical Society of Wisconsin, the Georgia Department of Archives and History, the Martin Luther King Jr. Center, the Bancroft Library at the University of California at Berkeley, the Hoover Institution, the *New York Times* Library, the Columbia University Oral History Office, the New York University Library, the Seeley G. Mudd Library at Princeton University, the University of Rochester Rare Books Department, the Robert W. Woodruff Library at Emory University, the Peace Collection at Swarthmore College, the Air Force Historical Research Center, the New York Municipal Archives, and the Philadelphia City Archives. Finally, I want to thank Jo Schweikhard Moss of Texas's Division of Emergency Management, who invited me to spend a few hours doing research in a bunker and experiencing a taste of the claustrophobic future that awaited government officials in 1962 in the event of nuclear war.

crisis week chronology
SNAPSHOTS OF FRIGHTENING DAYS

MONDAY, 22 OCTOBER 1962

Just a week after photo analysts determined that U-2 spy plane photos showed Soviet missile installations in Cuba, groundwork for war had begun. As President John F. Kennedy prepared to reveal the crisis to the American public, planes, trains, and trucks carrying thousands of troops and equipment streamed into South Florida, virtually transforming Key West into an impromptu military base. At the same time, the U.S. Navy and Marine Corps had doubled the nation's troop strength in Guantanamo, Cuba.[1] The U.S. military raised its level of Defense Condition from the normal peacetime level of DEFCON (defense condition) 5 to DEFCON 3. At the Pentagon, State Department and Department of Defense officials manned the Joint Chiefs of Staff National Military Command Center twenty-four hours a day.[2] The Soviet Union and Cuba also heightened their forces' alert status, but they did not issue a general alert, apparently for fear of instigating an American preemptive strike.[3] American officials did not know that nuclear warheads for the medium-range ballistic missiles already had reached Cuba.[4]

One hour before Kennedy's 7 P.M. speech, the Voice of America began lining up eleven southeastern radio stations to cancel regular programming and broadcast the address to Cuba,[5] and within minutes after Kennedy started speaking, U.S. ambassador to the United Nations Adlai Stevenson urged Soviet representative Valerian Zorin, chairman of the United Nations Security Council, to call an urgent meeting. As Kennedy promised Americans that he would not allow Soviet missiles to remain in Cuba, the Southern California Music Co. in Los Angeles tuned all of the TVs in its window to the president's speech, and a small, silent crowd gathered.[6] Throughout the evening, television networks interrupted regular programming with news bulletins on the crisis, and Manhattan's theater district was "practically deserted," according to television reports that called it "probably the quietest night since the night of Pearl Harbor."[7]

On this evening, just fifteen days before off-year elections in which the White House's party usually lost ground, two GOP leaders, New York governor Nelson Rockefeller and former vice president Richard Nixon, offered support to Kennedy. Former president Harry Truman called the plan to blockade Cuba "wonderful,"[8] and the Senate minority whip, California Republican Thomas H. Kuchel, declared, "Foreign policy is no longer an issue in this campaign."[9] The nation backed Kennedy: a Gallup Poll taken that evening found that just 4 percent of those who had heard the news opposed his plans; 84 percent supported Kennedy; and 12 percent voiced no opinion.[10]

In a press briefing, when asked what the government was doing to protect Americans, a Pentagon spokesman's answer—"civil defense"—drew a loud roar of laughter,[11] but for a handful of reporters, the possibility of living underground seemed all too near: the White House issued orders to those who would accompany Kennedy to a bunker outside Washington if war began. They were told to stay within fifteen minutes of the White House throughout the next few days.[12]

While Americans responded with outrage to the secret Soviet installations in Cuba, U.S. government officials guarded their own secrets. Just six days before, the head of the Central Intelligence Agency had recommended eight covert U.S. sabotage operations in Cuba as part of Operation Mongoose, the administration's intelligence operation to destabilize Fidel Castro's government. Included in the proposed actions were demolition of a railroad bridge, attacks on shipping and port facilities, and an assault on the Chinese embassy in Havana.[13] As the public phase of the crisis began, Soviet authorities arrested Oleg Penkovsky, a Soviet Military Intelligence Agency employee acting as a spy for the United States and Great Britain.[14]

TUESDAY, 23 OCTOBER 1962

The Soviet Union promised to defy a U.S. quarantine in the Caribbean, and across America, wary citizens saw signs of war, as the Strategic Air Command (SAC) dispersed bombers to civilian and military bases and navy ships streamed out to sea. An unofficial exodus of civilians and military dependents from Key West got under way. All civilian guests checked out of the Key Wester Motel, leaving only a dozen navy officers in the hotel's 100 rooms.[15] In one day, the local Western Union office handled more than $8,000 in money orders and a bank reported that withdrawals outnumbered deposits seven to one.[16]

As in wartime, the White House tightened security measures. Officials ordered visitors to leave packages in a van parked by the East Gate.[17] Besides tourists, the White House had 117 visitors on this day, including six employees of the Central Intelligence Agency, six military officers, and nine-teen nursery school classmates of four-year-old Caroline Kennedy.[18] In addition to signing a proclamation authorizing the naval blockade to commence at 10 A.M. the next day, Kennedy signed a $3.9 billion foreign aid bill that ended aid to any nation shipping arms to Cuba.[19]

Secretary of State Dean Rusk appeared before the Organization of American States seeking support for a resolution demanding that the Soviet Union immediately dismantle and remove the missiles and all other offensive weapons from Cuba. He needed only a two-thirds majority. No nation cast a vote against the resolution, while only two abstained. As the UN Security Council prepared to begin its first session on Cuba, a British delegate predicted, "The lights soon will be going out all over the world."[20] When asked whether the presence of Soviet missiles could mean war, Senate Majority Leader Mike Mansfield replied concisely, "It could."[21]

American pacifists rejected Kennedy's plans. "Last night President Kennedy announced an action which may be the beginning of the nuclear holocaust all of the arms of both sides were supposedly preventing," the Student Peace Union proclaimed. "President Kennedy is gambling hundreds of millions of lives that the Russians will not force him to go all the way."[22]

And around the globe, the crisis created a hunger for news. Buried just beneath Soviet condemnations of the blockade was a startled Soviet reaction clearly seen when *Pravda*, the Soviet Communist Party newspaper, rolled off the presses late, frustrating Soviet broadcasters who complained about a lack of adequate information.[23] At the State Department, an avalanche of diplomatic cables forced Rusk to ask for "cable silence" for all except urgent messages.[24]

In city after city across the United States, phone calls from people seeking information overwhelmed civil defense offices. As officials dusted off long-neglected plans, they found themselves unprepared to deal with nuclear war. Local and state leaders urged a mixture of calm and preparedness. Many cities experienced "a rush" on so-called survival supplies. Cincinnati's Western Union office processed a flood of telegrams to Washington,[25] and in Philadelphia, a mixture of youths and veterans kept armed forces recruiters busy.[26] Through the day and into the night a crowd sometimes numbering as many as 1,500 gathered on the corner of Telegraph Avenue and Bancroft Way at the University of California at Berkeley to debate the wisdom of the planned U.S. blockade.[27]

Ripple effects of the crisis affected tourism, too. When the Cuban government warned that any "airplane that takes off without previous permission will be shot down by our authorities," the only airlines offering service between the United States and Cuba, Pan American World Airways and KLM Royal Dutch Airlines, eliminated those flights. Other carriers announced plans to reroute flights so that they no longer crossed the tip of Cuba.[28]

WEDNESDAY, 24 OCTOBER 1962

At 10 A.M., the American naval blockade of Cuba officially began. In defiance, Nikita Khrushchev ordered Soviet ships to cross the blockade line.[29] Though he later withdrew that command, the Soviet leader remained angry. He held a three-hour meeting with U.S. businessman William Knox in Moscow and told Knox that he would order Soviet submarines to attack and sink any U.S. Navy vessels that attempted to stop and search Soviet ships.[30] For the only time in Cold War history, SAC raised its alert status to DEFCON 2, one step away from war footing, and within a day, its ready force increased from 912 to 1,436 bombers.[31] At the same time, U.S. submarines armed with Polaris missiles left their Holy Loch, Scotland, base on a secret course.[32] For the first time, the United States turned a radar tracking system southward in anticipation of a possible attack from Cuba.[33] And at the White House, news that the first Soviet ships were within a few miles of the blockade cast a pall over the morning's Executive Committee (Ex Comm) meeting, which Attorney General Robert Kennedy called one of the "the most trying, the most difficult, and the most filled with tension."[34]

With Florida becoming the focal point of U.S. military activity, the Federal Aviation Agency barred civilian planes from the state's southern half unless they were operating on approved flight plans and were in direct radio contact with air traffic controllers.[35] Two railway lines—the Atlantic Coast Line and the Pennsylvania Railroad—reported that nervous tourists were canceling reservations to Miami.[36]

American businesses outside the defense industry began joining the mobilization. American Telephone and Telegraph established lines at thirty-two bases in nine hours when dispersal of bombers created new communication problems.[37] In addition, chartered civilian airliners joined the effort to move thousands of troops into the Key West area.[38] The *New York Herald Tribune* reported that government planning for wartime economic controls was in the works,[39] and the *Wall Street Journal* proclaimed that American industry was much better prepared for war than it had been in the days leading up to the Korean conflict.[40] In the Motor City, optimism reigned as an auto forecasting expert for the Department of Commerce told the *Detroit Free Press* that the crisis would boost car sales.[41]

America's churches were less sanguine. The Presbyterian Church (U.S.A.) called on its 3.2 million members to make Sunday a day of prayer,[42] and in New England, telephone calls set off "prayer chains" for peace.[43] Birmingham, Alabama, organizers invited all downtown ministers to participate in a special prayer service dedicated to international peace.[44]

While President Kennedy held center stage in the global drama, Vice President Lyndon Johnson had a busy day that included attendance at an Ex Comm meeting, as well as an appointment with Scripps-Howard head Walker Stone, a meeting with the Office of Emergency Preparedness director Edward McDermott about operation of the government's legislative branch in an emergency, and a conversation with Pierre Salinger about potential candidates to head a wartime Office of Censorship.[45] From his national security aide, Howard Burris, Johnson received a proposal favoring emergency steps to improve U.S. oil readiness because the blockade heightened demand for petroleum products and war would expend even more.[46] Mail written to Johnson ran a wide gamut, including a tirade questioning Johnson's sanity for trusting Stevenson and a fearful woman's plea for U.S. concessions to the Soviet Union.[47]

By day's end, the gloom cast over the world had lifted a bit. Soviet ships nearing Cuba had begun slowing or reversing course. The threat had not ended, but as Robert Goralski of NBC News reported, "There is little doubt that we in this country—indeed, the entire world—have grasped the few slightly encouraging signs in the prayerful hope that war can be averted."[48]

THURSDAY, 25 OCTOBER 1962

The *Bucharest*, a tanker, became the first Soviet ship to reach the blockade line. After a visual inspection showed that it carried no weapons, the navy let the ship pass. Later in the day, the Pentagon revealed that twelve Soviet ships nearing the blockade had reversed course. During what newsman Walter Cronkite called "one of the most dramatic days in U.N. history,"[49] Stevenson delivered a fiery indictment of the Soviet Union in a Security Council meeting. Displaying photos of missile sites in Cuba, Stevenson told his Soviet counterpart that he would not proceed without an admission of the missiles' existence, saying, "I am prepared to wait for my answer until hell freezes over, if that is your decision."[50] Still seeking a peaceful outcome, UN secretary general U Thant urged both nations to avoid military contact.

On the domestic front, former president Eisenhower asked Americans to make sacrifices during the crisis.[51] In Washington, the Capitol tightened security and the White House canceled all social functions.[52] In a news briefing, presidential press secretary Pierre Salinger told reporters that the White House had received 48,000 telegrams since Kennedy's televised address and that the messages favored the president's action by a ratio of 22 to 1.[53]

In the American media, columnist Walter Lippmann made a suggestion that would serve as one basis for the crisis's peaceful resolution—a proposal to trade U.S. missiles in Turkey for Soviet missiles in Cuba.[54] In the Soviet Union, *Pravda* and *Isvestia* still made no mention of the missile installations in Cuba, although they became more explicit about ominous U.S. actions.[55]

War seemed especially close in South Florida. The army took over a 180-room Key West hotel, the Casa Marina, and servicemen filled the streets.[56] Among those on hand were antisabotage units to guard power lines, telephone poles, and the single water pipeline serving Key West.[57] Truck convoys delivered rocket launchers, generators, and other equipment to the potential invasion force, with one lost convoy tangling afternoon rush-hour traffic in Miami.[58] Meanwhile, Miami civilians kept phone lines busy; long-distance calls were up 25 percent.[59]

In the nation's biggest city, New York's Board of Estimate allotted $100,000 for mobile generators, and the school system ordered the city's 860 schools to hold air-raid drills at least twice over the next five school days.[60] To discourage sabotage in the cradle of American democracy, officials closed the pedestrian walkway on Philadelphia's Benjamin Franklin Bridge.[61] From Washington, Soviet ambassador to the United States Anatoly Dobrynin reported to his Foreign Ministry that "noticeably fewer people can be seen on Washington streets. Government offices are working until late at night. Preoccupation over the possibility of a major war is sensed in business circles too." Dobrynin added that African embassies had alerted students in the United States to prepare for evacuation. "In general," he wrote, "it is necessary to say that different sources in the journalist and diplomatic corps in Washington agree that currently the probability of a USA armed intervention against Cuba is great."[62]

On the West Coast, this was the second consecutive day of panic buying in Los Angeles supermarkets.[63] In San Francisco, overseas airlines enjoyed a boom, with a clear increase in the number of foreigners seeking flights out of the country and away from the potential war zone.[64] The County Committee of the Communist Party urged members to contact the White House and voice opposition to the blockade. According to a Federal Bureau of Investigation report, morale was high, although Albert Lima, chairman of the Northern California Communist Party, reported federal plans to establish concentration camps in the United States to house 250,000 Communist Party members and others who opposed Kennedy's policy.[65]

FRIDAY, 26 OCTOBER 1962

In communication with the navy, Kennedy chose the *Marucla*, a Soviet supply ship under Lebanese registry, as the first to be boarded on the blockade line. Because the ship was unlikely to carry arms, it offered a chance for a show of force without much danger of serious conflict. Ironically, a destroyer named for the president's late brother, Joseph P. Kennedy Jr., stopped the ship, and after an inspection revealed no missile parts aboard, the navy cleared it to pass.

Rapid completion of the Cuban missile sites was the topic before the Ex Comm, and after its morning session, a somber JFK responded to some participants' gung-ho attitude by asking Defense Secretary Robert McNamara, "Do you think the people in that room realize that if we make a mistake, there may be 200 million dead?"[66] The stress on Kennedy showed, and the Associated Press reported that he was working twelve- to seventeen-hour days, with about 90 percent of his time devoted to Cuba.[67] While Kennedy and his advisers considered future strategies ranging from air strikes on Cuba to a full-scale invasion, Kennedy ordered the air force to make low-level reconnaissance flights over Cuba every two hours.[68] At the same time, to provide added security at the White House, the administration barred cameramen from the west entrance.[69] Outside the executive mansion, 500 protesters, both for and against the blockade, filled the sidewalks.[70]

In the shadowy world of secret diplomacy, talks progressed. Robert Kennedy warned Dobrynin that unless the Soviet Union agreed to remove the missiles within two days, the United States would take further action. In addition, Alexander Fomin, counselor of the Soviet embassy, met with ABC reporter John Scali, and according to Scali, Fomin tried to find out whether the United States would pledge not to invade Cuba in return for the missiles' removal.[71] Despite the intensity of these exchanges, some Americans remained unconvinced that the nation faced imminent danger: frustrated members of the Republican Congressional Campaign Committee criticized the crisis's timing, claiming that Democrats were maneuvering for votes.[72]

Unfounded rumors continued to feed Florida's jitters. Some Floridians believed the governor had told visitors to stay away, while others thought the Florida Keys had been evacuated.[73] One embarrassed housewife explained her stockpiling of canned goods by saying that she and her husband had been dieting and "we're a little hungry."[74] In Jacksonville, Florida, a short circuit set off a civil defense siren, sparking 40,000 calls to the city police department.[75]

Across the United States, the crisis's effects were widespread. In Memphis, a thirty-five-car troop train rolled through at dawn, stirring memories of World War II. Many flatcars carried military equipment southward.[76] Near Rock Island, Illinois, the Army Corps of Engineers began closing access to the Mississippi River nightly as a security measure,[77] while New York City appealed for 49,000 volunteers to act as auxiliary firefighters "in event of an enemy attack."[78] In Philadelphia, the FBI got word that a Cuban had threatened sabotage if the United States attacked Cuba. Sources told the FBI that the man planned to fill a large pipe with shotgun ammunition to produce a bomb that he would place at one of the city's oil refineries.[79] And Scranton, Pennsylvania, post office officials promised to continue operating, even in nuclear war, but conceded that a direct hit would force the post office to relocate.[80]

In the isolation of life at sea, voyagers on the RMS *Queen Mary* awoke to news of the crisis in the *Ocean Times* and shared relief about their apparent safety from attack.[81] Seemingly a world away, at the heart of the action in Washington, Deputy Director of the U.S. Information Agency Donald Wilson later recalled that as he left his office that evening, "I literally wondered whether I'd come home the next night."[82]

SATURDAY, 27 OCTOBER 1962

On the darkest day of the crisis, a U-2 surveillance flight over Cuba brought the crisis's only combat death. A surface-to-air missile shot down the plane of air force major Rudolph Anderson, one of the first pilots to photograph the missiles in Cuba. Up until that moment, the United States had contemplated a military response to any Cuban or Soviet attack on a U.S. plane; however, officials took no action to avenge the twenty-five-year-old pilot's death.

The U.S. military effort to force Soviet submarines to surface reportedly led one Soviet captain to threaten to launch a nuclear torpedo. However, the vessel surfaced instead.[83] Under orders from President Kennedy, the U.S. military planned air strikes against Cuba on Monday. Bombers would target Soviet missile sites, air bases, and antiaircraft installations.[84] In all, the United States had about one million military personnel ready for battle.[85] In addition, the Defense Department activated twenty-four troop carrier squadrons and supporting units from the Air Force Reserve, disrupting the civilian lives of 14,000 part-time airmen.[86] Also, in preparation for a possible nuclear attack on Cuba, McNamara, who considered invasion "almost inevitable,"[87] recommended dropping pamphlets warning civilians to take cover. The government printed five million pamphlets that were never needed.[88]

On the opposite side of the potentially deadly crisis, tensions grew high in the Kremlin because a Soviet officer had downed the U-2 without consulting Moscow.[89] In addition, Soviet intelligence reported that a U.S. attack on Cuba would occur within days,[90] and for a few minutes, the Soviets' worst fears seemed to have been realized when an American plane entered Soviet airspace. Instead of being a bomber set on the destruction of the Soviet capital, the airplane was a U-2 reconnaissance plane that had drifted off course, leading Soviet fighters to scramble and intercept it. The American military ordered fighters from Alaska to escort the errant plane back to the safety of U.S. airspace.

On this day, Khrushchev dispatched two apparently contradictory messages to President Kennedy—one conciliatory and one bellicose. After some deliberation, Kennedy decided to respond to the first wire and ignore the second, more threatening message. Diplomat W. Averell Harriman privately said that Khrushchev's conciliation must be accepted cautiously: "If we think he is a black demon it makes no sense. We have to treat him halfway in between."[91] Meanwhile, Robert Kennedy continued backdoor efforts to achieve a resolution through secret meetings with Dobrynin. The attorney general offered a public promise that the United States would not invade Cuba, as well as a private agreement to remove outdated U.S. missiles from the Soviet Union's backyard in Turkey.

At the end of the crisis's grimmest twenty-four hours, McGeorge Bundy and several other Kennedy administration officials decided to sleep in their offices in case war began; however, a reportedly restless President Kennedy sought a distraction, so he watched *Roman Holiday*, a film starring Audrey Hepburn and Gregory Peck that chronicled a European princess's attempts to enjoy a break from the weight of official duties.[92]

In a report on National Civil Defense Readiness to the National Governor's Conference, Assistant Secretary of Defense Steuart Pittman proclaimed that Americans were ready for war, although civil defense facilities remained unstocked with food and woefully inadequate for the American population.[93] *Saturday Review* contended that the greatest threat to the United States was not the bomb but numbness caused by the bomb: "The beginning of the end is adjustment to the idea of the end."[94]

SUNDAY, 28 OCTOBER 1962

Early on this day, Nikita Khrushchev announced his decision to dismantle the missiles, dramatically easing tensions on both sides. Although many Americans interpreted this decision as capitulation in the face of U.S. military force, the Soviet leader did not come away empty-handed: He acquired two valuable concessions—a formal agreement not to invade Cuba and a secret promise to remove U.S. missiles from Turkey. Khrushchev later wrote that his fears of a military coup in the United States contributed to his decision to accept the deal and remove the missiles.[95] Although U.S. intelligence remained uncertain about the presence of nuclear warheads in Cuba, Soviet troops had completed work on all twenty-four medium-range missile sites at this point[96] and equipped them with warheads. As a result, the Soviet Union could have launched a nuclear attack from Cuba only eight hours after deciding to fire the missiles.[97] Counting warheads for IL-28 Soviet bombers, short-range rockets, and coastal defense rockets, there were a total of more than 100 in Cuba. The eighteen intermediate-range missile launchers had not been completed, and their parts were at sea between the Soviet Union and Cuba.[98]

Despite the apparent breakthrough, not everyone was celebrating. Rep. Howard W. Smith of Broad Run, Virginia, spoke for many Americans when he said: "The prospects are good . . . but we must remember that dealing with Khrushchev is like negotiating with a rattlesnake."[99] Republicans also worried that successful resolution of this crisis would help Kennedy's standing, and GOP senator Hugh Scott of Pennsylvania proclaimed, "The Republicans, in my judgment, by their firm attitude of immediate action helped greatly in fixing the climate of readiness for action in Cuba."[100]

In the aftermath of Khrushchev's decision, U.S. defenses remained on alert. The Joint Chiefs of Staff ordered ships on the blockade line to hold their stations while avoiding contact with Soviet vessels. For some Americans, the crisis still intruded on family life. Air force reservists in troop transport squadrons bid farewell to their families and reported to duty with less than eight hours' notice. At 4:15 A.M., honeymooning bridegroom and Airman Second Class David Heward, twenty-four, of Merchantville, New Jersey, woke to news that he was among reservists being called up. He broke the news to his wife, canceling their honeymoon trip to Bermuda, reporting, "She cried like the dickens."[101] A Massachusetts couple learned from the car radio that their honeymoon was over. The groom left his bride with relatives in Natick and continued on to Hanscom Field.[102]

In the largest peace demonstration ever held in New York, thousands of pacifists rallied near the United Nations building,[103] and in the spirit of peace, church attendance was up 10 to 20 percent across the nation.[104] In Rome, U.S. Catholic bishops, who were attending the Second Ecumenical Council, called for making the day a national day of prayer, and the minister at the Lowes Marsh Creek Presbyterian Church near Gettysburg, Pennsylvania, told the congregation that "so long as you are right[,] God is on your side. Right always conquers in spite of insurmountable odds and armaments."[105] In Key West, church congregations found their numbers increased by men in uniform, and the congregation of Holy Innocent Episcopal Church responded to news of Khrushchev's decision by going out into the bright Florida sunshine to kneel in prayer on the church's lawn.[106]

A wave of relief rolled over the nation. The pall of nuclear war had receded.

AWAITING
armageddon

introduction

During the Cuban Missile Crisis, it was literally true that when the president of the United States went to sleep, he did not know whether he would ever wake up in the morning to anything left on Earth.—Journalist Peter Lisagor

For a precarious week in 1962, all Americans got a taste of life on death row. The Cuban Missile Crisis represented the most dangerous confrontation in almost fifty years of Cold War between the United States and the Soviet Union, delivering the world to the precipice of nuclear war. It unfolded as a Cold War game of "chicken": one side had to flinch or both would lose. A misstep by either side could have launched a catastrophic bloodbath.

Perhaps 10 million Americans fled their homes after President Kennedy revealed the presence of Soviet nuclear missiles in Cuba and threatened war to remove them. For days, the nervous nation held its breath. In some cities, wary crowds gathered outside appliance stores to get the latest news from television. Elsewhere, citizens carried newly marketed transistor radios to follow the day's events. As anxious civilians listened for warning of a nuclear attack, troops prepared for battle, congregations bowed their heads in prayer, families stocked fallout shelters, and parents in some cities bought dog tags to make identification of their children's bodies simpler. What Americans saw in the missile crisis was not pretty. As Spencer R. Weart wrote in *Nuclear Fear: A History*, "When the crisis ended most people turned their attention away as swiftly as a child who lifts up a rock, sees something slimy underneath, and drops the rock back."[1]

Faced with the prospect of imminent war, politicians and journalists rallied around Kennedy like frightened children, offering almost unqualified support. Federal, state, and local officials scurried here and there, trying to implement civil defense plans, and the public realized that the emperor wore no clothes: the U.S. civil defense program was meaningless. A year earlier, Americans alarmed by the latest crisis over control of Berlin had shown heightened interest in civil defense, but that crisis never reached the horrifying stage at which Americans actually felt that, within minutes, they might have to seek refuge in their basements, crouching there to hide from a monster called nuclear war. For years, American exceptionalism, a pervasive belief system that celebrated the unique and special nature of the United States, clouded a basic truth—the United States was fallible and vulnerable. In an age when the struggle for civil rights was a defining issue, nuclear weapons offered the ultimate equality. Rich or poor, black or white, all would die if a missile struck nearby.

This crisis forced Americans to examine civil defense and other elements of the Cold War after years of averting their eyes from the sticky details. During this era, schools ludicrously had taught children to hide from nuclear war by ducking under their desks or crouching in hallways, and Cold War literature routinely had assured Americans that their government and their way of life would survive a nuclear war. Civil defense was not a topic for serious political discourse: it was a shell game in a war of words with the Soviet Union. The sudden possibility that civil defense might be needed immediately to save lives compelled Americans to take a harder look.

In reality, plans to save the president and other officials were inadequate, and strategies to protect the public were even worse. Unwilling to finance an elaborate civil defense program, the government had stocked virtually no public shelters with food and survival supplies. If war came, most Americans would be on their own.

To date, literature on the crisis has made no investigation of its civilian impact. My goal is to fill that gaping hole in the history of a pivotal Cold War event by examining responses during the week between Kennedy's announcement that Soviet missiles had been planted in Cuba and Soviet premier Nikita Khrushchev's decision to withdraw those missiles. This approach emphasizes actions and reactions outside of military and diplomatic circles, although some review of that story is necessary to provide perspective for the most dangerous week of the nuclear age.

Though an almost-exclusive focus on diplomatic and military events has been a consistent factor in previous missile crisis studies, the tone of those narratives has changed over the years. During the 1960s, accounts produced by Kennedy loyalists, such as Theodore C. Sorensen's *Kennedy* and Arthur M. Schlesinger Jr.'s *Thousand Days*, celebrated the heroic president who faced down the bullying Khrushchev. Revisionist accounts in later years took a tougher look at Kennedy's own culpability in heightening the crisis and his later, almost-desperate efforts to bring it to a peaceful end. For instance,

Barton J. Bernstein has argued in numerous writings, including an article in James A. Nathan's 1992 collection of essays, *The Cuban Missile Crisis Revisited*, that a more prudent president would have avoided the provocative 1961 Bay of Pigs invasion in Cuba and would not have pursued clandestine efforts to overthrow the Cuban government, actions that helped to set the stage for Khrushchev's gamble in the missile crisis. Michael Beschloss's *Crisis Years: Kennedy and Khrushchev, 1960–1963* contended that Kennedy's hard line toward Khrushchev demonstrated little understanding of the pressures faced by the Soviet leader, and Beschloss suggested that in the early months of his administration, Kennedy left the impression that he "was at once more passive and more militant than [his predecessor Dwight D.] Eisenhower."[2] Beschloss noted that during the missile crisis, Kennedy's tough stance became surprisingly flexible when the nearness of war became almost palpable. In 1997, Ernest R. May and Philip D. Zelikow provided fascinating insight into White House deliberations during the crisis in *The Kennedy Tapes: Inside the White House during the Cuban Missile Crisis*, a book that demonstrated how individuals' preconceptions shaped their responses to the myriad of details flowing from the crisis. Also in 1997, Aleksandr Fursenko and Timothy Naftali offered new perspectives by probing American, Soviet, and Cuban archives to uncover the motivations of Kennedy, Khrushchev, and Castro in *"One Hell of a Gamble": Khrushchev, Castro, and Kennedy, 1958–1964*. In Naftali and Fursenko's account, all three leaders receive a share of the blame, but the forces driving each man are clearer. The archival work of Naftali and Fursenko significantly clarified and amplified the oral recollections that emerged from a series of forums beginning in the 1980s in which representatives of one or more of the three involved governments reminisced about the crisis. The meetings, documented by James G. Blight and others, demonstrated official fallibilities on all sides.

In the final analysis, the Cuban Missile Crisis was an almost inevitable product of a Cold War culture that considered negotiation equivalent to appeasement, compromise equivalent to treason. While neither this crisis nor the Cold War itself was a figment of the American imagination, blinding fear of Communism as a monolithic and insidious menace to freedom heightened the threat of war throughout this period. And because of the American image of Communism as a single and unified threat, many thought the crisis's high stakes rose even higher when the other Communist superpower—the People's Republic of China—simultaneously fought an undeclared border war with India, possibly opening the door to a massive world war with nuclear weapons in the arsenals of both sides. Although previous crises over Berlin had threatened to ignite a nuclear conflict, none had mobilized the military on both sides to such a high state of readiness.

As a tool for stopping war, the atomic bomb had helped to bring a triumphant end to World War II for the United States and its allies. It had saved American lives that might have been lost in an invasion of Japan, but it had introduced the world to a new and perilous age. The atomic bomb that hit Hiroshima offered a stark preview of what could be mankind's own destruction—instant suicide in the shadow of a mushroom cloud. After the Soviet Union joined the United States as a nuclear power in 1949, that threat became a submerged part of the American consciousness. While Joseph McCarthy rabidly pursued his Communist-hunting witch trials of the 1950s, American tensions grew. As the United States faced a totalitarian enemy, it acquired some of the enemy's attributes, including suspicion of those who did not fall into line and behave like their neighbors. When Soviet triumphs in space surpassed American achievements, fears multiplied, and the Cold War played an expanding role in daily life. Countless government projects, from education to highways, came to be seen as weapons in an invisible war against a looming Communist giant.

To many Americans, the complicated field of foreign affairs became a simple morality play matching good against evil. In a nation that prided itself on religiosity, Communism was not just an opposing economic or political system; it was Satan in a new form, and like the snake in the Garden of Eden, it could invade our blessed land, seduce the weak, and destroy our way of life. Americans, who sometimes viewed themselves as God's chosen people and routinely interwove patriotism with Christianity, feared being cast out of Eden again.

At the same time, the Cold War generated hyperbolic rhetoric that fired passions on both sides. From Khrushchev's promise to bury Western democracies to Ronald Reagan's description of the Soviet Union as an "evil empire," this overblown oratory framed how both sides viewed each another. Everything was black or white, evil or virtuous. There was little room for nuances of gray. This stark perspective fed America's trepidations, fanning the flames with anti-Communist diatribes in civic programs and news publications, as well as Sunday school lessons and comic books. Anti-Communism became an all-encompassing way of perceiving the world. Every foreign encounter had one measuring stick: would it provide opportunities for the spread of Communism or bolster the position of the United States and its allies? The fates of independent nations in Africa, Asia, and Latin America became inconsequential details when weighed against potential harm to the United

States. Even the cause of spreading democracy in the Third World became lost in the desire to stop Communism and protect one's self.

During an era when optimism and pessimism vied for dominance of the American spirit, Americans remained hopeful about man's ability to achieve great things through science and through his own ingenuity. Before an American had even orbited the Earth, John F. Kennedy boldly promised that the nation would land a man on the moon by the end of the decade—a goal that, in some ways, seemed more easily attainable than peaceful coexistence with Communism or the enrollment of one black man at the University of Mississippi. The future's scientific challenges had become more manageable than prejudices born in the past, and many Americans were doubtful about the fate of man himself. Some felt that science's potential had outgrown humanity because where the worlds of technology and human frailty meshed, science provided one final solution to any international dispute between superpowers—simply wiping out the opposition.

The missile crisis represented a dangerous intersection between Cold War culture and nuclear politics. Eisenhower had seen the existence of vast nuclear stockpiles on both sides as a deterrent to war, but in a culture dominated by unmalleable anti-Communism that demanded tough responses to Communist actions, the prospect of war seemed to many people to be an acceptable alternative to acquiescence. During the crisis, Kennedy danced along a razor's edge that separated rigid Cold War dogma from the concrete devastation of nuclear war. It should come as little surprise that after this crisis, he sought to make American culture more pliable and peaceful coexistence more palatable. His constituents emerged from the crisis like convicted felons who receive a reprieve after being strapped into the electric chair: they sighed with relief but could not shake the near-memory of sudden death.

It is difficult to identify a single moment when the nation left behind the jubilant Americanism of the immediate postwar era and began to pull apart at the seams, but the missile crisis represented one notable and often-unexplored juncture in the shattering of domestic calm. Public responses to this crisis demonstrated nascent cracks in the nation's facade of prosperous stability that had characterized the 1950s and early 1960s. Confronted with the reality of defenselessness in the nuclear age, some Americans recognized the faulty underpinning of their boundless belief in the nation's power and could not avoid seeing dangerous flaws in the nation's reigning Cold War culture. It made catastrophic war almost unavoidable and wholly acceptable to many Americans who feared Communism more than annihilation. Many of the issues that would create rifts in society during the late 1960s emerged at the time of the crisis. The government's credibility, for example, suffered during and after the crisis, both because officials could not protect the population at large and because they sought to use the American media as a propaganda tool. In addition, the newborn peace movement demonstrated declining faith in foreign policy driven by an overpowering fear of Communism and a willingness to sacrifice everything to assuage that fear. Children of this era, who later would form the nucleus of the militant antiwar movement, grappled with the possibility of global annihilation as they learned to read and write. In some ways, the missile crisis itself and the threat of nuclear war helped to lay the groundwork for divisive problems that arose later in the decade.

I believe that the domestic experience of the Cuban Missile Crisis is an important starting point in the effort to understand the sixties. As a ten-year-old, I saw my world come perilously close to dying. I remember the look on my fifth-grade teacher's face when she told us that nuclear war might begin at any minute. The first Soviet ship was approaching the American naval blockade around Cuba, she explained, and, soon, we might be dismissed from school, presumably to die at home with our housewife mothers. Parents at the dawn of the twenty-first century justifiably bemoan the influences of video game violence and internet pornography on their children, but I wonder what could be worse than telling a child that both he and his country might be obliterated within minutes.

WHY AMERICANS NEVER EMBRACED CIVIL DEFENSE
Although the threat of nuclear war had existed since the Soviet Union detonated its first atomic bomb thirteen years earlier, the Cuban Missile Crisis represented the first time many Americans truly faced the nation's susceptibility to devastating nuclear attack. An irreconcilable Cold War conflict between America's hopes and its fears made it difficult for the nation's citizens to confront this awful prospect. The Cold War created an immobilizing stalemate between two driving forces in American culture, and because that deadlock could not be overcome, neither the American people nor the American government ever developed a value system or coherent policy related to survival in nuclear war.

Throughout the nation's history, a hopeful orientation has kept Americans looking ahead to the promise of a new frontier, whether geographic, technologic, or economic. Generation after generation has directed its gaze toward the next town, the next job, the next child. This mind-set began with the first European immigrants who boarded wooden ships to find a new home on a continent far from their homeland.[3] The American abundance that they found fed this optimism. As David Potter argued in his 1954 study, *People of Plenty*, the presence of vast natural resources and the ever-expanding frontier gave Americans a life without boundaries, in which the future always held promise. After World War II, rapid technological leaps reinforced Americans' tendency to anticipate a better life than their parents had.

The nation's geographic distance from foreign powers strengthened Americans' sense of impregnability. Remoteness from Britain had benefited settlers in colonial America, allowing freedoms to blossom at a rate that accelerated the urge for total independence. Of course, from colonial years through the Civil War, thousands of soldiers shed blood on American soil, but many civilians never were threatened. Even when bloody war ruptured the nation in the 1860s, much of Union territory was outside the reach of Confederate troops. In the twentieth century, geographic isolation from enemies in Europe and Asia made a promising future attainable. This enabled Americans to bury the fear of massive war deep inside, as a nightmarish prospect unlikely to touch their lives. America was a sanctuary. Men "went away" to war "over there." War did not threaten Americans in their homes.

Counterbalancing this sense of security at home, many Americans over the years have embraced a nagging fear of infiltration, subterfuge, chaos, and a loss of civilization to "the other." Seventeenth-century Puritans settled in New England hoping to live in isolation from alien forces in a purified "City on the Hill," but "the other" lurked in the woods just outside their settlements. Native Americans represented an obvious counterpoint to European culture. Settlers feared that the natives' lifestyles might have a subversive influence on their own culture—and they coveted valuable lands controlled by neighboring tribes. Because Native American cultures lacked the work ethic, Judeo-Christian heritage, and trappings of European culture, it became easy for many white settlers to see themselves as good Christians and the natives as lazy, heathen savages, thus providing an excuse for a holy war against "the other." African slaves also were "the other" in early American culture, and long after slavery ended, many white Americans continued to see African Americans as alien and potentially seditious influences. Other immigrants, such as the Irish and Eastern European Jews, and political movements, such as labor and civil rights campaigns, have spurred similar fears and have been assigned the role of "the other."

Following participation in two world wars and especially after witnessing Adolf Hitler's ominous blitzkrieg across Europe at the start of World War II, Americans began to look outside for the next threat to their lives, their livelihoods, and their civilization. In the 1940s, the Communist and totalitarian government of the Soviet Union assumed the role of "the other." Although the Soviet Union never directly sought world domination through military conquest, Soviet leaders did expect a gradual evolution to Communism, and fearful American politicians convinced the public that Communists favored aggressive action to reach that goal.

Historian David Campbell has identified the Cold War as a response to "the need to discipline the ambiguity of global life,"[4] and the Cold War did provide a simple framework for interpreting world events and setting U.S. priorities. Although the Cold War led the United States away from traditional isolationism, most Americans confined the ideological conflict's meaning to a simple issue—American survival. The United States entered Third World battlefields to contain Communism and, therefore, to protect itself. In many ways, viewing every international instability as a threat to the United States amounted to isolationism writ large across the globe.

Identification of a common enemy offered one tool to retard the disintegration of societal bonds and reduce American fears of disunity and destruction, according to historian Richard Polenburg in *One Nation Indivisible*. Anti-Communism created an age of insecurity in which perceived threats lurked around every corner, but it produced a fear-driven sense of unity. This was the unity of conformity, the unity that says people who are different warrant suspicion. As economic change transformed the entrepreneur's son into a cog in the wheel of a large corporation, willingness to conform became both a political and an economic imperative. In 1944, theologian Reinhold Niebuhr warned Americans that self-love and the desire to dominate "the other" were the root of all sin,[5] but for many Americans during the Cold War, opposition to the Communist "other" became a defining virtue. The Cold War mentality also served as a convenient deterrent to social change. As Stephen Springarn, an aide to Harry Truman, commented in April 1949, "the consuming fear of communism has led many sincere persons into the belief that . . . change (be it civil rights or a compulsory national health program) is subversive and those who urge it are either communists or fellow travellers."[6] At the same time that the United States was bound together by fright, it was barren of community because the suspicion-driven Cold War did not nurture trust, and in this long period of crisis, no circling of wagons could save American lives. The postwar era perpetuated terror toward the unseen Communist within the United States, and thus, it did not engender a sense of community.

Even if it had, community action offered little defense from the most likely conflict with the Soviet Union—nuclear war. On the frontier, when Americans confronted trouble, they found safety in a joint effort, and as late as World War II, civil defense drills bolstered a sense of shared dangers and common goals. However, the World War II narrative, which promised victory as a result of unity, fell apart in the face of nuclear war because no rallying of civilians could save America.[7] In reality, if nuclear war came, most Americans in target areas would die alone or with their families, hiding in dark basements, as their ancient ancestors must have huddled in caves for security. In these years, frightened Americans abdicated responsibility for thinking about nuclear war to their leaders, men who shared their internal conflicts and never seriously addressed the issue of civil defense. Margaret Mead had written during World War II that "total war stretches out the human beings who form a nation into a great straggling chain, as strong as their ability to join hands rapidly again if one drops out";[8] America's planning for total nuclear war offered no hope of a human chain at all.

By the early 1960s, Americans no longer wrapped themselves in a cloak of self-confidence. "The placing into orbit of the first earth satellite [Sputnik] by the Soviet Union appears to have radically altered the prevailing worldwide estimate of the relative balance between the United States and the Union of Soviet Socialist Republics in many fields, but particularly in science and military power," the Eisenhower administration concluded in 1960,[9] and during the Kennedy administration, the Soviet advantage seemed to widen through the launching of the first man in space. For Americans, Yuri Gagarin and Sputnik created a foretaste of slippage into second place. John F. Kennedy realized the actual contest was not to determine which system of government was best. In a press conference after Gagarin's flight, he said, "We are in a period of long drawn-out tests to see which system is . . . more durable—not better, but more durable."[10] After Soviet successes in space, there was a growing sense among Americans that good guys did not always finish first. The rightness of American democracy was never in doubt for most Americans, but in a battle based on durability, many feared a Soviet victory.

This changing attitude even made an impact on popular culture. Pre-Sputnik television programming had offered a plethora of Westerns confirming what Americans knew after World War II—that the good and the just always triumph. By the early 1960s, science fiction programs, such as

The Twilight Zone and *Outer Limits*, offered a vision of a darker existence in which all that was good about America could be meaningless. Similarly, Perry Mason's flawless court record was juxtaposed with a father-son lawyer team that sometimes lost on *The Defenders*. During the week of the missile crisis, a two-part episode concluded notably with the heroes' defeat in an effort to broaden the scope of insanity pleas in murder trials.[11] It was in this new world, where the hero's victory could not be assumed, that Americans confronted the real possibility of nuclear war.

During this period, even the hero's modus operandi was open to question. While the good and the bad remained easily identifiable on TV Westerns, a growing shift away from labeling Indians as "the enemy" reflected a burgeoning recognition of the dark stain on frontier history presented by the white race's treatment of Native Americans. At the same time, Americans witnessed a corresponding imperfection of American ideals in the treatment of African Americans and Native Americans. In addition, the cult of the gunfighter, represented in TV series such as *Have Gun, Will Travel* and *Wanted: Dead or Alive*, and in the popular 1960 film *The Magnificent Seven*, introduced heroes driven by "idealism as to ends, and cynicism as to means," according to Richard Slotkin's *Gunfighter Nation*. And in many ways, Slotkin pointed out, the New Frontier embraced toughness without sentimentality, an attitude in sync with the code of the gunfighter.[12] The same could be said about the administrations of other Cold War presidents, which used American power to counter Communism in Third World nations through U.S.-inspired coups, assassinations, and support for corrupt governments.

While the conflict between hope and fear has colored American history since colonial days, destruction of "the other" did not carry the threat of self-destruction or destruction of the much-prized American future until 1945. In the Cold War, the clash between these two impulses could not be resolved because nuclear conflict with "the other"—the Soviet Union—could eradicate a key tenet in the American creed, the belief in tomorrow. Anti-Communism, with its quasi-religious zealotry, enraptured many Americans enough to make them accept a war that risked the next generation, but Americans' natural optimism made it impossible to address the prospect of futurelessness. Arthur Schlesinger Sr. contended in a 1942 presidential address to the American Historical Association that a key part of American character was a willingness "to die for their conception of life so that their children might live it."[13] Now, Americans encountered the possibility of erasing their children's lives in a gamble to defeat a feared enemy.

This change coincided with a growing sense of uneasiness among people who felt they had lost control of their fates. The Depression had shaken many Americans' faith in the cycle of success, but the nation regained confidence through its victorious role in World War II. In the postwar nation, control again seemed fleeting. Life had always been subject to the unpredictability of death and disease; however, new man-made variables—the military draft for possible service in foreign wars, the economic insecurity of a nascent global economy, and the prospect of massive nuclear war—further encroached on individual autonomy at this time. No matter how carefully a family planned, there was no promise that tomorrow would be a better day or that tomorrow would even come. For many, it became easier to forge ahead, focusing on the parts of life that were controllable and ignoring the overwhelming threat of nuclear war.

The conflict between hope for the future and sometimes-suicidal fear of the Soviet Union caused a sort of paralysis, all too apparent as many Americans sleepwalked through the Cuban Missile Crisis. Because they had neither committed to a strong civil defense plan nor accepted the fact that minimal and haphazard planning would save few lives, Americans could not cope with the real prospect of war. President Kennedy benefited from and perhaps even relied upon this incapacitating glitch in the American psyche, which enabled him to take action without facing the challenging questions that a more clear-thinking populace might ask. Like youngsters, unprepared Americans panicked or denied the danger around them as they followed their daily routines numbly listening for the sound of a shrill siren, a flash of light, and the end.

KENNEDY, KHRUSHCHEV, AND CUBA

Fidel Castro's rise to power in a 1959 Cuban coup and his subsequent embrace of Communism had raised the specter of Communist regimes materializing throughout Latin America, and to many Americans, Cuba's closeness made Castro's government seem like an insidious foreign virus infecting the United States' sphere of influence. The reality that Castro was, in fact, Cuban often became lost in Cold War rhetoric. With Cuba seen as a base for Communist expansion in the Americas, the United States' historical preoccupation with the island ballooned—and that contributed to Soviet concerns about Cuban security. Americans feared the devil at their doorstep, and, as a result, leaders such as Kennedy and Eisenhower encountered great political pressure to oust Castro's government. At the same time, Soviet leaders felt an equally important obligation to protect their foothold in the West.

Almost as soon as he assumed the presidency, Kennedy confronted a formidable challenge in Cuba. The Central Intelligence Agency presented him with a proposal developed during the Eisenhower administration to bolster an invasion of Cuba by a refugee force. Kennedy approved the plan with a proviso that no U.S. military forces would participate under any circumstances. After training the would-be invaders, the CIA launched the operation on 17 April 1961. A 1,400-man force made an amphibious landing at Cuba's Bay of Pigs. The outcome was disastrous: Castro's forces quickly overwhelmed the exile group. The CIA begged Kennedy to authorize air and naval support for the invaders, but he refused. Ultimately, 1,000 exiles surrendered to Cuban armed forces. Worsening the defeat's sting, government efforts to obscure the American role in the operation disintegrated when refugee pilots flying easily identifiable CIA planes landed in Miami after missing many of their Cuban targets and requested asylum in the United States. So complete was this failure that in the years that followed, "Bay of Pigs" became a metaphor for an utter fiasco. In the wake of this disaster, two CIA leaders, Allen Dulles and Richard Bissell, lost their jobs, but Kennedy publicly accepted complete blame for the debacle. "There's an old saying that victory has a hundred fathers and defeat is an orphan," he told reporters at a news conference. "I am the responsible officer of this government."[14]

Although Kennedy's approval rating soared to record levels after this admitted catastrophe, the loss at the Bay of Pigs dogged much of the president's thinking and led to the institution of a covert program known as Operation Mongoose in November 1961. This venture, driven by the zeal of Attorney General Robert F. Kennedy, sought to incite anti-Castro uprisings in Cuba and to delineate strategy for the use of an American military force if clandestine operations succeeded in launching a rebellion against Castro. Operation Mongoose hatched a number of elaborate and unorthodox schemes to unnerve Castro's government. For example, there were plans to institute prayers for Cuba in U.S. military units that included Cuban personnel, with the idea that photos of these sessions would create invasion jitters in Havana.[15] Other scenarios mapped out destruction of Cuban bridges, port facilities, and oil tankers[16] and sabotage of sugar production enterprises.[17] While covert operations took shape, the White House asked the military to prepare contingency plans for invasion of Cuba at some future date, and the Pentagon conveniently had completed those blueprints for action by the time U-2 planes spotted Soviet missiles in Cuba in October 1962.

In response to the apparent American threat to Cuba and to enhance his nation's standing in the arms race, Khrushchev formally decided in late May

1962 to instigate a major arms buildup, including nuclear missiles, in Cuba. According to Fursenko and Naftali, Khrushchev was responding in part to an erroneous leak from the U.S. government in early 1962 that Kennedy had planned a preemptive nuclear strike against the Soviet Union in 1961 and that he had changed his mind only after two massive Soviet nuclear tests late in the year.[18] The secret Soviet initiative, code-named Operation Anadyr, originally called for installation of twenty-four medium-range missiles and twelve intermediate-range missiles.[19]

U.S. intelligence noted large shipments of Soviet materiel to Cuba in mid-July, and preparatory work apparently began on missile sites by 1 August;[20] however, the United States remained unaware of the operation's true intent. To conceal the nature of the shipments, the Soviet military transported missile parts on ships carrying Soviet troops dressed in civilian clothes, and officers hid valuable information on the missile project among files of general information on nations friendly to the Soviet Union.[21] When the luxury liner *Admiral Nakhimov* departed on the Black Sea, a news item in a Soviet newspaper reported the first tourist cruise to Cuba, but the ship carried 2,000 soldiers.[22] In all, the Soviet merchant marine and navy made 185 trips to Cuba during this period. The Soviet military assigned 42,000 troops to Cuba[23]—four times as many as the Central Intelligence Agency estimated at the time. By mid-September, the missiles themselves began arriving, and the first warheads reached Cuba on 4 October.[24] Soviet troops in Cuba also had access to tactical nuclear weapons for use against a possible American invasion force, and General Issa Pliyev, commander of the Soviet forces in Cuba, had permission to use them.[25]

In the late summer and early autumn of 1962, the United States kept a wary eye on Soviet arms shipments. A U-2 flight on 29 August spotted no nuclear missiles but showed some structures later identified as eight surface-to-air missile sites in Cuba, evidence that future surveillance flights would be in danger of attack. On 4 September, Soviet officials claimed that a U-2 flight violated Soviet airspace over the island of Sakhalin in the north Pacific and within a few days, Communist China downed a U-2 plane. These developments, plus discovery of the surface-to-air missiles, led to a decision to restrict U-2 flights to international waters, where photo coverage was limited because of the need to shoot at a slanted angle. In addition, cloud cover over the island made flights impossible or rendered them useless throughout most of September.[26]

Conclusive evidence of a threat to the United States did not arrive until mid-October. Almost a week before the nation and the world learned that a crisis existed, two U-2 pilots shooting photos as they soared high above the Caribbean captured the evidence that would ignite American passions and lead to a dangerous encounter between the United States and the Soviet Union. Shown in the photos taken by Majors R. S. Heyser and Rudolph Anderson were launching sites under construction that soon would be capable of hurling Soviet nuclear missiles at much of the United States. When the National Photographic Interpretation Center analyzed the film on 15 October, construction of Soviet missile sites was clear.

The next day, this critical information reached the president, and he quickly assembled key leaders, later to be labeled the Executive Committee of the National Security Council, to search for a strategy guaranteeing removal of the missiles. This group was not merely a logical subgroup of the cabinet; it included longtime Kennedy confidantes, and Robert Kennedy carried special influence. Meeting at times with the president and at other times without him, the Ex Comm gathered repeatedly in secret over the next few days to consider a slew of questions, starting with the most basic: how did the missiles in Cuba alter the arms race?

While the U.S. nuclear arsenal still dwarfed Soviet armaments, the missiles in Cuba offered the Soviet Union a strategic advantage. The United States' nuclear stockpile held an estimated 27,305 nuclear warheads, including both strategic and tactical weapons;[27] the Soviet Union's stockpile could claim only 3,322 warheads in all.[28] To deliver that payload, the United States had 284 missiles, 1,450 strategic bombers,[29] and 9 operational Polaris submarines. American allies bolstered the United States' position: French and British forces claimed 230 nuclear bombers, while Great Britain, Italy, and Turkey shared joint control with the United States of more than 100 intermediate-range missiles.[30] In contrast, the Soviets had only 20 intercontinental ballistic missiles; 700 medium-range missiles; and 1,200 medium- and long-range bombers. At that time, most Soviet missiles had an effective range that ended within 2,500 miles of Soviet territory. Placing missiles in Cuba instantly enabled the Soviet Union to make shorter-range missiles do the work of intercontinental missiles by threatening the United States with nuclear attack.[31] At the time of the crisis, Raymond Garthoff of the State Department's Bureau of Political/Military Affairs concluded that the additional weapons in the Soviet arsenal meant that the United States would lose an additional 30 percent of its weapons in a surprise Soviet attack, leaving the nation with only 15 percent of its pre-attack military force.[32]

Meeting behind closed doors, the Ex Comm worked its way through options ranging from using nuclear weapons against Cuba to seeking mediation by the United Nations. In the initial meetings, most participants favored air strikes on the missile sites, although Robert Kennedy strongly dissented. Continuing air surveillance of Cuba provided more information about the installations as the Ex Comm deliberated, revealing that intermediate-range, as well as medium-range, missiles were present. The intermediate-range missiles could strike targets 2,200 nautical miles from the launch site, more than twice the distance a medium-range missile could cover.

During this period of secrecy, Kennedy maintained his official schedule of meetings and public appearances, including an 18 October meeting with Soviet foreign minister Andrei Gromyko at the White House. The president gave Gromyko no inkling that U.S. intelligence had spotted the missiles, but he did reread a 4 September statement warning against Soviet deployment of offensive weapons in Cuba. Gromyko, who like his government asserted that the Soviet Union was placing only defensive weapons in Cuba, accused the United States of "pestering" a tiny country. Though angered, Kennedy cannily maintained a cordial mood. On the same day, Robert Kennedy met with KGB agent and "back-channel" contact Georgi Bolshakov, who assured the attorney general that surface-to-surface missiles would not be sent to Cuba.[33]

As the Ex Comm's debates continued, the president honored previous commitments to campaign for Democratic candidates around the nation until 20 October, when he cut short a six-state campaign sweep and canceled an appearance at the closing of the hugely successful Seattle World's Fair. By that time, the majority of the Ex Comm members had shifted their views and now favored a naval quarantine as the most effective first step to challenge the Soviets while minimizing the likelihood of nuclear war. After considering the international implications of making a surprise attack, President Kennedy agreed. His decision was reinforced in an 21 October briefing by the Tactical Air Command's General Walter C. Sweeney, who said that several hundred bombing sorties would be necessary for an air strike and that 10 percent of the Soviet missiles probably would survive even that heavy bombardment.[34]

As a result, the navy started assembling a blockade, and the military as a whole began mobilizing for a possible second step—an invasion. Kennedy planned to reveal the discovery of the missiles as well as his response in a televised address to the nation on Monday, 22 October. The quarantine, scheduled to take effect 24 October, would stop any Soviet ships likely to be carrying offensive weapons, especially missile parts, to the island. The legality of the quarantine was questionable and confusing, even to the president of the United States. Kennedy asked his advisers whether it would be necessary to make a declaration of war to back up the blockade.[35] Normally, international law considers blockades to be acts of war; however, the administration traced its legal justification to the Inter-American Treaty of Reciprocal Assistance of 1947, known as the Rio Pact, which authorized the use of military force to maintain "the peace and security of the continent."[36]

Over the weekend leading up to the president's speech, the White House summoned congressional leaders and sent jets to return them to Washington for a briefing, scheduled just two hours before Kennedy's televised address—enough time to demand their loyalty but too little to factor their input into the administration's plans. Tracking down most of the congressional leaders was easy: it was the campaign season, and most were in their home states. The sudden appearance of a U.S. Air Force plane surprised Rep. Hale Boggs, who was fishing in the Gulf of Mexico. As the plane circled above his boat, an air force crewman tossed a bottle down. When Boggs fished it out of the waves, he found a note inside telling him to contact the president.[37] Soon, he and the other leaders were on their way back to Washington.

Kennedy also dispatched a team of diplomats, led by Truman secretary of state Dean Acheson, to Europe to brief American allies. Upon Acheson's landing in Great Britain, U.S. ambassador David Bruce startled him, arriving with a bottle in one raincoat pocket and a revolver in the other. Bruce had orders to provide an armed escort for Acheson. "There was nothing said about shooting me, was there?" Acheson asked.[38] On 22 October, the State Department transmitted a special "go" message, authorizing American envoys to brief foreign heads of states or foreign ministers on American plans. Through quiet diplomacy and political persuasion, Kennedy sought support for his action, which would create worldwide fears of a nuclear confrontation. A few journalists learned about the military mobilization over the weekend leading up to Kennedy's speech, but the president managed to suppress those reports.

By the time Kennedy reported to the nation that the Soviet Union had placed missiles in Cuba, the American military effort was well under way. Days before, military leaders had begun to deploy their forces. The need for quick mobilization triggered "almost a panic" in the Pentagon, according to air force general Horace Wade. "People started to worry about moving divisions. They started to worry about preparing plans for an invasion, mobilizing the forces, Reserve forces, the Guard forces, were they going to get congressional support, and they knew they couldn't mobilize the Guard and the Reserve without congressional support."[39] As Pentagon officials issued orders, some ground units reported they were at 95–100 percent of authorized strength just twelve hours after mobilization and all were ready to perform their duties within thirty hours.[40] Trucks carrying troops and ammunition rolled southward on America's highways.

Special assignments for the air force began 16 October, with orders to increase surveillance flights over Cuba. To protect the nation's nuclear weaponry, the Strategic Air Command dispersed 183 B-47s to thirty-three civilian and military airfields. The air force also positioned 183 interceptors in Florida to stop enemy planes from entering U.S. airspace. At all times, four interceptors were in the air over the state.[41] Meanwhile, the potential invasion force of 140,000 assembled.[42] By 19 October, the military had airlifted 7,000 bombs, 40,000 rockets, 3 million rounds of ammunition, and 3,000 fuel tanks, pylons, and launchers to Florida, with some materiel arriving from bases as far away as Turkey and the Philippines.[43] On 21 October, many naval vessels received orders to take to sea immediately as part of the quarantine. Some left port with as little as 50 percent of their crews; there was no time to await absent crew members.

Swift evacuation of 2,432 women and children from the Guantanamo Bay base in Cuba was also one of the navy's top priorities. "As we were driving home [from school], there were suitcases on everybody's lawn. . . . My mother said, 'We're leaving in about five minutes. Go up to your room and take anything you can carry,'"[44] recalled one woman, who was eight years old in 1962. Though the order to evacuate was sudden, it was not entirely unexpected: wives had orders to keep a suitcase packed at all times. When the word came, many rushed from their homes without time to finish household chores or tell their husbands goodbye. Base officials distributed handouts to all dependents. High on the list of directions was, "Please do not ask questions or request exceptions." The navy urged wives to be calm, and indicating a lack of faith in the wives' ability to follow instructions, the handout closed this way: "God Bless you. We will all miss you. PUT THIS IN YOUR PURSE. DO NOT LEAVE IT LYING AROUND THE HOUSE OR YARD."[45] Four ships took the dependents on a three-day voyage from Cuba to the home of the Atlantic Fleet, Norfolk, Virginia, a voyage they began with no idea of why they were leaving.

PARADISE LOST

The military dependents at Guantanamo were not the only Americans in the dark as the United States prepared for war. When President Kennedy spoke to the nation, millions listened in stunned silence. How they responded in the following days is largely an untold story.

For six days, ordinary Americans lived their daily lives under the shadow of nuclear war. The succeeding chapters will examine the crisis's unsettling impact on American life and its role in shaking America's confidence in its invulnerability. The combination of unyielding Cold War dogma and the equally indomitable reality of nuclear war brought America to a crossroads in 1962: the nation had to decide whether the fears of today merited abandoning hopes for tomorrow. Clearly, exaggerated American anxieties about Cuba's ability to subvert Latin American governments had helped to mobilize a chain of events that threatened the nation's future, and Americans found themselves surprisingly unprepared to face the prospect of war.

When the crisis ended, Americans rejoiced. This time, there had been no Armageddon, but the nation could not easily reclaim the sense of security lost during a week under the threat of war. Unavoidably, life had changed, and that change may have contributed to growing instability that would shake the nation's foundation before the decade's end.

CHAPTER ONE
the shadow of death

As time passed, the radioactivity would also; with a cobalt half-life of about five years these streets and houses would be habitable again in twenty years at the latest, and probably sooner than that. The human race was to be wiped out and the world made clean again for wiser occupants without undue delay.—from Nevil Shute's *On the Beach*

By the 1960s, most Americans had a vision of nuclear war: towering mushroom clouds, sudden devastation, an eerily empty landscape, and death, perhaps even mankind's end. Many of their perceptions sprang from news reports, military and civil defense propaganda, novels, television, and movies—all of which were based on snippets of scientific fact with imaginative fiction filling in the gaps. Most information about nuclear weaponry was secret, and because all-out nuclear war had never occurred, guesswork played a major role in predicting its results.

Since the bombing of Hiroshima, total nuclear war had been a distant threat—a nightmarish prospect with little more likelihood than H. G. Wells's Martian invasion. While Americans had a mental picture of nuclear war, they had yet to recognize American vulnerability. As Eisenhower's director of the Civil Defense Administration said in 1955, "The American people have simply not accepted yet the possibility of an enemy attack on the United States from the skies by intercontinental bombers carrying these tremendous nuclear weapons. It is something that still appears fantastic."[1] Extremely rapid advances in science, such as the development of missiles capable of carrying nuclear warheads in the late 1950s and early 1960s, made it no easier for Americans to accept the truth or for scientists to conceive solutions. Nuclear war's image, part fact and part science fiction, had become a part of the American psyche without being integrated into the real world through acceptance of its inevitably tragic outcome or through solid actions aimed at prevention or protection. In fact, American civil defense plans of this era could be compared to installation of a flimsy chain lock to protect the nation from a multimegaton monster named nuclear war. This chapter examines Americans' expectations of nuclear war when they found themselves on the brink in the Cuban Missile Crisis.

By the time Kennedy became president, the Soviet Union's technological advances had made the threat of nuclear war more real. Once confident, Americans now had "an image, born of *Sputnik*, of 10-foot-tall Russians who rarely do anything wrong," reported a 1963 Rand Corporation report.[2] When the Soviet Union planted missiles in Cuba, Democratic senator Richard Russell of Georgia, chairman of the Armed Services Committee, warned that nuclear war could start within ten days,[3] and privately, Kennedy set the odds "between one out of three and even."[4]

On an often-unspoken level, nuclear war haunted Americans, and none more than the Ex Comm's members. Like an army private who justifies his actions by claiming that he was just following orders, Secretary of State Rusk asserted, "We ourselves are not moved to general war, we're simply doing what we said we would do if they took certain action." In a macabre twist, he noted that America could "eliminate the Cuban problem by actually eliminating the island."[5] Cold War politics and anxiety about war drove the Ex Comm, but National Security adviser McGeorge Bundy said, "It wasn't the fear of the foot soldier, afraid of being killed when his time comes to hit the beach or go over the top. It was rather the fear of the commanding officer who, having ordered his men to 'charge,' suddenly feels that he has given the wrong order."[6]

Nuclear weaponry placed new burdens on world leaders. As Secretary of Defense Robert McNamara later hypothesized, "If you go to nuclear war, and the other side retaliates, and only a few—maybe even only one—bomb gets through to an American city, you—the one who just initiated the nuclear war—will have had to shoulder the responsibility for the worst catastrophe in the history of this country."[7] Khrushchev and Kennedy were all too aware of the dangers inherent in their course. A month before the Hiroshima bombing, Kennedy wrote in his diary, "The clash [with the Soviet Union] may be finally and indefinitely postponed by the eventual discovery of a weapon so horrible that it will truthfully mean the abolishment of all nations employing it."[8] And in September 1959, Khrushchev declared in Moscow, "Those who say that they do not understand what peaceful coexistence is, and are afraid of it, are wittingly or unwittingly helping to further the Cold War which is bound to spread unless we intervene and stop it. It will reach a point of such intensity that a spark may at any moment set off a world conflagration."[9]

For many Americans, nuclear warfare's destructive capacity seemed unimaginable, but nuclear war's potential was not wholly unknown. The U.S. bombings of Hiroshima and Nagasaki in 1945 left behind ghostly images: "The streets were deserted except for the dead," Dr. Michihiko Hachiya wrote in his diary after the Hiroshima bombing. "Some looked as if they had been frozen by death while in the full action of flight; others lay sprawled as though some giant flung them to their death from a great height. Hiroshima was no longer a city, but a burnt-over prairie."[10] The bomb destroyed industries, eliminated phone service, and disrupted other utilities. Debris and casualties cluttered the streets, making automobile travel impossible. Accompanying these dark scenes in many American minds was a stain of guilt: "A sense of impending doom and helplessness hangs over us. We fear that another nation might initiate an atomic attack on us, and we know, in our heart of hearts, that we would not be in a position to pass judgment on their deed," a Presbyterian minister in Syracuse, New York, told his congregation in 1958.[11]

And the threat of destruction radiated almost from the moment of the Hiroshima blast. "In that terrible flash 10,000 miles away, men have seen not only the fate of Japan, but have glimpsed the future of America," the *New York Times*'s James Reston wrote in August 1945.[12] One day after the Hiroshima attack, the *St. Louis Post-Dispatch* warned that scientists may have "signed the mammalian world's death warrant."[13] When the Soviet Union set off an atomic bomb in 1949, the United States began a blueprint of life after nuclear war. Civil defense officials even scripted what a president might tell his battle-scarred nation: "Within the hour the aggressor has launched a brutal unprovoked nuclear attack on our country and the homelands of our allies. Some of our cities have been hit and heavy casualties have been suffered by the civilian population."[14]

Why would Americans accept the prospect of such a fate? For many, it was a potentially tragic end to a noble cause. Others felt like helpless victims in a world apparently barreling toward self-destruction. Nuclear war was a part of daily life, and a nightmare waiting to happen.

AMERICA'S FEAR

Many Americans believed nuclear war was an acceptable risk in the Cold War battle against Communism. Following World War II, fear of Communism often seemed to outweigh fear of nuclear war. Historian Marc Trachtenberg has labeled this phenomenon "the 'heroic' phase in American attitudes about nuclear war" because nuclear war's potential for destruction

A new portrait of the American family: Harry A. Thomason, his wife, and five children gather in the family's tiny fallout shelter in District Heights, Maryland, in 1955. The family faced the prospect of spending days or weeks in this cramped structure built with reinforced concrete and accessible through the basement. This potential living space for a family of seven was five feet wide, twelve feet long, and just under six feet high. *Washington Star* photo, National Archives.

was not considered adequate to rule out its use.[15] As Spencer R. Weart has noted, it is almost as if the United States and the Soviet Union had joined in an "apocalyptic suicide pact,"[16] and as he also stated, suicide was not foreign to Americans who, statistics show, are far more likely to kill themselves than to be murdered.[17]

In World War II, "civilized" nations accepted the idea of exterminating enemy civilians through massive bombing—whether nuclear or conventional. Blanket bombing of Dresden and Tokyo followed the same logic that justified the atomic attacks on Hiroshima and Nagasaki. And at times after the war, zealous anti-Communism became intertwined with this willingness to exterminate the enemy or even risk one's own civilization. By 1962, although both sides talked about restricting nuclear attacks to military targets, that was no longer an advantageous strategy because many missile sites had been hardened, or shielded by steel and concrete. Ten to thirty missile hits would have been required to destroy one hardened installation, according to Secretary of the Air Force Curtis LeMay.[18] Also, the United States' Polaris missiles on submarines were too weak to destroy hardened sites and, therefore, were clearly intended to target Soviet cities.[19] LeMay's definition of war represented some Americans' willingness to accept extermination: "I'll tell you what war is all about—you've got to kill people, and when you've killed enough they stop fighting."[20] However, there were opponents of this point of view. Social philosopher Lewis Mumford condemned anti-Communism's infatuation with extermination in 1959, writing, "Those who believe that any country has the right to make such a decision share the madness of Captain Ahab in Moby Dick. For them Russia is the White Whale that must be hunted down and grappled with."[21]

As Mumford suggested, anti-Communism was often obsessive, and it had contradictory effects on the United States. As a force that led neighbor to suspect neighbor, it was divisive. During the early 1950s, Senator Joseph McCarthy's ugly witch-hunt for Communists reflected paranoia about Communist infiltration, which was embraced by many Americans. And yet, anti-Communism also fortified solidarity at a time when civil rights issues opened huge rifts.

As the U.S. government's efforts to protect African Americans' rights conflicted with states' rights, fissures between black and white and North and South widened. Just over a month before the Cuban crisis, America's attention was riveted on Oxford, Mississippi, where federal troops interceded to enroll James Meredith as the University of Mississippi's first African American student. Cries of "states' rights" mingled with outrage over Mississippi's refusal to obey a federal injunction to integrate. On such issues, southern Democrats responded to federal intervention by creating legislative obstacles for Kennedy's administration, often joining Republicans to block social legislation. On foreign policy, however, anti-Communism reigned as the almost unquestioned voice, and most liberals joined conservatives of both parties in backing strong action whenever faced with Soviet aggression. Therefore, a president unable to find consensus on domestic issues could expect solid support for tough action against Communism.

After *Sputnik*, appealing to people's fears of Soviet superiority became a strong political strategy: Kennedy himself capitalized on a nonexistent Soviet advantage in nuclear missiles as a theme in his 1960 presidential campaign. As Philip Nash has concluded, "He chose to believe the most dire assessments of the strategic balance and disregard the rest"[22]—a common phenomenon in the Cold War. Thus, public fear of Communism nourished a willingness to support large defense budgets and to accept leaders' bold and sometimes dangerous stands against the Soviet Union.

In addition, leaders, perhaps too readily, drew Cold War lessons from World War II. Facing the Communists, Eisenhower saw brinkmanship as a necessity that went beyond political posturing.[23] While measuring his responses to avoid allowing a dispute over Hungary or Berlin to mushroom into nuclear war, Eisenhower recalled Great Britain's conciliatory response in Munich[24] to Adolf Hitler's 1938 annexation of Sudetenland and concluded that anything less than a firm stand would open the door to disaster: "The last thing we were going to use was appeasement, because we had [Neville] Chamberlain still to look at. . . . There's no possible way of winning in negotiations against a man or a people of the attitudes and deportment of the Communists."[25] Eisenhower believed preparation for massive retaliation through development of a huge nuclear arsenal would deter an attack, and by building foreign policy around nuclear weaponry, he hoped deterrence would make war so dangerous that no one would contemplate it.[26] The retired general knew the surest way to avoid a catastrophic emulation of World War II's Pearl Harbor would be a preemptive strike, but he hoped that the nuclear stockpile's existence alone would make an attack unnecessary. (Despite that stockpile, Kennedy admitted in 1962 that "in some circumstances, we might have to take the initiative" and launch an attack before the enemy.)[27]

In another echo of World War II, U.S. politicians stressed the evils of a totalitarian state, a tactic that let them use that war as a foreshadowing of World War III, linking Communism with Fascism and Soviet leaders with Hitler. That tortured linkage made nuclear war seem potentially necessary and almost palatable. In a nation that feared a monolithic enemy, slogans like "Better Dead Than Red" found receptive audiences. Such zealous feelings, however, were dangerous. As journalist Walter Lippmann told the Women's National Press Club in 1962, "However lunatic it might be to commit suicide, a nation can be provoked and exasperated to the point of lunacy where its nervous system cannot endure inaction, where only violence can relieve its feelings."[28]

To some, war seemed inevitable. In 1962, 34 percent of Americans believed peace with the Soviet Union was impossible.[29] As the Presbyterian Church (U.S.A.) argued in 1954, "The goal of Communism is world domination. No one of us should be so naive as to suppose that anything short of such a goal fits into the pattern of this atheistic philosophy."[30] This anti-Communist attitude permeated Cold War culture. It appeared in melodramatic television series, such as *I Led Three Lives,* a 1950s syndicated drama that chronicled the life of a U.S. double agent supposedly helping the global Communist conspiracy. Spy novels, whose audience included Kennedy, also shaped Cold War expectations. Kennedy repeated a rumor of a Communist plot to journalist Hugh Sidey: Soviet envoys, Kennedy said, reportedly had smuggled parts of an atomic bomb in diplomatic pouches and assembled the weapon in their Washington embassy. Sidey was doubtful, but Kennedy, who loved Ian Fleming's James Bond thriller *From Russia with Love,* seemed to think such a scheme fit nicely into the Soviets' modus operandi.[31]

Strangely, while each side perceived dramatic differences with the other, Cold War dueling employed similarly overdrawn rhetoric on both sides of the ideological divide. When JFK revealed the missiles in Cuba, he said, "The path we have chosen for the present is full of hazards . . . but it is the one most consistent with our character and courage as a nation and our commitments around the world. The cost of freedom is always high—but Americans have always paid it. And one path we shall never choose, and that is the path of surrender or submission."[32] The Soviets responded in kind: "We want peace. But we never have feared, and do not fear, threats. We realize that the aggressive actions of the United States constitute a serious danger to the peace of the whole world. And we will do everything to prevent this danger and to smash the aggressor if he dare attempt to accomplish his mad plans."[33]

In truth, when American or Soviet leaders sought to back away from tough rhetoric and explore peaceful relations, they faced attack from militant factions at home. Threatening to destroy their own civilizations became almost de rigueur. In nations gripped by often irrational fears, taking foolish risks sometimes was a sure route to political success.

LIFE AND DEATH IN THE NUCLEAR AGE

Everyone was vulnerable to nuclear war—the bold politicians, the daring generals, even the frightened kindergartners. No one had an exemption, and the Cuban Missile Crisis brought that message home. "The crisis was unique in the sense that it was the first time that there was a real, imminent, potential threat to the physical safety and well-being of American citizens," Douglas Dillon, Kennedy's secretary of the treasury, noted many years later.[34] The Cold War had caused other scares, most recently 1961's Berlin standoff that concluded with Soviet construction of the Berlin Wall;[35] however, this crisis forced Americans to take a fresh look at nuclear war's potential. Many hoped that mankind was too rational to follow that suicidal path, but Kennedy, the man who could order a U.S. missile launch, believed that nuclear war was quite possible.

On a daily basis, testing of multimegaton bombs by the United States and the Soviet Union imprinted the mushroom cloud on the American consciousness. These tests, mostly conducted in the Earth's atmosphere, generated radioactive fallout that was a recurrent reminder of the weapon's potential. Plants that absorbed the radioisotope strontium 90 were devoured by cows and eventually consumed by humans through milk. It remained in the human body for about forty years with unknown effects.[36] To subdue consumers' fears, President Kennedy captured headlines one day by publicly drinking a glass of milk and announcing that it would be served at every White House meal.[37] Fallout also tainted wheat supplies,[38] and adults even warned children not to eat winter's almost-magical heralds—snowflakes— because they contained fallout.

In 1959, scientists had produced a congressional study outlining the dangers of nuclear weapons and showing that only 25 percent of those killed at Hiroshima and Nagasaki could have been saved by the kind of shelter program planned during the Eisenhower and Kennedy administrations.[39] At the same time, researchers had reported that an attack using 1.5-megaton bombs would destroy about 25 percent of the nation's homes and seriously damage 18 percent. About 5 percent of undamaged buildings would require evacuation because of fallout.[40] Scientists estimated that neutral nations would experience an increase in birth defects to about 5 percent of births. In warring nations, such defects would rise to 12–20 percent.[41] Scientists said a single one-megaton bomb detonated at satellite altitude could incinerate six

In what could be a scene of children at play, members of the John C. Leger family of Bronxville, New York, crouch in an escape tunnel and prepare for war. The family had an elaborate bomb shelter as early as 1952, before introduction of the hydrogen bomb heightened the potential for destruction in a nuclear war. © Bettmann/CORBIS.

western states in the United States,[42] and that one ten-megaton bomb could send searing heat over 5,000 square miles, an area about the size of Connecticut. Unless nations made plans to protect animals, those who survived would find a land devoid of horses, cattle, pigs, and chickens, the prophets of doom warned. In addition, radiation would kill birds, and insects would overpopulate this brave new world.[43]

Obviously, nuclear war carried many threats. A secret report written for Kennedy in 1962 outlined what could be expected in an attack. First, blast effects such as collapsing of buildings, winds over 150 miles per hour, and flying debris would kill anyone close to the explosion. In coastal areas, flooding would heighten casualties.[44] Second, heat and light would cause flash blindness, retinal and skin burns, as well as deadly firestorms.[45] Third, radioactive fallout would drift to Earth, widening the circle of casualties.[46]

In the first day of war, urban residents and those near military installations would face the biggest threat. Based on the 1950 census, scientists predicted that in Philadelphia, 36 percent would die that day, with an additional 24 percent fatally injured. Most survivors would be hurt, but almost 3,000 of the area's 8,110 doctors would be dead and, thus, unavailable to help.[47]

While some experts warned about nuclear war's costs, others provided a more optimistic view of the morning after Armageddon. In his 1960 book, *On Thermonuclear War*, weapons strategist Herman Kahn suggested that the nation would not be crippled by all-out war because weapons would strike specific locales, thus allowing people outside of major cities to rebuild.[48] If only 2 million perished, Kahn saw the economy rebounding in one year; if 40 million died, reducing the nation's population by more than 20 percent, recovery would take twenty years.[49]

Similarly, Edward Teller, an American nuclear scientist, predicted in a 1962 *Saturday Evening Post* article "that our present industrial complex, if replaced, could reproduce all we have in about three years." He contended that the nation could rebuild its industrial base in only five years.[50] In a reply to Teller, other scientists stated, "It is arrant nonsense to suppose that we could rebuild a destroyed world with tools of production that have been lost."[51]

To believe that civil defense was worth the effort, Americans had to trust that it was possible to survive nuclear war and that life would be worth living in a ravaged land. At the same time, they had to accept a truth they desperately wanted to discount—that the U.S. military could not protect them.[52] Public disbelief would guarantee that little effort would be made to provide fallout protection, even in rural areas, where the chance to escape direct hits was greatest. If Americans really had faced how slim their chances were, they probably would have become less supportive of the Cold War brinkmanship and arms buildup embraced by both major political parties. Scientists, generals, and politicians were powerfully motivated to sell the idea of survival.

Support for shelter programs waned and ebbed as crises occurred. This stop-and-start brand of enthusiasm discouraged support from lawmakers, some of whom feared that it could be a government-building program, such as the New Deal.[53] This up-and-down cycle, all too apparent in the Kennedy years, began in 1957 when a panel of defense experts released the Gaither Report, which spotlighted the issue of preparedness. Subsequent crises piqued the public's interest; nevertheless, Congress remained hesitant to make a big investment in shelter programs. Lawmakers were not alone in their doubts: in 1957, Eisenhower's secretary of state, John Foster Dulles, argued in a cabinet meeting that it would be defensible to tell the nation that no truly effective means of protection existed; however, it would be politically incorrect, to say the least. Eisenhower rejected Dulles's argument, saying that even minimal civil defense would make the nation's chances of survival better,[54] though the president himself wondered how much America could withstand.[55] Most of those who believed civil defense was pointless made their objections quietly, but a November 1959 article in the *Milwaukee Journal* quoted Wisconsin's civil defense chief as admitting that Governor Gaylord Nelson was unconvinced such programs were realistic.[56] In 1960, New Jersey governor Robert B. Meyner crusaded against big civil defense expenditures, arguing that "we are fostering a cruel deception on the American people if we try to persuade them that they can have civilian defense through underground shelters in the next war."[57]

Although officials in the Eisenhower administration realized that nuclear attack drills frightened many people, nationwide alerts were held annually in the 1950s to test readiness.[58] Some believed the annual drills would minimize panic if a real attack occurred, and that was a priority because a 1953 Federal Civil Defense Agency report had warned that "mass panic, if not quickly quelled, can in itself be a lethal weapon."[59] In 1955, forty-six states participated in Operation Alert, and 8.5 million people, about 5 percent of the population, were presumed killed in the make-believe attack. Three of the fifty-three participating cities avoided disaster by assuming that all attacking bombers had been shot down.[60] Eisenhower and 15,000 government employees took refuge at secret locations, but one cabinet member was late because she stopped for lunch before reaching the shelter.[61] Afterward, Eisenhower told high-ranking officials that he was becoming convinced that if nuclear war occurred, the country would have to be run "as one big camp" with complete regimentation.[62] In war's aftermath, experts predicted imposition of martial law,[63] but a report prepared in 1956 concluded that "a massive nuclear attack on the United States resulting in casualties of the order of 50,000,000, without drastically improved preparation of the people, would jeopardize support of the National Government and of the war effort, and might well result in national disintegration."[64] Operation Alert 1956 simulated 15 million deaths,[65] despite Secretary of Defense Charles Wilson's continuing concern that the yearly exercise would "scare a lot of people without purpose."[66] When cabinet members boasted about the drills' efficiency, Eisenhower reminded them that in a real attack, some evacuees would be "absolutely nuts."[67] From a distance of forty years, sociologist Guy Oakes called Operation Alert "an elaborate national sociodrama that combined elements of mobilization for war, disaster relief, the church social, summer camp, and the county fair."[68]

If that first missile were launched, reality would allow little time for saving lives: the government believed that the United States could expect no more than fifteen minutes of warning before a Soviet missile attack hit home.[69] Caught between the desire to save themselves and the fear that no protection existed, Americans felt preparedness was the only answer, but existing civil defense plans seemed like ludicrous attempts to quiet public fears. For example, some planners argued for a new living pattern that would scatter the nation's industrial centers as well as its population to make it harder to wipe out American civilization by attacking its urban centers.[70] However, such a big change in residential patterns was hard to sell and too expensive to implement.

Another conceivable escape plan—evacuating cities at the first threat of war—became impractical as advances in missile technology shrank the anticipated warning time. In addition, the geography of some urban areas made evacuation problematic. For instance, San Francisco, which resides on a peninsula, and Manhattan, which is an island, both offer limited evacuation routes because of the need to use a handful of bridges or tunnels.[71] Evacuation, according to the District of Columbia's civil defense director, was most useful as a bargaining chip with the enemy: if weeks of pre-attack tension allowed time to evacuate, an attack on urban areas would be less useful.[72] However, planners feared that premature evacuation could cut industrial production, creating a shortage of manufactured goods.[73] A third option—building blast-proof underground shelters to house almost 200 million people—was never a serious choice either. For politicians, its cost was too high, and its effectiveness was questionable because experts doubted that any bunker could protect people near a blast site. Only the nuclear weapon's slow and silent killer, radioactive fallout, left an opportunity for saving lives, and whenever possible, officials promoted construction of family shelters. In fact, Eisenhower rejected putting the director of civil defense in the cabinet because he did not want Americans to expect the government to "do it all."[74]

With almost 40 percent of Americans living outside key target areas in towns of fewer than 50,000 people, many could expect to escape blast effects.[75] Therefore, the government embarked on a plan to shelter Americans from fallout and to link the entombed survivors through special radio frequencies. Still, as a pamphlet titled *How to Survive an Atomic Bomb* told readers in 1950, those who rode out a nuclear war in a shelter would have to accept that "things are probably going to look different when you get outside."[76]

In 1959, a booklet produced by the Office of Civil and Defense Mobilization explained the strategy by revealing that an attack on scattered military and civilian targets would blanket virtually the entire East Coast with fallout within twenty-four hours, thanks to west-to-east weather patterns. The booklet urged families to set up underground shielded fallout shelters, allowing ten square feet for each family member.[77] (This advice ignored the reality that while 80 percent of homes in the North had basements, only 10 percent of homes in the South offered underground refuges.)[78] Another guide urged families to turn their homes into shelters by buying a long list of foods, medical supplies, flashlights, and portable radios and making their homes more like "Grandma's Pantry."[79] Officials knew that one nuclear test over the Pacific produced a radioactive cloud large enough to cover an area from Washington, D.C., to Manhattan,[80] and yet, because of government insistence on making civil defense a private initiative, the United States had shelter space to house no more than 1 percent of the population by 1959.[81]

In July 1961, President Kennedy added impetus to the do-it-yourself shelter movement. In a nationally televised address, Kennedy said, "In the event of an attack, the lives of those families which are not hit in a nuclear blast and fire can still be saved if they can be warned to take shelter and if that shelter is available. . . . We owe that kind of insurance to our families and to our country. . . . The time to start is now."[82] Although Kennedy tried to carefully calibrate the speech to avoid setting off a panic, it shocked Americans, generating more than 6,000 letters a day to the federal civil defense agency, more than it usually received in a month.[83]

Two months later, *Life* published a letter from Kennedy urging every family to build a shelter or to guarantee access to one. An accompanying how-to article declared: "As the warlike rattle rolled out of Moscow and as small amounts of fallout from the daily succession of Soviet nuclear tests floated over the U.S., the people woke up to the fact that they ought to be doing something to protect themselves." *Life* warned its readers that nuclear attack would be preceded by a three- to five-minute blast of a warning siren or whistle. They were advised to bury their heads, await the flash that indicates a nuclear blast, count the number of seconds until a shock wave was felt, and divide that number by five to find out how many miles away the bomb had hit. Fallout would travel at a minimum speed of one mile in three minutes, thus allowing time for people to seek better cover if they lived some distance from the bomb site. Only 3 percent of Americans would die in a nuclear attack if Americans took proper precautions, *Life* reassured its readers,[84] but that estimation was based on the assumption that a Soviet attack would be relatively small and limited to military targets, not major cities.[85]

In the spirit of Kennedy's new mobilization, the government forged ahead with scattered efforts. "Prepackaged disaster hospitals" and dry, packaged meals were among the wonders being made for survival, and enterprising merchants sold survival supplies such as air blowers, filters, flashlights, chemical toilets, plastic fallout-protection suits, and first-aid kits.[86] An August 1961 survey promoting civil defense reported finding more than a million family fallout shelters of some kind among 50 million American households;[87] however, later counts suggest that at most, 200,000 families had a shelter area.[88]

By 1961, doomsday preparations were becoming business opportunities. Luxury retailer Hammacher-Schlemmer of New York City sold a $14,000 shelter, with a television and food guaranteed to stay fresh for fifteen years.[89] In December of that year, Dallas hosted a Fallout Survival Show, where 100 exhibitors displayed their wares. The event's organizers assured anxious Cold Warriors that "high officials of our government estimate that 97 out of 100 people can be saved in the event of an atomic attack if advance preparations are adequate." Among the exhibitors were shelter manufacturers, including Peace O' Mind Shelters, Living Inc., and A-One Bomb & Storm Shelter Co.[90]

To bolster family shelters, the Federal Housing Administration made fallout shelters eligible for rehabilitation and home improvement loans, and the Veterans Administration agreed to make direct loans to veterans adding fallout shelters to their homes.[91] The government also gave shelter financing to key radio stations so they could continue broadcasting war news and fallout conditions after an attack.[92]

When the Soviet Union intensified Cold War tensions over Berlin in the last half of 1961, interest in fallout shelters peaked, but even then, a Gallup Poll showed that only 5 percent of Americans claimed to have made the most minimal effort to create shelter space in their homes.[93] By the fall of 1961, the Survey Research Center of the University of Michigan found that only .4 percent of those polled actually had built their own shelter areas. Although congressional appropriations for civil defense jumped 400 percent in August 1961,[94] the idea of family fallout shelters never truly won over the civilian population, and between the fall of 1961 and the spring of 1962, 600 shelter companies failed nationwide.[95] Building such a shelter simply was too costly for many Americans. A prefabricated model sold for $150 but had just a four-foot diameter. More livable shelters cost thousands of dollars.[96] "For most homeowners, the $1,000-and-up price tags on shelters are apparently too steep," *Newsweek* reported in November 1961.[97] Kennedy's ambassador to India, John Kenneth Galbraith, denounced the Defense Department's 1961 booklet promoting expensive shelters. Writing to Kennedy, he said, "The present pamphlet is a design for saving Republicans and sacrificing Democrats. . . . I am not at all attracted by a pamphlet which seeks to save the better elements of the population, but in the main writes off those who voted for you."[98]

In addition, the presence of family shelters raised the unpleasant specter of desperate neighbors attempting to break into a family's shelter, setting neighbor against neighbor in a battle for survival. A Jesuit priest editorialized in the magazine *America* that any man had the right to use violence to protect his family's shelter from encroachment. "Nowhere in the traditional Catholic morality does one read that Christ, in counseling nonresistance to evil[,] rescinded the right of self-defense, which is granted by nature and recognized in the legal systems of all nations," the Rev. L. C. McHugh wrote.[99] Endorsing the every-man-for-himself philosophy and labeling his shelterless neighbors as "stupid," a suburban Chicago homeowner boasted that he would mount a machine gun at his shelter's entrance,[100] and Las Vegas's civil defense director sought 5,000 volunteers to protect Nevada from Californians fleeing nuclear attack.[101] The neighbor-versus-neighbor scenario surfaced in a September 1961 episode of television's *Twilight Zone*. It depicted a neighborhood shattered when people responded to a reported alien attack by trying to break into the block's only private shelter. Although the warning was a false alarm, the event destroyed something precious — the bond tying neighbor to neighbor. Writer Rod Serling summed up the lesson simply: "For civilization to survive, the human race has to remain civilized."[102]

Questions of morality aside, there was rampant skepticism about whether home shelters would save many lives. The American Association for the Advancement of Science's Committee on Science in the Promotion of Human Welfare said that "any shelter system short of one that places the nation's entire population and industry permanently underground can be negated by a corresponding increase in the attacker's power."[103]

Finally, the quality of bunker life raised concern. Eisenhower reportedly had experienced claustrophobia during brief stays in European bunkers during World War II, and in 1961, he admitted, "If I was in the finest shelter in the world all alone, with all my family somewhere else, I just think I'd walk out. I wouldn't want to live in that kind of world."[104] For many, spending at least two weeks underground sounded worse than death.

PUBLIC FALLOUT SHELTERS

Although some historians report that the fallout shelter craze ended after the Berlin crisis, a 1962 Elmo Roper poll revealed support for a public fallout shelter program. Sixty-eight percent of those surveyed favored including shelter space in new buildings; 77 percent backed a federal shelter incentive program encouraging schools and hospitals to provide shelter space; and 86 percent favored stocking shelters in existing buildings.[105]

And by 1962, the Kennedy administration had begun to focus on the gargantuan task of setting up public shelters. What the administration hoped to do was to find space that was either shielded or underground in public buildings, such as office buildings, schools, churches, apartment buildings, and stores. Once shelter spaces were identified, they would be marked and stocked with survival supplies, but implementing the plan was not easy. Locating adequate space for a healthy population would be difficult; however, allowing for the extra space needed to treat victims of radiation sickness made the task more formidable. Outside, many would die, but inside, conditions might be worse, as frightened and sick people wondered about their loved ones. Testifying before members of the Joint Atomic Energy Committee, John Wolfe, an Atomic Energy Commission scientist, painted a grim picture: "I visualize those people unsheltered in heavy fallout areas after three months to be dead, dying, sick, or helpless; those sheltered, if they can psychologically withstand confinement for the period, would emerge to a strange landscape."[106]

McNamara, whose department oversaw civil defense planning in the Kennedy administration, conceded that shelters were not foolproof, because "in a nuclear attack, several million Americans—perhaps several tens of millions—might be killed." He added, "No program of civil defense could save all of these people, at least no program that is financially practicable."[107] However, in the spring of 1962, the Defense Department outlined a $6 billion plan to locate and stock facilities that could serve as public shelters against fallout.[108] Congress allocated only $75 million for fiscal 1963. By October, when the Cuban Missile Crisis occurred, less than a month's work had been invested in this project.

Philadelphia's Independence Hall appears to be lighted by the flames of massive destruction as part of a civil defense drill in 1959. This drill represented one of America's many dress rehearsals for nuclear devastation. *Philadelphia Bulletin* photo, Temple University Libraries, Urban Archives, Philadelphia, Pennsylvania.

Plans for the shelters, largely located in commercial areas, drew opposition from many directions. Some businesses refused to make space available because they wanted to use it for storage or sales. Others worried about unknown insurance consequences. Some people pointed out that shelters seemed likely to save only one part of the population: men.[109] Since many women worked alone at home, they would be less likely to reach a public shelter in time. Children's ability to reach a shelter depended on the location and construction of their schools.

Despite these shortcomings, the effort to provide shelters continued for obvious reasons: a report from the Weapons Systems Evaluation Group showed that if Soviet weapons with the power of 200 megatons hit American cities, there could be 30 million fatalities, even with a fallout shelter system. Twenty million more probably would die without shelters. American scientists predicted that by 1965, enhanced Soviet technology would enable Moscow to order an attack that could kill 80 to 90 percent of the American population without shelters, 50 to 75 percent with shelters.[110] In short, shelters could save more than one-quarter of the population.

Nevertheless, civil defense preparations maintained a helter-skelter reputation. The shortcomings of civilian preparedness were made clear in real-life tests of the system. In 1955, an unidentified squadron of bombers was spotted approaching the California coast and air-raid sirens sounded in Oakland. Despite warning of an attack, most residents took no action because they assumed it was a practice exercise or a mistake.[111] When sirens mistakenly sounded in the early morning of 22 July 1957 in Schenectady, New York, only one family acted, evacuating without appropriately waiting for an order to do so; others, including the mayor, just went back to sleep.[112] Similarly, in 1958, when an incorrect telephone tie-in set off sirens in Washington, D.C., only 4 percent of those who had heard the alarms recalled feeling frightened.[113] However, in September 1959, when air-raid sirens blared one night to celebrate a Chicago White Sox victory that clinched the American League pennant, most of those who heard the sirens admitted to being frightened. Many Chicagoans used telephone lines to confirm the attack—a step that would unnecessarily jam the lines in a real emergency.[114] All in all, these incidents show that Americans were ill-prepared to take advantage of the minimal civil defense options available to them.

There were other gaps in America's use of its advanced technology. More than any weaponry that preceded it, nuclear arms provide the opportunity to launch a devastating war unintentionally. While the fictional madman with his finger on the button offers a grand opportunity for drama, the United States by 1962 had established layer upon layer of procedures to prevent that scenario from coming true; nevertheless, accidents remained possible. For instance, in 1961 when Kennedy took office, he could not find the phone linking him with the command and control system. The reason: Eisenhower had kept the special phone in a desk drawer and when Jacqueline Kennedy chose another desk for her husband, Eisenhower's desk was removed and the phone was disconnected.[115]

In addition, nuclear weaponry was never foolproof. The first atomic bomb tested by the United States one month before Hiroshima had yielded a sixteen-kiloton explosion—four times its anticipated strength. Furthermore, the first air-dropped, multimegaton hydrogen bomb landed almost four miles off target, and in 1962, a range safety officer was forced to destroy three malfunctioning Thor missiles and their warheads when a test went awry.[116]

The Pentagon has acknowledged twenty accidents involving nuclear weapons between 1950 and 1962. The most frightening accident occurred in January 1961, when a crashing B-52 jettisoned two weapons near Goldsboro, North Carolina. Five of the six interlocking safety triggers on one bomb apparently failed, leaving only one to save that spot in rural North Carolina from becoming another Hiroshima.[117]

It seems almost a matter of luck that the United States never stumbled into nuclear war through overzealous emotions, inadequate safety measures, or sheer indifference. America's civil defense programs of the 1950s and 1960s were, in many ways, a product of vivid imaginations that reached only an indifferent audience. Because they were exploring new territory, planners' best hope was to engage in well-informed speculation. Meanwhile, most Americans approached civil defense as many airline passengers respond to the safety instructions at the start of each flight: they listened without giving their full attention because they really did not want to focus on the potential danger implied. And many of their leaders followed the same strategy.

THE IMAGINED FUTURE

Colored by bleak truth and morbid speculation, fiction of the 1950s and 1960s painted a stark portrait of life in the nuclear age and did nothing to assuage the fears of Americans. Some works pictured a dead or dying planet. Others sketched the broad outlines of Earth's long recovery from man's foolish blunders. None offered hope for those uneasy about vague government promises and low spending commitments to Americans' survival.

In 1957, Nevil Shute's *On the Beach* took readers to a dying world, as radiation from a war in the Northern Hemisphere drifted southward and slowly killed the globe's last human inhabitants in Australia. A lone U.S. submarine represented all that was left of America, now a wasteland strewn with death. The sub's crew joined Australians in confronting death—whether their chosen ending came on a racetrack, careening wildly around untenable curves, or at home with the aid of government-issued suicide pills. Two years after the novel's release, a movie based on it offered the planet's epitaph: "The war started when people accepted the idiotic principle that peace could be maintained by arranging to defend themselves with weapons they couldn't possibly use without committing suicide. . . . The devices outgrew us. We couldn't control them."[118] The film distressed the Eisenhower administration. At a cabinet meeting, Special Assistant to the President Karl G. Harr Jr. urged officials to avoid support for its "erroneous themes," such as the idea that a nuclear war in the Northern Hemisphere might create fallout sufficient to kill humans in the Southern Hemisphere.[119] The United States Information Agency produced an "Infoguide," classified until 1994, which urged officials to reassure constituents that nuclear war would never wipe out the planet's entire population.[120] An Office of Defense and Civilian Mobilization official warned, too, that *On the Beach*'s theme of hopelessness might deter civil defense efforts.[121]

During the Cuban Missile Crisis, as man faced his closest brush with nuclear war, excerpts from *Fail-Safe* by Eugene Burdick and Harvey Wheeler appeared in the *Saturday Evening Post*. This thriller explores whether the atomic bomb had become more powerful than man—like a monster freed from its cage, now impossible to restrain. "We're at the mercy of our monster and we are at the mercy of theirs," one character proclaims. "They toy with us as the Olympian gods toyed with the Greeks. And like the gods of Greek tragedy, they have a tragic flaw. They know only how to destroy, not how to save."[122] As the plot unfolds, U.S. bombers, out of touch with their base, mistakenly destroy Moscow, and the president makes a stunning peace agreement: he sends U.S. bombers to obliterate New York City, killing thousands, including his own wife. This novel was inspired by real-life concerns. Much to Eisenhower's dismay, a 1958 Pentagon news leak outlined the elaborate safety mechanisms in place to avoid miscommunication with U.S. bombers.[123] Although the military precautions in place in the early 1960s should have made accidental war impossible, the novel raised Americans' awareness of the possibilities.

Seven Days in May by Fletcher Knebel and Charles Bailey, which ranked number two on the *New York Times* best-seller list at the crisis's start, offered a different Cold War parable: military men plot a coup when the president makes a peace pact with the Soviets. Again, nuclear arms add a sense of doom. "Civilization can go with a moan and a whimper overnight. Everybody knows it. But how can an individual feel anything but helpless?" the president asks. "He can't grab a rifle and rush out to defend his country. He probably can't even help much by joining the Navy and serving on a missile submarine. He'd know that if we ever got an order to fire, it would mean that his home was probably already a pile of ashes—or would be in 15 minutes."[124]

Mordecai Roshwald's 1959 novel, *Level 7*, describes the destruction of human life by missiles launched from deep underground shelters. In these tombs, pushing the button to fire weapons becomes almost routine and can be done without emotion by flesh-and-blood automatons forced to abandon their humanity. Leaders tell the bunkers' residents that they will remain safe, and in hundreds of years when radiation subsides, their progeny will repopulate Earth's surface. At first, the entombed feel trapped, then bored, and finally fortunate. However, scientific advancement has led the way to suicide: all die, and, ironically, the last to perish is the man who thoughtlessly has obeyed orders by pushing the buttons that kill mankind.

Another 1959 novel, Walter M. Miller Jr.'s *A Canticle for Leibowitz*, envisions Earth in nuclear war's aftermath. For centuries, there is only barren land and water. A primitive society of loners has outlawed the literacy that led to such devastation, but gradually, scholarship reemerges. Almost inevitably, mankind again unleashes nuclear war. Only slightly more optimistic was Pat Frank's *Alas, Babylon*, in which the United States wins the war but a band of Floridian survivors battle with primitive, horrifying conditions to survive.

As the medium of television developed, it, too, sought to open a window into a dark future. In October 1959, *The Twilight Zone* foresaw a world in which a lone man survives nuclear war by an accident of fate. A bank teller, Henry Bemis, lives because he has closeted himself in a bank vault during lunch so he can read, a beloved pastime discouraged by both his wife and his supervisor. When Bemis emerges, he is devastated by the destruction until he finds the wreckage of a library. Gleefully, he sorts through books, mapping out his future through the pages of literature; however, a small accident—the destruction of his eyeglasses in a place no longer populated by optometrists—ends his literary exploration of the now-dead world.[125]

Helplessness and fear permeated portrayals of nuclear war and cast a shadow over American society—not as a constant topic for conversation but as an unending threat hovering in the background of daily life. Children absorbed its meaning before they learned to read. In the American home, televised tests of civil defense broadcast frequencies made nuclear war a part of family life. Like people living for generations near a long-dormant volcano, Americans proceeded from day to day with the realization that tomorrow their world might melt away.

GRIM EXPECTATIONS

How ready were most Americans for war? Between 1945 and 1948, the percentage of them expecting a third world war grew from 32 to 73 percent,[126] and a 1956 survey of college students showed that more than 70 percent considered another world war likely. Eighty percent of those young Americans expected war within ten years. Only slightly more than 60 percent of the students believed they would survive such a war, and only a small percentage of those said they felt certain of that.[127] Nevertheless, because nuclear war remained unthinkable to many, fear was by no means unanimously felt. A 1961 American Institute of Public Opinion survey showed that while 59 percent of Americans were very worried or fairly worried about nuclear war, 38 percent of those polled described themselves as "not worried at all."[128] However, a pilot study in mid-1962 showed that more than 50 percent of the residents of a small midwestern college town believed that nuclear war would destroy most of civilization.[129] Whether they were in denial or convinced that nothing could save them, civilians enabled government officials to opt for a cheap, shallow, and ineffective shell game that offered little protection. Few politicians seemed willing to tell voters that this sort of civil defense would save a proportionately small number of lives.

For those civilians unable to cope with the idea of nuclear holocaust, *Esquire* offered an escape in its January 1962 issue: experts named nine locations as safe hideaways. These sites were chosen because of their distance from targets, their position in west-to-east weather patterns, and their willingness to accept immigrants. Eureka, California, was the only U.S. site to make the list. Other winners were Cork, Ireland; Guadalajara, Mexico; the central valley of Chile; Mendoza, Argentina; Belo Horizonte, Brazil; Tananarive, Madagascar; Melbourne, Australia; and Christchurch, New Zealand.[130]

For those who planned to ride out a nuclear war, the odds of having good government leadership or stable finances were not good. The federal government planned to guarantee its own survival through a vast communications network, but officials expected they would need at least a month to regain control after an assault. Eight regional government shelters were readied to keep federal agencies at work across the country. Smaller relocation sites also were planned. In fact, by 1961, thirty federal agencies already were at work round-the-clock in some alternative offices.[131] In what truly would be a capitalist's worst nightmare, the government planned to reallocate American wealth after nuclear war. Heavy taxes were on the drawing boards to finance reconstruction, and the government intended to take the property of those who died without heirs. Neither businesses nor individuals would lose money deposited in destroyed banks: the Federal Reserve System had stockpiled cash around the nation and planned to operate through a regional bank. Debtors would not be excused from repaying loans, but creditors could not foreclose on war victims. The insurance industry inevitably would go bankrupt because claims would exceed company holdings.[132] Businesses were expected to avoid decimation in part because about 400 corporations and governments kept duplicate records in the Western States Atomic Vault.[133]

For those who dared to investigate the details, there were grisly realities for Cold Warriors to absorb. A government drill using Univac computer projections allowed the Office of Emergency Planning's National Resource Evaluation Center to predict on 1 October 1962, just three weeks before the Cuban Missile Crisis, what would have happened if the Soviet Union had launched a massive attack against the United States on 21 September 1962. In a forty-eight-hour attack, 355 nuclear weapons would strike. In this exercise of wishful thinking, the hypothetical Soviets would reduce casualty figures by targeting military sites over cities, but about fifty urban centers nevertheless would suffer some blast damage. Despite fallout, most areas would be accessible within two days. Fifteen days after the attack, more than 164 million people would be counted as survivors, but 34.8 million would lack a water source. Military casualties would be high, and both air and naval operations would be severely hurt by losses of personnel and equipment. Nationwide, 2.6 million hospital beds would be needed to treat casualties, but only 1.1 million would exist. About 75 percent of the industrial workforce would survive, while 48 percent of pre-attack industrial production facilities would be either lost or seriously damaged. Most survivors would have telephone service, but no route would be intact for transcontinental or north-south traffic. Heavy damage to radio stations would leave some areas with little or no daytime coverage, and radiation and blast effects would make it impossible for twenty-five state governments to function in their capitals for at least ninety days.[134]

Against this backdrop of fears and hopes, John F. Kennedy and Nikita Khrushchev confronted each other over Cuba. Wary Americans contemplated the ghosts of Hiroshima as they faced the two superpowers' flirtation with mutual destruction. And they knew they were not ready.

bunker mentality

I am afraid that we are living in times when we don't have much time.—Pierre Salinger, 26 October 1962 News Conference (the statement was quickly taken off the record)

Most accounts of the Cuban Missile Crisis offer a familiar view of Kennedy and his advisers rationally working toward a consensus on how to oust Soviet missiles from Cuba without provoking a war; however, recently de-classified documents on the nation's civil defense preparations tell a different story. What emerges is a clear sense of a bureaucracy on the verge of panic as it confronted a problem too huge to fathom—the immediate threat of nuclear war in a nation poorly prepared to endure an attack on its own soil. While military preparations proceeded with a decent level of efficiency and foresight if not total consistency, planning to preserve the civilian government and the civilian population was haphazard and, in some cases, almost comical.

As administration officials struggled to convey a sense of preparedness to a worried public, they confronted challenges on several fronts. Planning for continuity of government was incomplete and unrealistic. In addition, public fallout shelters, which lacked necessities such as food, medical supplies, and identifying signs, could house less than half of the population.

Early in the crisis, Kennedy asked his two emergency-planning agencies, the Defense Department's Office of Civil Defense and the Office of Emergency Planning (OEP) to enhance the existing state of readiness.[1] However, White House tapes show that Kennedy invested most of his time in weighing military and diplomatic solutions, allocating surprisingly little attention to civil defense—a possible sign that he did not believe civil defense could save many Americans if the crisis became the trigger for World War III. As he attempted to bolster civil defense in 1961, he had given the Office of Civil Defense and the Office of Emergency Planning separate missions: the Office of Civil Defense took responsibility for protection of the population, while the White House's Office of Emergency Planning handled government planning and operations for any kind of emergency, including natural disasters and nuclear wars—an arrangement that inevitably led to time-consuming conflicts and overlapping efforts. Thus, as officials tried to reformulate outdated plans, organizational rivalries threatened to make a difficult situation impossible.[2]

In many ways, the administration found itself in a dilemma of its own creation. The U.S. threat to the Soviet Union was self-evident: remove your missiles from Cuba or expect an attack. Yet, JFK had to know that the United States was not ready for the war he had risked starting. As a realist, he probably considered it impossible to be prepared for such a conflagration, but he also must have recognized that U.S. precautions had not reached even minimally acceptable levels.

Despite intensified activities prompted by the crisis, an Office of Emergency Planning memorandum admitted, "The vulnerability of emergency operating centers, tenuous transportation plans for relocation of employees, and dependence on adequate advance warning pose tremendous threats to our continuity-of-government capability."[3] At the same time, drastic moves to bolster public shelters left millions unprotected. In short, the government was extremely susceptible to devastating losses and chaos in a massive surprise attack, and even with warning, millions would have no chance of survival.

During the crisis, ragged nerves set the tone as gaping holes in government preparedness became obvious. Some agencies expressed dismay because they were unable to stock and equip shelter areas using already-appropriated funds; others complained that emergency shelters provided inadequate space and fallout protection.[4] Often, officials found themselves trapped between the need to make immediate upgrades and the desire to avoid creating a panic. Therefore, Office of Emergency Planning officials advised regional workers that "the present situation calls for a review of readiness and not for substantial public actions to improve readiness,"[5] and Kennedy told civil defense officials not to place state or local programs on alert.[6]

Working on three fronts, the government prepared for war. First, steps to preserve the government required re-examination. Second, the military raised its alert status to bolster its ability to move quickly. Third, the government sought to improve the protection available to civilians. All three areas demonstrated troubling problems in the United States' readiness for war.

SCENARIOS FOR SURVIVAL

Merging brutal reality with the miraculous potential of science fiction, intricate scenarios promised to save the U.S. government in nuclear war. Just as the military had strategies for launching attacks, the civilian government had plans for surviving them. According to defense outlines, if U.S. radar provided only a few minutes of warning that enemy aircraft or missiles soon would hit Washington, the president would take shelter in the White House bunker, and the military would spring into action to rescue him. Outpost Mission, a special group of helicopter pilots and rescue workers from Olmstead Air Force Base in Pennsylvania, would travel to Washington after the attack to dig through the rubble, break into the bunker, and transport the president to a safer location. Extensive destruction might make locating the president difficult, but disaster planners believed that the rescuers had the heavy equipment needed to extricate the chief executive.[7] (In a never-never-land view of a postattack capital, the strategists left little room for the truth that a hydrogen bomb attack on Washington probably would kill the president, even if he was in the White House bunker—obviously a recognized fact because a great deal of money had been invested in building deeper bunkers outside the metropolitan area.) If the government received hours or days of warning before an attack, plans called for military helicopters to pick up the president and other key officials on the White House's South Lawn[8] and transport them to Mount Weather, a bunker hidden away in the Virginia mountains, or to an unidentified ship at sea.

Neither plan allowed for the possibility that an attack might elude U.S. radar, which is what would have occurred if the Soviet Union had attacked from Cuba early in the crisis, when no U.S. radar units scanned southern skies.[9] In reality, there could be little certainty of anyone's survival in a war powered by weapons of mass destruction. Thus, a report written four months before the crisis warned that "the survival of the presidency could be in doubt during a critical decision-making period if the elected president were lost, since all eligible successors normally live and work in the Washington, D.C., area and could be casualties of the same attack."[10]

Even if the president reached a bunker, he faced governing a devastated nation from an underground prison.[11] Many citizens would be dead, dying, wounded, or ill. Even those far from enemy targets might experience radiation sickness and almost certainly would find themselves cut off from the national economy and from the media that helped to generate a sense of American identity. In the days after the attack, fallout would keep the president and other leaders marooned in reinforced tombs while panic and chaos gripped an apparently leaderless land.

Life underground would not be easy. Mount Weather was a 434-acre site located forty-eight miles from Washington. The facility contained twenty office buildings, a hospital, dining and recreation areas, sleeping quarters, reservoirs of drinking and cooling water, an emergency power plant, a radio and television studio hooked up to the Emergency Broadcasting System, and—ominously—a crematorium. This superbunker could accommodate 200 people for up to thirty days.[12] Constructed between 1954 and 1958, Mount Weather offered private rooms for the president, cabinet members, and Supreme Court justices, but other government employees could expect barrackslike conditions. Because Kennedy suffered from back injuries, officials installed a therapeutic mattress in the presidential living area, and since stress reactions could be expected among officials holed-up in a shelter buried under 600 feet of stone, the bunker was stocked with sedatives and included a padded isolation cell.[13] During a war, leaders at Mount Weather could follow military actions above ground using the Bomb Alarm System, sensors on telephone poles strategically placed near ninety-nine cities and military installations. These sensors would alert officials to nuclear blasts around the nation. With a design guided by wishful thinking, the alarm network was dependent on continued commercial telephone and telegraph service to register nuclear detonations and could be incapacitated by power outages.[14]

The congressional bunker, buried 720 feet in a hillside under the Greenbrier resort in White Sulphur Springs, West Virginia, could house 1,100 members of Congress and staff members for up to sixty days and could withstand a modest nuclear blast fifteen to thirty miles away, thanks to its underground location and its twenty-five-ton doors.[15] Two large rooms within the bunker would serve as House and Senate chambers, while other areas would be assigned to staffers so that lawmakers could try to stay in touch with their surviving constituents. The daunting task of moving 1,100 people from Washington to a small town in West Virginia was no less onerous than solving the conflicts likely to arise when four members of Congress were assigned to a cubicle with two sets of bunk beds. Sixty-two dormitory residents would share six showers and toilets. Meal options would include dehydrated foods, and residents would eat in a dining room with an intentionally dizzying floor pattern, installed to discourage diners from lingering beyond assigned mealtimes. All residents would receive a uniform consisting of military fatigues and tennis shoes. An incinerator would dispose of all refuse, including corpses. Hospital facilities would be available for physical and psychiatric care, and a well-stocked weapons room would house explosives, guns, and riot batons to maintain order.[16]

While the protection and relocation of the nation's leaders remained in doubt, schemes for moving more than 1,000 other government employees to relocation sites were even less certain. Organizers assigned pick-up points to staffers, but reasonable questions remained about their ability to reach those sites when an attack was imminent or already under way. As a result, the workers who were needed to govern a war-ravaged nation had little chance of surviving a surprise attack.

Beyond saving key officials, federal evacuation plans encompassed the rescue of cultural treasures. Planners assigned certain officials to save priceless documents and works of art by moving them to a bunker that included vault areas. The National Gallery of Art also owned a windowless $550,000 facility at Randolph-Macon Woman's College in Lynchburg, Virginia, which would offer a safe haven for works of art, carried there by two-and-a-half-ton trucks.[17]

To govern from an underground tomb, the elected president—or the highest ranking surviving person in the chain of command[18]—would need a sophisticated communications system to allow contacts with other nations' leaders and to receive reports on weather, firestorms, and air traffic. Consequently, establishment of an advanced communications network was a high priority;[19] however, if communications failed or the federal government ceased operations, each governor possessed authority to take necessary actions to maintain order and aid survivors.[20]

While these plans sound truly tenuous, the reality that existed in 1962 was even worse. U.S. leaders had never faced the problems involved in relocating government. State leaders could act as backups if the U.S. government was wiped out by surprise attack. However, state officials, too, were vulnerable, and they relied on the U.S. government for needs like civil defense supplies.

THE REAL WORLD IN 1962

In October 1962, when federal officials took a hard look at continuity-of-government plans, they saw a cascade of problems. Most plans required advance warning before attack; some departmental policies were out of date and did not conform with current staffing and equipment needs; guidelines designated some staff members and consultants to be evacuated too late; many officials did not understand the levels of military alert status; communications at relocation sites were inadequate; some relocation sites lacked fallout protection; no plan existed to maintain computer resources; and some of the individuals slated to move into bunkers were reluctant to leave their families unprotected. Although the existing guidelines had many weaknesses, the administration did not have time to devise new procedures. In fact, the time constraints imposed by the fear of imminent nuclear war forced officials to grapple with the materials at hand and seek the most realistic responses to current circumstances.

Some high-ranking officials immediately left Washington to guarantee that a nuclear strike would not eliminate all top officials in any agency.[21] The Office of Emergency Planning asked all departments and agencies to plan for a civil defense buildup under the assumption that the crisis would last up to six months,[22] but agencies did not have the luxury of a well-reasoned planning process. They had to identify procedural snags and act to resolve them immediately.

Long-standing plans called for relocating small cadres of government staffers to safe areas only when the entire military instituted DEFCON (defense condition) 2, which was one step away from war; however, recognizing the many weaknesses in preparations and realizing that missiles fired from Cuba would hit their targets with little warning, officials began exploring the possibility of accelerating that schedule by starting relocations while still at DEFCON 3. Consequently, the Office of Emergency Planning asked each agency to plan for that contingency.[23]

With government workers on pins and needles, maintaining calm and executing evacuation procedures in an orderly fashion were difficult tasks. Within twenty-four hours of Kennedy's announcement of the blockade, two agencies—the Civil Service Commission and the Department of the Interior —reported receiving the heart-pounding news that the military as a whole had adopted DEFCON 2 status, though later investigations could find no source of those false alarms.[24] At the same time, some agencies surrendered to an overpowering sense of urgency and a lack of readiness by violating guidelines and prematurely placing staffers in relocation facilities. The Small Business Administration, for instance, reassigned four workers to a relocation site, and without consulting the Office of Emergency Planning, the Department of Labor expanded its special facility staff with an expert on wage stabilization and another on manpower issues.[25]

In all, the government had ninety-three prearranged evacuation sites within a 300-mile range of Washington.[26] In addition to having a specified number of reserved spaces in an underground relocation facility, each agency had a mandate to maintain its own relocation site at some distance from Washington. The Department of Agriculture's relocation plan was typical: it called for three employees to take shelter in one of the large government bunkers and three more to travel to the department's own emergency site.[27] Such evacuation obviously would preserve only a skeletal government, but that was the most planners expected.

In many cases, those relocation sites did not provide special fallout protection, a detail that did not seem critical until war became a real possibility. During the crisis, the Department of the Interior startled the Office of Emergency Planning by revealing that it had given up its relocation site and had nowhere to house workers who were to be assigned there.[28] Clearly, up until this point, continuity-of-government planning had lacked realism.

With the immediate possibility of war, some Kennedy administration staff members and their secretaries slept in the bomb shelter beneath the White House during the crisis.[29] Meanwhile, the Office of Emergency Planning adopted round-the-clock shifts in Washington and in its regional offices,[30] urged employees to reevaluate out-of-town engagements,[31] and granted unlimited overtime.[32] In preparation for evacuation, the government gave special identification cards to federal employees designated to assume wartime duty assignments.[33]

The overnight journal written by Office of Emergency Planning officials offers a window into a confused and confusing world. On the night of 22 October, when Kennedy delivered his address, an official of the Railroad Retirement Board called at 8:35 P.M. to say "Civil Defense" had phoned and given him a code word, and he wanted to know whether he should go to his office, where his code words were locked up, to find out what it meant. After some checking, the officer on duty, Ralph E. Spear, confirmed that the mystery call had been the board's official notification that the military had gone to a DEFCON 3 status. At 10:10 P.M., a United Press International reporter called seeking details on still-unwritten plans for rationing. Five minutes later, Spear learned that the Office of Civil Defense and the Office of Emergency Planning feverishly were seeking the same preparedness information from state agencies and regional federal offices, thus creating a bureaucratic overload when duplicated effort could cause a disastrous loss of time. Shortly after midnight, Spear got word that while staffers in the Office of Emergency Planning had upgraded their alert status to DEFCON 3, officials in the Office of Civil Defense were not changing operational status because they believed DEFCON 3 did not apply to the civilian government.[34]

And at 4:50 A.M., a regional OEP official called asking for clarification on the need to clear all statements through the federal office and expressed concern about lack of fallout protection at regional relocation sites.[35] Questions, both answerable and unanswerable, embattled the Office of Emergency Planning with little time before nuclear war might begin.

While Washington mobilized, workers in the large federal bunkers prepared for the possibility that important guests might arrive soon. Most records of what happened in these bunkers during the crisis are still classified or lost,[36] but a few documents provide insights. One still partially classified 1964 report provides a day-by-day account of events at an unnamed bunker, apparently Mount Weather because the site's director, J. Leo Bourassa, authored the document. Within minutes of JFK's 22 October speech, the facility adopted DEFCON 3 status, and supervisors called key personnel to their stations to begin making the bunker ready for "the arrival of emergency assignees."[37] Officials ordered enhanced staffing and the relocation of "medical cadre" workers to emergency duty stations. In all, the Office of Emergency Planning called about 150 key staff people and representatives of other agencies to the facility.[38] The next day, an employee assigned to Emergency News Service Duty[39] moved into quarters in the bunker. On 26 October, to fine-tune communications from the site, the Defense Communications Agency ordered lowering the volume level of electronically transmitted uncoded messages to reduce the possibility of Soviet or Cuban interception, and, the following day, officials devised potential DEFCON 2 personnel reassignments.[40]

In another partially declassified document, officials at an unidentified bunker sought added military support and asked for chaplains to address the prospective occupants' spiritual needs. That document reviewed available recreational and exercise equipment, as well as plans for group calisthenics. In addition, it identified detention rooms set aside for both men and women.[41]

Inside and outside the bunkers, communication issues bedeviled the administration. Work was under way to connect one undisclosed federal relocation facility—probably Mount Weather—with the four major broadcast networks in Washington and New York, and with ten Washington radio stations, which would serve as broadcast outlets for national leaders driven underground. (Of course, this plan could have proven problematic if both the president and vice president had been killed, leaving the new president—the former Speaker of the House—in the congressional bunker in West Virginia.) To disseminate national news, workers installed a teletype connection tying the National News Center within the bunker with the headquarters of the Associated Press and United Press International in New York, as well as both agencies' Atlanta regional offices. Arrangements for the Atlanta connection apparently reflected concern about possible destruction of the New York offices in an attack. Officials also planned to tie one relocation site to FM radio stations in Washington's periphery to assure that communication with the capital area would not be lost even if an attack disrupted transmissions from the city itself.[42]

Unraveling wartime transportation issues kept the Office of Emergency Transportation and the Maritime Administration in almost continuous meetings throughout the crisis, and the Federal Aviation Agency, the Interstate Commerce Commission, the Bureau of Public Roads, the Civil Aeronautics Board, and the Maritime Administration assumed alert status.[43] At the same time, the Office of Emergency Planning encountered travel problems of its own. Many key officials were traveling when the crisis broke, making it difficult to execute emergency plans. Office of Emergency Planning officials quickly identified a problem that had eluded them until then: government officials needed some kind of special credentials to give them "high travel priority" in an emergency.[44]

To bolster the government's wartime workforce, federal officials alerted members of the 2,800-person "executive reserve," a group of former government employees who would be called into service in an emergency. These experts would serve as consultants on such previously unaddressed issues as rationing and price controls.[45] Procedures stated that all of these reservists should be notified at DEFCON 2 that their services would be required at DEFCON I, but when faced with a real crisis and obvious gaps in preparedness, officials acknowledged that they needed the services of some reservists before war and called them in under DEFCON 3.[46]

During the crisis, administration officials also worked with regional offices to make sure measures were in hand to preserve federal operations within the states and territories. The crisis's urgency brought to light significant shortcomings in regional planning for alternative sites of government. For instance, there was no consistent provision made for communication between relocation sites;[47] therefore, officials might survive, but they would have no way of coordinating action. In addition, the OEP's contacts with government agencies' regional offices in the Northwest revealed that at least half were unaware of the DEFCON stages' meanings, and besides the Federal Reserve Branch Bank in Seattle, which planned to turn its basement vaults into shelters, only one regional office had its own relocation site.[48]

"In the absence of any funds to the individual agencies, none is equipped to establish emergency communications, to secure a relocation area in which operating records can be cached, or to take other measures which would enable the agency to move quickly and resume some form of operation in a relatively secure area," a regional OEP report declared.[49] At the same time, the Office of Emergency Planning learned that its own regional offices had a vulnerability: no encrypting capacity to allow for secure communications between regional offices in wartime.[50]

The federal government attempted to guide state and local governments to achieve self-preservation, too.[51] While the Office of Civil Defense helped states to refine plans for sheltering the public, the Office of Emergency Planning reviewed governmental lines of succession, evaluated the adequacy of plans for records relocation and preservation plans, and supported establishment of emergency operating centers. Officials also worked with a Council of State Governments task force to review state laws from previous wars and draft necessary postwar recovery legislation.[52]

The biggest task in maintaining continuity of government—federal government evacuation—remained the highest priority because civilian leadership was necessary to supervise the military during war and to restore order afterward. As a result, federal officials tinkered with the mechanics of transporting the nation's leaders, a process fraught with complications.[53] Planners assigned new evacuation pick-up points to congressional leaders and the Supreme Court,[54] and they worked out new logistical arrangements for Vice President Lyndon Johnson. A military helicopter was to pick up the easily identifiable vice president at any one of eighteen sites in the Washington area, including such public locations as the Athletic Field at American University, the traffic circle on the Virginia side of Memorial Bridge, and the parking lot at D.C. Stadium.[55] The laughable nature of such plans is clear when one imagines how Washingtonians trapped in rush-hour traffic and aware of a threatening international crisis would respond to seeing a helicopter swoop down and pick up the vice president from a traffic circle.

As the U.S. government edged closer to evacuation, difficult choices awaited the few individuals with places in government bunkers. On 25 October, these people got official word that relocation of their dependents was their own responsibility.[56] Almost two years earlier, Kennedy's top aides had received their introduction to evacuation plans, and presidential press secretary Pierre Salinger recalled later what he learned: "If the order ever comes for you to evacuate with the president, you'll face the toughest thing you've ever had to do in your life. You're going to have to tell your family,

'Goodbye—you're on your own.'"[57] After one such briefing, an aide privately told Kennedy that he did not believe he could abandon his family, and to his surprise, the president responded, "That's OK. Neither do I. I'm staying right here."[58] (In fact, during the crisis, JFK advised his wife to take their two children and leave town for the weekend, as the wives of some cabinet members had done; however, Jacqueline Kennedy chose to stay with her husband.)[59] Beyond sentimentality, there was another side to the evacuation issue. As Dean Rusk later wrote, "I am convinced that government leaders . . . are simply not going to say good-bye to their colleagues and possibly their own families and then board a helicopter and whirl away to some cave. Even if we did, and if the president and secretary of state survived . . . the first band of shivering survivors who got hold of them would likely hang them from the nearest tree."[60]

To allay officials' personal misgivings, the administration quietly worked out plans during the crisis to move evacuees' families to safe locations, but the exodus of these families would not be inconspicuous. All family members would rendezvous at the Reno Reservoir, just off the Washington beltway, and evacuate the capital via motorcade. Obviously, this scenario created the possibility that dependents would become trapped in a traffic jam of confused and frightened people, but it offered some solace to government employees.[61]

On 26 October, Office of Emergency Planning director Edward A. McDermott met with Supreme Court chief justice Earl Warren to review plans for the Supreme Court's evacuation to Mount Weather. McDermott urged Warren to be aware of the justices' locations throughout the crisis. He also asked Warren to consider whether the court needed its extensive records in the bunker. McDermott's apparent point was that the court might not need the ability to remain fully functional during or immediately after a nuclear war.[62] Thus, the highest court in the land and the highest ranking component of the government's judicial branch might be rendered ineffective because the task of moving its records was too daunting for a government caught unprepared.

The following day, Kennedy urged those who had been living in the White House all week to go home for the night.[63] The United States and the Soviet Union appeared to be sliding into war on 27 October. An American pilot had been killed, and Kennedy was frustrated by receiving conflicting signals from the Kremlin. Pierre Salinger recalled many years later. "I went home that night for the first time, and, I often thought, for the last time—as I walked out of the White House, I was handed a sealed envelope, and I was told to give it to my wife and to tell her that the next day, if I disappeared—because if there had been a military situation, the White House would have disappeared into a security place—that she was to open this envelope which would tell her where to take her children and herself to be safe."[64]

Fortunately, that prospect never became reality. The Soviet Union agreed the next day to remove the missiles, and a day later, all departments reported that, if necessary, they could begin dispatching employees to bunkers.[65] That move would allow relocated workers to tackle some of the issues that remained unresolved. Perhaps after a few more weeks, some important issues would have been resolved and others would have been set aside and acknowledged to be unsolvable. Still, as a 1958 White House memo had predicted, "Government which goes on with some kind of continuity will be like a one-eyed man in the land of the blind."[66] Clearly, if the attack had come 27 October, as many had feared it would, continuity of the government would have been a grand ambition that remained unfulfillable.

MILITARY MOVES AND MISHAPS

When two nations are poised for battle, the slightest misstep can have tragic results. Heightened states of alert can worsen chances for disaster. While the Strategic Air Command moved to DEFCON 2 and the rest of the military stood at DEFCON 3, Kennedy did not order forces in Europe to DEFCON 3, but some individual commanders followed that course anyway. And although the United States conceded internally that the Jupiter missiles in Turkey and Italy were outmoded, the U.S. Air Forces Europe raised all missiles to a heightened state of readiness.[67] Despite U.S. law and official policy, which required separate storage of their warheads, Thor and Jupiter missiles in Great Britain, Italy, and Turkey already were armed with nuclear warheads.[68]

The Strategic Air Command made its shift in DEFCON status "in the clear" without permission from the White House or Pentagon, so the Soviet Union was aware of the U.S. alert status.[69] Soviet and Cuban military forces, as well as those of their allies in the Warsaw Pact nations, also adopted higher alert statuses, although it is difficult to say how high an alert they reached.[70] By 22 October, all of the nuclear warheads for the medium-range missiles and nearly 100 more for other weapons had reached Cuba.[71] Also among Soviet hardware were IL-28 bombers capable of striking targets such as Cape Canaveral, New Orleans, or Mexico City.[72]

At all times during the crisis, sixty American B-52s were airborne, with fifty-two carrying 196 nuclear weapons. On the ground, 271 B-52s and 340

With the scent of war in the air, the army recruiting station in Miami processes Cuban exiles volunteering for military service on the day after President Kennedy's speech announcing a naval blockade of Cuba. © Bettmann/CORBIS.

B-47s were on alert, as well as 136 Atlas and Titan missiles. The Strategic Air Command kept 1,962 weapons in the air or capable of being in the air within fifteen minutes.[73] The bomber alert alone required 20,000 officers and airmen on combat crews to remain at their alert stations for four weeks. It also affected 100,000 SAC aircraft and missile maintenance personnel, 20,000 security police, and 6,000 refueling specialists.[74] Strategic Air Command crews worked long hours, with eighty-hour work weeks becoming the norm.[75] Secretary of Defense Robert McNamara canceled all SAC leaves and recalled men already on leave.[76]

Twenty-four hours before institution of the blockade, twenty-six Soviet and Eastern bloc ships reportedly were en route to Cuba. Within twenty-four hours, however, sixteen had turned back. While the Pentagon had vowed to "use force if necessary to halt" ships,[77] confrontations unfolded differently. Official accounts indicated that the first ship to pass through the quarantine line was the *Bucharest*, a Soviet tanker obviously not carrying weapons parts.[78] However, according to Gen. David Burchinal, then working for air force chief of staff Curtis LeMay, the first ship to reach the quarantine line was a Swedish vessel that ignored the signal to stop. Under Pentagon orders,

As part of the Cuban Missile Crisis's military mobilization, U.S. Air Force troop carrier planes arrive at Miami International Airport on 22 October 1962. Massive numbers of men had to be moved to man the blockade and to prepare for a possible invasion of Cuba. © Bettmann/CORBIS.

the navy let it pass without inspection, he said. On 26 October, under the direction of McNamara, the navy stopped the *Marucla*, a ship of Lebanese registry contracted to carry Soviet supplies to Cuba and unlikely to be carrying missile parts. Five men from two U.S. destroyers boarded the ship. They found no missiles parts, but they did discover electronic military gear.[79] Nevertheless, the navy cleared the ship to cross the blockade line.[80] Ironically, at the same time peace advocates believed that the Kennedy administration was unnecessarily heightening tensions by enforcing the blockade, high-ranking military officials were dismayed by the administration's great efforts to avoid conflict, as well as its micromanagement of the military operation. White House tapes of deliberations during the crisis show LeMay himself declaring that the blockade was "almost as bad as the appeasement at Munich."[81] Afterward, looking back at the crisis, Gen. Leon W. Johnson said that administration officials "were very good at putting out brave words, but they didn't do a bloody thing to back them up."[82]

Although the administration sought to avoid potentially provocative actions by the military, the navy engaged in a dangerous game of hide-

and-seek with Soviet nuclear submarines, some of which were armed with nuclear torpedoes, without the White House's knowledge. Near the ninety-ship quarantine line,[83] navy ships and planes detected and tracked two submarines, ultimately forcing them to surface.[84] U.S. ships also located and targeted Soviet submarines in other parts of the world.[85]

Since Soviets continued to work on readying the missiles in Cuba, planning for an invasion and air strikes remained essential. A complete amphibious task force of U.S. Marines was at sea in the Caribbean by 28 October.[86] McNamara had told the Ex Comm that invasion preparations would take seven days because of the need to move more army and marine units across the nation. Such an incursion would require the aid of more than 100 merchant ships.[87] Invasion plans called for three waves of 100 fighter bombers to cross the Caribbean at an altitude of only fifty feet so that they would not be visible on radar until they ascended to 1,500 feet over Cuba. Their goal was to obliterate missile sites and runways that Soviet bombers could use.[88] The Pentagon expected 90,000 men to land, while 250,000 men would take part in the overall operation.[89] Marine logistical support anticipated fifteen days of combat.[90] The largest drop of paratroopers since the 1944 invasion of Normandy would have been the invasion's centerpiece. The Pentagon estimated that 18,500 Americans would die[91] and that U.S. forces would take 50,000 prisoners.[92]

For marines in the potential invasion force, information was scarce. Vincent Maggio, then twenty-two, recalls, "We left not knowing where we were going or what it was all about. We almost knew nothing. . . . Then, it came down to the nitty-gritty where we were all lined up in the proper formation where the helicopters were ready. All you heard was the helicopters and the chaplain came over, over the air, and blessed us all and wished us the best of luck." By then aware that Cuba was the target, Maggio believed an invasion was imminent, and suddenly, "everything shut down . . . the motors went quiet—the ship, the helicopters—and it was all over."[93] Khrushchev's withdrawal of the missiles brought a sudden, unexpected reprieve.

During the crisis, with so many units on alert, several incidents within the U.S. military came close to sparking accidental war. The military's biggest single mistake during the week occurred on 26 October, when Maj. Charles Maultsby, a U-2 pilot making a transpolar reconnaissance flight on a new route, strayed into Soviet airspace. As soon as the blip appeared on Soviet radar screens, MiG-interceptors took off. Maultsby called a U.S. base on an unscrambled frequency to explain his predicament. He received orders to return to U.S. airspace as quickly as possible, but the pilot soon realized that he was running out of fuel and losing altitude. U.S. interceptors launched from Galena Air Force Base in western Alaska to escort the U-2 to safety and keep the Soviet planes out of U.S. airspace. The American interceptors, which carried nuclear missiles, met the U-2 over the Bering Straits and guided it to safety.[94] That same day, U-2 pilot Rudolph Anderson had been shot down over Cuba, so tensions were high.

In the United States, there were other brushes with accidental warfare. After discovery of the missiles in Cuba, the military had turned some nuclear missile detection units southward to spot any weapons fired from Cuba, and the air force took this action hastily. The personnel who began scanning southern skies for incoming missiles in the "Falling Leaves Project" had received no special training.[95] Scott D. Sagan's *Limits of Safety* cites several instances in which the precarious peace was threatened by false alarms in the missile detection system. First, on 26 October, a missile was launched from Cape Canaveral, Florida, when only one U.S. nuclear missile detection unit was pointed toward the south. Since no one had notified radar operators of the planned test, the sudden appearance of the missile on the radar screen startled them and made them believe a missile had been launched from Cuba. The radar team had been told that the United States could get as little as five minutes' warning between the launch of a medium-range missile from Cuba and its impact in the southern United States—and now suddenly a blip flickered, possibly indicating imminent devastation. Several tense minutes passed before the missile was clearly seen to be heading southeast and not toward the United States.[96] Second, a missile launch from Cuba was reported by a radar station over the voice hotline with the NORAD (North American Air Defense) command center in Colorado on 28 October. According to the radio operators, the missile appeared to be headed toward impact near Tampa. The rest of NORAD was alerted to the attack, which appeared to be unmistakable. Since the missile seemed moments from its target, NORAD waited to confirm impact through the bomb alarm network. After the sensors registered no detonation near Tampa, NORAD learned that a test tape mistakenly had been running at the radar station.[97] Later that same day, a radar station reported unidentified flying objects somewhere over Georgia but later recognized that the blip represented a satellite orbiting the Earth.[98] In addition, a prowling bear sparked sabotage alarms at all bases in the upper Midwest and unexpectedly triggered a nuclear war alarm at Volk Field, Wisconsin. Officers at Volk caught the error just before planes took off.[99] Also, on 24 October, a Soviet spacecraft set to deliver the first payload to Mars exploded on the launchpad at Baikonur in the Soviet Union.

U.S. radar detection registered the explosion, and because Soviet space-craft and nuclear missiles shared the same launchpads, there was momentary concern about a missile launch; however, U.S. officials quickly realized that the blast had occurred on the ground.[100] In each case, nuclear war was avoided because humans refused to accept what the military's technology told them.

While civilians generally were not aware of these close calls, the military mobilization affected the lives of many Americans in diverse ways. Because full-scale war was a possibility, the Pentagon announced on 23 October that it had extended all navy and marine tours of duty for one year.[101] Military officials had planned to announce similar extensions for army and air force members on 28 October, but news of Khrushchev's agreement to withdraw the missiles made that move unnecessary.[102] Also during the crisis, Defense Secretary Robert McNamara called up twenty-four troop carrier/assault squadrons from the Air Force Ready Reserve. A total of 14,200 men reported for duty, anticipating a year of service,[103] though the air force released them from active duty less than a month later.

Troop movements snarled the nation's transportation systems. To bolster the invasion force, the army moved its 1st Armored Division from Fort Hood, Texas, to Fort Stewart, Georgia, on 23 October. That relocation alone required 2,000 flat cars, 299 railroad cars of other types, and 200 passenger cars to transport about 5,000 troops.[104] Tensions were high on troop trains. Thirty-five years later, a former soldier recalled an anxious captain yelling at an anguished subordinate, "Damn it, lieutenant, don't cry in front of the private!"[105] Many young men feared they were riding a train to death.

Witnesses saw long lines of flatcars and sometimes entire trains loaded with jeeps, water tank trucks, other trucks of all sizes, and supplies moving across the country toward the Southeast.[106] Gen. Herbert Powell, who commanded the army component of the missile crisis mobilization, recalled later that the military "tied up all of the flatcars in the country," delaying shipment of the fall harvest to market. Troop movements also put extra pressure on commercial airlines since many armored divisions traveled by plane, not train.[107]

On military bases, rather than following standardized procedures, leaders set their own tone in the treatment of military dependents. At some bases, the crisis barely received notice beyond its direct military effects. Elsewhere, the threat of war became palpable as base officials distributed information on evacuations and shelter space. Transfers of military personnel on short notice created problems for families on some bases, and the mobilization also derailed what some couples had viewed as the most momentous event of their lives—their weddings. Stories about tearful brides whose grooms ran off to war appeared in newspapers across the country.

Despite many years of preparation for the possibility of nuclear war, the military's response often revealed a good deal less regimentation than might be expected. Individual officers apparently exercised significant initiative in some cases, while in others, the White House and the Pentagon directly oversaw minute details. At the same time, massive movements of military troops and equipment unavoidably impacted the day-to-day existence of American civilians.

SHELTERING THE PUBLIC

In the 1950s, neither the Eisenhower administration nor Congress ever had much enthusiasm for turning civil defense into a major expenditure. In response to the 1961 Berlin crisis, Kennedy had declared a national emergency and sought a $3.25 billion increase in defense spending,[108] including a $207.6 million supplement to the civil defense budget.[109] Because Kennedy's Berlin speech had created a civil defense mania among some Americans, Congress gave approval for the full amount in civil defense. That supplement alone was twice as much as Eisenhower had ever sought for civil defense.[110] Whereas Eisenhower saw civil defense primarily as a deterrent to war and feared creating a panic, Kennedy perceived a "hotter" Cold War that required concrete steps to protect the population. His main emphasis at this time was on private shelters. During the Berlin crisis, the administration received more civil defense inquiries in a single day in August than it had counted for the entire month of January 1961.[111] In September, the White House reported receiving 6,500 inquiries per day, and civil defense was the number one topic of letters to the editor in the *Washington Post* and the *New York Times* for September and October.[112] Producers of survival products also reported a surge in sales after Kennedy's 25 July 1961 speech. Between that speech and 31 October, the Cincinnati division of the Bendix Corporation, which had developed a device to measure radiation in the air, reported selling more than 200,000 devices after distributing fewer than 5,000 in the previous twenty months. Similarly, a producer of food survival kits reported sales of $8,000 in the five months preceding Kennedy's speech, and sales of almost $100,000 in the four months afterward.[113] Unlike the Cuban crisis, which carried the threat of immediate war and which was public for only a week before its resolution, the Berlin crisis lasted for months and offered a sense of pending, though not imminent, danger.

After the Berlin crisis ended, administration officials became uneasy about the near-stampede the crisis had generated and recognized that emphasis on home shelters, which were too costly for many Americans, rankled nerves and generated panic. As a result, officials agreed in November 1961 to tone down civil defense literature and to begin emphasizing public rather than private shelters[114] as part of a five-year program.[115] As Berlin tensions eased, however, support for civil defense waned.[116] In 1962, Kennedy sought $695 million to institute a shelter incentive program, to create shelter areas in new federal buildings, and to accelerate locating, marking, and stocking public shelters. However, Congress acted on neither the incentives nor the federal building proposal, and it slashed funding for existing programs to about half of the previous year's level.[117]

At the same time, the Soviet Union apparently had a more extensive civil defense program, although it, too, recognized the improbability of saving the entire population. In the 1950s and 1960s, all Soviet citizens between the ages of sixteen and sixty received orders to attend several training sessions. Family shelters were acceptable in the suburbs but were not favored.[118] Subway systems in many Soviet cities were expected to house millions during a nuclear attack.[119] In addition, urban apartment buildings, factories, schools, and other public buildings commonly maintained basement shelters.[120] The amount of space allotted for each individual in a public shelter was five to ten square feet.[121] Reports estimated that the Soviet Union invested $500 million to $1.5 billion annually in civil defense[122]—considerably more than the $75 million allocated by the U.S. government in fiscal 1963.[123] A 1958 Central Intelligence Agency report, which remained classified until 2001, concluded that "it is impossible to determine the precise state of civil defense readiness in the USSR";[124] however, it noted that Soviet planning seemed geared toward controlling the population and that the government apparently had set no deadline for completion of preparations. The CIA report's tone clearly suggested that the Soviet Union was expected to seek readiness by a specific date to make a Soviet first strike feasible.

Other nations also seemed more willing than the United States to look squarely into the face of nuclear war and address its dangers. In Sweden, an elaborate program comprised fourteen underground shelter areas to serve as command posts that would oversee evacuation of 90 percent of Sweden's urban population to rural areas up to 250 miles from likely targets. Starting in 1945, this neutral nation required that every new building contain a reinforced-concrete shelter with an air-filtering system. Urban businesses routinely stored records in underground storage areas. A law passed in the 1940s also subjected all Swedes to a draft for civil defense service.[125]

Similarly, Switzerland, another neutral nation, had been better prepared than the United States since the mid-1950s. Most households kept a food supply adequate for several weeks in an emergency, and underground public shelters were equipped with emergency hospitals as well as government and military stockpiles. Under the 1962 Federal Civil Protection Law, all able-bodied males could be drafted into civil defense duty, which served as an alternative to military service during peacetime. As in Sweden, all new structures were required to contain shelter areas. In addition, each shelter had to provide protection against nuclear weapons and against chemical and biological agents. All employers with more than 100 employees were required to establish tactical units among workers to play a role in the community's civil defense program.[126]

U.S. paralysis on civil defense could be credited to an inability to face the prospect of nuclear war or simply to a sense of futility. Kennedy's first director of civil defense, Frank Ellis, saw it this way: "Certain people seem to be afflicted by a new and dreadful disease which has been called 'nuclearosis' of the brain. It's a malady wherein one is so overawed by the destructive power of nuclear weapons that he can no longer think objectively on the subject of national defense."[127] One thing is clear: the cause of that apathy was not sheer ignorance. Hiroshima and Nagasaki were not-too-distant memories, and Americans knew something about fallout's dangers because they consumed radioactive material regularly in milk as a result of atmospheric nuclear tests.

Intellectually, Americans knew the hazards of nuclear war, but America was not ready—and much of its citizenry was surprised by that realization during the crisis. The United States simply had refused to accept that war might erase or, at the very least, devastate the future. As a result, civil defense was kept on a back burner, partially because the nation's leaders failed to tell the public the truth—that the United States had little means of protecting its citizens from total war. This disconnection in the American psyche—an inability to face the loss of the future that could result from rabid anti-Communism—left the nation vulnerable to war and to false claims of safety. Cold War culture taught Americans to fear, but it did not offer a refuge from the deadliest threat, nuclear attack. The federal government often used assertions about civil defense preparedness as a public relations weapon to deter a Soviet attack, but public shelter designations barely had begun. And only 1 percent of U.S. companies had taken civil defense actions in their facilities,[128] although the survival of manufacturing capability was considered crucial to the nation's recovery.

When the crisis developed, people who had never given public shelters any real thought suddenly started to wonder why the government had not done more. Failing to invest in civil defense could be a rational response if the nation's leaders believed there was no way to protect the population and advised the populace to accept that reality. However, U.S. leaders achieved little while pretending to do a great deal, neither accepting the pointlessness of limited civil defense preparations nor spending the money to make civil defense viable. Apathy, fiscal conservatism, and the absence of workable plans lay the groundwork for a lack of preparedness. When U.S. planes spotted Soviet missiles in Cuba, conditions provided the breeding ground for fear and little chance for hope, but the White House decided to continue the civil defense charade.

QUEST FOR SAFETY

On the day after he announced the Cuban Missile Crisis to the nation, Kennedy turned his attention to civil defense and received an update on survival prospects for the population. He learned that existing shelters could house only 60 million Americans—less than a third of the population; however, the government had not marked most of those shelters or stocked them with necessary supplies, like food, water, medicine, sanitation equipment, and radiation monitors.[129] Assistant Secretary of Defense for Civil Defense Steuart Pittman told him that 92 million Americans and fifty-eight cities with populations of more than 100,000 were within range of the missiles in Cuba.[130] Pittman, who just three days before had given the U.S. Civil Defense Council an optimistic report on the adequacy of shelters,[131] suggested that the United States should consider lowering the protection factors governing selection of shelter sites. By reducing the level of protection, the government could move quickly to approve more buildings as shelters.[132]

At that time, JFK expressed interest in another option: evacuation of key areas within the United States. "If we are ever going to carry it out all the way we ought to have those cities evacuated," he told Deputy Secretary of Defense Roswell Gilpatric in an 23 October telephone conversation.[133] However, civil defense experts already knew that evacuation of cities was impractical in many cases and likely to set off a nationwide panic. The fact that Kennedy would explore this option after it had been rejected by the

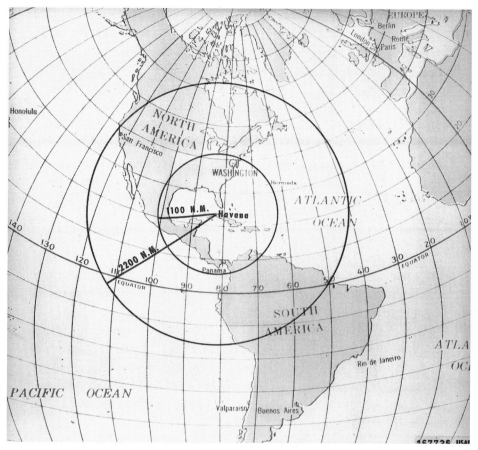

An air force map shows the ranges of medium- and intermediate-range Soviet missiles in Cuba. Mapping the missiles' potential reach helped the Kennedy administration's rushed efforts to provide minimal civil defense protection, with special attention going to the areas closest to Cuba. National Archives.

experts indicates how little real thought and discussion had gone into the administration's civil defense plans.

Kennedy continued to push shelters despite a lack of preparedness because he knew what the public did not: even before the Soviet installation in Cuba, U.S. intelligence estimates predicted that with shelters, 135 million out of 185 million Americans would be killed or injured if the Soviet Union attacked urban areas with only low-yield weapons. Casualty projections rose to 145 million with a mix of high- and low-yield weapons. Estimated casualties dropped if the Soviet targets were assumed to be only military sites, but even then, 55 million to 85 million casualties were expected with a shelter program.[134] Without shelters, even more would die. Ironically, the military's decision to scatter bombers at civilian airports may have guaranteed higher civilian casualties because the Soviet Union could not afford to limit an attack to military bases.[135]

In the current crisis, Kennedy was most concerned about the Southeast, parts of which might be vulnerable to Cuban attacks using conventional weapons and all of which lay within range of Soviet missiles in Cuba. He asked Pittman to produce a regional plan to be mobilized if the United States invaded Cuba,[136] and he expected that plan to evaluate the possibility of some evacuations.[137] *The Army War Room Journal* shows military opposition to any evacuation,[138] and Pittman feared that evacuations in that region could create panic elsewhere, causing "a hell of a mess."[139] In addition, he explained, a nuclear attack would create fallout that would contaminate rural areas as well as the urban centers they surrounded. Fallout shelters primarily were in cities, and those who fled to the "safety" of rural areas would have no fallout protection.[140]

While federal authorities attempted to assemble emergency plans, the nation's governors expressed concern about the status of civil defense, and during the crisis week, representatives of the Civil Defense Committee of the Governors' Conference met with administration officials. Alarmed that the federal fallout shelter program just had begun, the governors, led by New York's Nelson Rockefeller, heard reassurances of federal commitment to the program.[141] The governors urged federal officials to work through them in accelerating preparations,[142] and they resolved to hasten construction of emergency operating centers for state and local governments.[143] After the governors' meeting, the top leaders and civil defense committee chairmen of the U.S. Conference of Mayors, the American Municipal Association, and the National Association of Counties brought similar concerns to a meeting with federal officials.[144] Fearful that state and local governments would appear to be taking the initiative in civil defense and probably aware that the outspoken Rockefeller was a likely Kennedy rival for the presidency in 1964, Pittman scheduled regional conferences so that all fifty governors could be briefed on federal plans.[145]

By sparking newfound interest in civil defense and generating political heat from the governors and others, this crisis created a new sense of urgency within the Defense Department's Office of Civil Defense. In light of the program's obvious shortcomings, officials moved quickly to provide additional training for the general population in radiological monitoring, shelter management, and medical self-help. At the same time, the federal government expedited civil defense aid to states through direct allocations, matching funds, and rapid distribution of surplus federal property.[146] To keep up with public demand, the government also printed 10 million copies of two civil defense booklets.[147] Meanwhile, in the Soviet Union a similar scramble apparently was under way. Although Americans knew little about what was happening within the Soviet government, former Soviet journalist Melor Sturua much later reported, "There was [a] sense of . . . hysteria" about civil defense during the crisis.[148] However, because of censored news accounts, most of the Soviet population had no idea how serious the Cuban crisis was.

Although Pittman had misgivings about evacuation, transportation agencies devoted valuable crisis hours to outlining contingency plans for the evacuation of Florida,[149] and by midweek, he proposed several steps to enhance U.S. preparedness. Telling his coworkers that he was "under a great deal of pressure from the press and the public to say something," he backed swift unveiling of an intense three-month effort to make a dramatic increase in shelter space.[150]

In addition, he produced two plans intended to provide extra protection to vulnerable areas during any American military engagement in Cuba. The first focused on areas, such as South Florida, that were close enough to Cuba that they might fall victim to a Cuban attack using conventional weapons. It called for activation of National Guard units, police and fire departments, and emergency casualty centers, and it recommended selective evacuation in Florida and New Orleans, noting that officials in both areas had experience in executing evacuations because of the areas' vulnerability to hurricanes. What Pittman envisioned were limited evacuations of downtown areas, which would lead people into suburban motels—short getaways suitable for avoiding conventional weapons attacks that would serve little purpose if a nuclear missile hit the same area. The plan also urged that the target areas receive shipments of federal supplies, such as emergency water systems, portable hospitals, processed food, and medical stockpiles.[151] Pittman, moreover, favored a cautious approach to implementing this plan, saying that he would meet quietly with regional civil defense officials and help to coordinate local planning when Kennedy decided to activate the plan. After that, he argued, the president should make a second ruling as to whether he really wanted to proceed with the mobilization.

In his second recommendation, Pittman proposed stepping up civil defense preparations in the arc that fell within a 1,000-mile range of medium-range nuclear weapons in Cuba. This proposal called for doubling the number of shelters in the arc, in part by reducing shelter protection levels; launching a crash program to mark shelters within a week; getting individuals to stock public shelters with a three-day supply of food per person; and encouraging building owners to make minor plumbing changes to assure that shelter areas would have a guaranteed three-day water supply. (Fallout danger was expected to last at least fourteen days, but sheltering people for three days was better than not sheltering them at all.) Under this plan, the Corps of Engineers would work with officials to identify caves and mines within twenty-five miles of population centers in the hope of designating 5 million additional shelter spaces. Pittman also endorsed a plan to bolster preparation of rural home shelters. He favored relocating emergency supplies at six strategic locations, activating 350 portable hospitals, and positioning food stockpiles within the arc. Standby reservists and the Third Army, which had served under Gen. George Patton in World War II, would be available to assist civil defense workers, and the U.S. government would step up dissemination of civil defense information. In addition, within a week, a two-hour course would teach 14,000 architects, engineers, and contractors what they needed to know to prepare shelter areas. By donating surplus equipment, the federal government also would help local governments to set up emergency operating centers in public shelters.[152]

On 28 October, the day Khrushchev apparently ended the crisis by announcing his intention to remove the missiles, Kennedy approved the accelerated civil defense program,[153] and the federal government soon would urge state and local civil defense directors to enhance this mobilization by developing partnerships with national voluntary agencies, such as the American Red Cross, the Boy Scouts of America, and the Salvation Army, all of which had approached the White House with offers of help.[154] The president also authorized discreet consultation with state and local authorities in areas within striking distance of Cuba's conventional weapons, and he gave qualified approval to the plan for the arc. However, to avoid public upheaval, he ordered that no steps be taken in the arc that would have significant public impact, and he specified that any special effort in that area should be restricted to any continuation of the current crisis.[155] In essence, with the crisis's end, acceleration within the arc became part of a national plan for better protection.[156]

The president also supported Pittman's proposal to lower standards for public fallout shelters from a 100 protection factor to a 40 protection factor, meaning that instead of cutting radiation exposure 100 times, a building would be required only to cut radiation 40 times. This move would double the amount of easily identifiable shelter space available[157] and raise potential occupancy to between 110 million and 120 million people.[158] At the same time, the protection provided obviously would be less, although experts debated how much impact that would have. Even with this change, more than 60 million people would have no chance of finding space in a public shelter.

As the crisis ended, American civil defense planning remained in disarray, and members of the public had become increasingly aware of that fact as they witnessed civil defense deficiencies in their own communities. Many loose ends remained, ranging from the basic need to pay civil defense workers to the more complex implementation of a proposal to eliminate tax duties on emergency supplies coming into the country after a nuclear war.[159]

Like many civil defense measures, lowering the shelter standards to make more buildings qualify was a sleight-of-hand maneuver intended to provide the illusion of safety to a vulnerable nation. As long as those shelters were unmarked and unstocked with supplies, they offered little refuge from war, and if lowering the standards caused more radiation sickness, that would add to the human misery within crowded shelters. In promoting civil defense, the government relied on a small investment and questionable planning to accomplish an almost impossible feat, and as the possibility of nuclear war grew, it became clear that there was simply no magic to protect the United States. At the same time, flaws in the military mobilization raised further questions about the likelihood that the nation would survive war. The missile crisis had galvanized the public's attention on the prospect of nuclear war and raised civilian anxieties.

ready or not...

The city of West Covina, 36 miles west of Los Angeles, gave way to what its CD director, Mrs. Cleo Boschoff, termed temporary panic. Raids on West Covina supermarkets ex-
hausted all stocks of canned goods repeatedly for periods of two to four hours—until
new deliveries were trucked in.—Associated Press report on the missile crisis

If nuclear war came with some warning, high-ranking government officials
could find relative safety in secret bunkers carved into the mountains of Virginia, West Virginia, and Pennsylvania, but for most Americans, there was
nowhere to hide. When the Cuban Missile Crisis occurred, vulnerability to
attack became a stark reality for many civilians, and well-publicized civil
defense programs offered little solace from the sense of impending doom.
The situation created fertile ground for doubts about the individual's safety
and the government's dependability.

Some Americans responded with drastic action—leaving their homes behind to find relative safety in areas distant from likely Soviet targets. Although the government did not implement any formal evacuations, government analysis indicates that many Floridians fled to areas that seemed
safer,[1] and it has been estimated that as many as 10 million Americans left
the nation's urban areas, taking "vacations" in rural areas far away from nuclear targets.[2] Anecdotal evidence supports this contention. About a dozen
women reportedly left husbands in Washington and Baltimore to take refuge
in Cumberland, Maryland,[3] and entire families from spots as far south as
Chicago are reported to have taken refuge in Wisconsin.[4] Col. David H.
Hackworth, who was with the 101st Airborne Division at that time, recalled
in his memoirs that he sent his family to a cabin in the mountains during
the crisis.[5] And in South Florida, word spread about a woman who told a
military policeman, "I've got to get out of here. My husband's in the Navy
and his ship has gone to sea, and he wants me to take the kids home to my

While some civilians flooded stores, others watched in wonder as the nation's military arsenal became part of the civilian landscape. Here, civilians assemble on George Smathers Beach in Key West, Florida, to see soldiers position antiaircraft missiles. © Bettmann/CORBIS.

mother." After looking in the car, the officer asked, "What kids?" and the red-faced woman gasped, "My God, I forgot them."[6]

At a time when the middle-class home had become a sanctuary from the evil outside world, many Americans left that comfortable refuge and sought safety in the great unknown. They fled not only the prospect that Khrushchev might attack but also the possibility that Kennedy or some nameless U.S. military officer inadvertently might spark a chain of events that would obliterate their world. These fugitives found themselves adrift in a world of ambiguity. As an eighth-grader wrote a little over a year later, "If Kennedy wasn't killed, he might have become the greatest president ever. He also might have started atomic war and destroyed the world."[7] A youngster could see the ironic truth: in this age of uncertainty, even a potentially great leader could, by a simple error in judgment, end life on the planet. On the front lines of the Cold War, a split-second error by a military leader could be equally disastrous.

Most Americans lacked the will or the resources to run and hide; therefore, they sought answers, however tenuous, in their own communities. A deluge of frantic calls swamped civil defense offices across the country as many Americans felt the threat of imminent nuclear war for the first time. On 24 October, callers seeking updates on the crisis jammed phone lines at the *New York Times* with 15,000 calls in nine hours.[8] Where is the nearest shelter? How can I turn my basement into a shelter? What supplies should I buy? What should I do if I hear an air-raid siren? All these questions and more reflected an explosion of previously contained public anxiety.

Worried citizens who contacted civil defense offices found little good news there. U.S. civil defense preparations were in disarray, and the missiles in Cuba, which lay within easy striking distance of 92 million Americans, were so close that there would be little warning before they hit their targets. As civilians contemplated their chances of surviving nuclear war, the phones were "ringing like mad" in Chicago's civil defense office.[9] In New Orleans, more than 2,000 citizens dropped by the civil defense office between 24 and 27 October.[10] In Miami, Cincinnati, Richmond, Cleveland, Oklahoma City, and Atlanta, understaffed civil defense offices struggled to keep up with the calls, many of which came from citizens too frantic to wait for instructions to arrive by mail. The West Covina, California, office received an average of one call per minute.[11] To handle 400 to 500 calls a day, Memphis added new phone lines,[12] and Texas's civil defense office distributed half a million pamphlets during the short crisis period.[13]

In Philadelphia, where women and children reportedly had run into the streets in a panic following Orson Welles's *War of the Worlds* 1938 broadcast,[14] this real-life threat prompted requests for "hundreds and thousands" of pieces of civil defense literature, and one report concluded that "the near panic exhibited by many, many citizens bespoke the neglect they had followed in terms of their individual preparedness."[15] The city's African American newspaper reported that "more than 250,000 Philadelphians—the vast majority of them Negroes—are living on the bull's-eye of a potential atom bomb attack" with no shelters available.[16] Equal opportunity to live or die became an issue in New Orleans, where the crisis prompted city officials to end a policy of segregating fallout shelters. Now, all could compete equally for inadequate shelter spaces.[17]

Many cities found themselves overwhelmed by the sudden demand for information. In North Carolina's southern piedmont, Charlotte's civil defense director begged citizens not to jam phone lines by calling his office whenever they heard strange noises; instead, he urged them to tune their radios to civil defense channels.[18] To answer citizens' questions, the Los Angeles office offered speakers to address civic groups.[19] Des Moines ordered

85,000 copies of the area's civil defense emergency plan for distribution to residents,[20] and cities from Roanoke to North Las Vegas, Bangor to Miami, scheduled survival-training classes. For fifty cents, the *Washington Star's* readers could buy a booklet titled "You Can Survive Atomic Attack,"[21] and in Houston, a local TV station found an eager audience for a rerun called "Education for Nuclear Survival."[22]

Despite the obvious frenzy of activity, many Americans quietly continued their daily lives. Although it is hard to document inaction, there are bits of evidence. Some towns reported no increased civil defense activity at all, and in Waterford, Connecticut, civil defense director Marshall Rubin quit in disgust after only five of the city's 16,000 residents called for information at this time.[23] In Delaware County, Pennsylvania, residents paid a price for failing to name community shelter directors: the civil defense director refused to issue information on shelters in fourteen areas until those communities named directors.[24]

Some Americans apparently did not act because they did not expect the crisis to expand into war. Why should they? Their newspapers were filled with the usual mix of recipes, sports scores, and department store ads. There were experts to back up the strong sense that Khrushchev never would use nuclear weapons against the United States. The Soviet Union "will do a lot of yelling" but will not risk war, retired army general Mark Clark told the Iowa Bankers Association convention in Des Moines. "The last thing on Russia's schedule is a shooting war," the veteran of World War II and the Korean conflict proclaimed.[25]

Others believed there was a very real danger but saw no viable protection from nuclear weapons. As a child, Otto Reichert-Facilides had lived in Bremerhaven, Germany, which was a target of Allied bombers during World War II. He moved to Philadelphia in 1957, and at the time of the crisis, he was a thirty-seven-year-old husband and father of two small sons. He remembers clearly why he made no civil defense preparations in 1962: "I had gone through the whole war period with bombing in the city where I lived. Our house was totally bombed out, totally destroyed. And so was Berlin, where I was for a short period." Consequently, the principles of mass destruction and psychological warfare against civilians were familiar to him. Given the power of nuclear weapons, Reichert saw no value in preparing a shelter or providing hopeful fairy tales for his children. "I know what it means to be bombed. I know what it does—total destruction of the physical environment—and the bombs that were thrown at that time killed not so totally as an atomic bomb." After hearing about the installation of Soviet nuclear missiles in Cuba, he recalled, "I was horrified. . . . I knew that this was absolutely horrendous, that these [weapons] were much stronger than Hiroshima, which was a very strong recent memory. That was the promise of the Cuban Missile Crisis—a ten- or hundred-fold Hiroshima coming to American cities. What it would have done to American society can only fill one with absolute horror because it wouldn't have been only the death of the people, but it would have been the psychological impact."[26]

To get information into the hands of those who wanted it, many newspapers published lists of designated shelters, with the bad news that most citizens would find no room in the shelters if war began. Even more critical was the lack of supplies in designated shelters. None had been stocked with supplies in New York,[27] Chicago,[28] Buffalo, Camden, Newark, Louisville, St. Louis, Green Bay, St. Paul, Little Rock, Albuquerque, Oklahoma City, El Paso, Denver, Des Moines, Wichita, Salt Lake City, Long Beach, Sacramento, Phoenix, or Seattle. The District of Columbia, with a population of 784,000, had enough stocked shelter spaces for 5,514. With a population of more than 900,000, Baltimore could feed only 1,246 shelter occupants.[29] In Los Angeles, residents learned that shelter space was available for 1.3 million people—about half of the population, but supplies were available for only 40,000.[30] The state of Arizona had stocked shelters in only one county,[31] while Indiana had a total of only one marked shelter.[32]

The unwelcome truth was clear to New York's director of civil defense, Lt. Gen. Francis W. Farrell. "As far as shelters for the majority of our citizens is concerned—of course, we don't have any. But I think that the thumbnail is this—we are in good shape to conduct the affairs of the State at the Capitol in Albany."[33] In other words, New York could preserve the government but not the citizenry. In Wisconsin, where one underfunded county civil defense director spent his own money to purchase emergency supplies,[34] the state sent newspapers a list of potential shelter areas, although they were neither marked nor stocked with supplies. As a precautionary step, officials mailed television and radio stations information to broadcast at the start of nuclear war.[35]

Clearly, civilians' prospects were not good, particularly in target areas, such as cities and areas near military bases, and after listening to a White House discussion about what steps could be taken to improve the situation quickly, CIA director John McCone wrote in his notes: "I got the conclusion that not very much could or would be done; that whatever was done would involve a great deal of publicity and public alarm."[36]

In some places, officials reassured residents by reminding them that they were far from target areas. This logic worked well in isolated spots like Duluth, Minnesota,[37] but for residents of Jacksonville, Florida, which was ringed by three naval bases, there was no way to hide the ugly truth. The city, which had no stocked shelters, would be high on the Soviet list of targets.[38]

Ironically, while there was an inadequate supply of stocked shelters, the various levels of government had been very efficient about installing air-raid sirens in major cities and most small towns across the country. As a result, Americans could be alerted to an attack but most could find no shelter.[39] This is typical of the kind of haphazard planning that marked civil defense preparations. Highly visible steps were taken, but the crucial actions—the ones that could save lives—often were considered too costly. New York City alone had more than 700 sirens[40] to work hand in hand with thousands of unmarked, unstocked shelters.[41] If missiles approached, a national warning system would alert every city with a population exceeding 20,000,[42] but for most people in target areas, this would provide only a few moments for desperate measures and prayers.[43]

In this tense week, siren malfunctions and tests caused several scares. One night, residents of Harrisburg, Pennsylvania, heard a loud explosion followed by a siren. About 1,000 calls poured into police switchboards, and operators could offer no reassuring words until learning fifteen minutes later that a construction blast had set off the siren.[44] In Des Plaines, Illinois, a nighttime drill sent many suburbanites into a panic,[45] and two accidental siren blasts in one day jolted citizens of Tampa.[46] San Antonio residents flooded phone lines after one siren's accidental sounding. "This place went plumb haywire," said the fire alarm operator who cut off the siren.[47]

On the other hand, residents of Little Rock, Arkansas,[48] and Olathe, Kansas,[49] learned from drills that several of their sirens were not operational, leaving some parts of both cities with the prospect of getting no warning before an attack. In Green Bay, Wisconsin, a test showed that although sirens worked, they could not be heard inside more than half of the city's schools.[50] Midland, Texas, residents learned that no air-raid sirens were functioning, so if war began, police cars would ride through the city with sirens blaring.[51] At the University of California at Berkeley, where officials urged students to become familiar with the meanings of various alarm signals, one student summed up the exercise's usefulness: "The air raid siren is preceded by a bright flash."[52]

Despite the possibility of a malfunction, some cities canceled scheduled siren tests to avoid unnecessarily frightening the public.[53] At this time, almost anything unusual became a cause for alarm among nervous citizens: when a power failure silenced a Columbia, South Carolina, radio station, some listeners feared war was responsible for the eerily dead air on their favorite station.[54]

Americans who sought a reprieve from bad news in a movie theater heard a newsreel commentator call the crisis "the most critical threat of global war since the surrender of Germany 17 years ago,"[55] and as tensions built, many locales began reevaluating their survival strategies. In most areas, widespread civil defense training was on hold, and with little adequately stocked shelter space, South Carolina's civil defense director admitted: "In event of nuclear attack each community must rely principally on its own preparedness and means of survival."[56]

Even in shelters that had been marked and stocked with food, the quality of life would be horrendous. In addition to overcrowded, claustrophobic conditions, survivors in most areas could look forward to life sustained through a diet of "survival biscuits," products of the National Biscuit Company[57] or the Nebraska Department of Agriculture. The biscuits tasted like graham crackers and would provide 2,000 calories per day. Both had an expected shelf life of five years and were low in protein to minimize the amount of water needed to support renal activity.[58]

Despite estimates that fallout would remain dangerous for at least two weeks, the federal government planned to stock each shelter with just 10,000 calories of food per person per shelter space—a diet of 2,000 calories a day for five days or 714 calories a day for fourteen days.[59] Thus, even in a stocked shelter, hunger could become an added source of stress. New York considered these allocations "austere" and hoped to augment the federally supplied food to offer at least 20,000 calories per person, but those plans were still on a wish list when the crisis began.[60]

A reporter checked one of Denver's "stocked" shelters and found two dozen chairs, twelve empty 17.5-gallon water cans, several hundred boxes of survival crackers, fifteen stretchers, first-aid and radiation-detection kits, and civil defense literature. The shelter, which supposedly was stocked to serve 2,620 people, had access to water but no cots and no working generator.[61]

As they tried to hasten preparations, Atlanta, Tulsa, and Miami officials reported problems getting building owners to provide shelter space because they had no insurance liability protection.[62] In Washington, the crisis's nerve-jangling power prompted at least fifty building owners to offer shelter space,[63] but the capital still had far too few shelters.[64] Gastonia, North

Carolina, on the other hand, had designated 232 shelters, but none had been marked.[65]

In addition to finding shelter space, authorities across the country attempted to contribute to national defense and reinforce civil order. In New York, the city's police officers and firefighters ended two weeks of picketing city hall.[66] Governor Nelson Rockefeller announced that he was moving to bring the state's civil defense "to a maximum posture of readiness,"[67] and a day after Kennedy's speech, state officials began planning for mobilization of the state militia because the U.S. government would take over the National Guard in wartime.[68] In the Miami area, federal authorities openly maintained surveillance of the Cuban population.[69] Philadelphia canceled all vacations and leaves for police officers, firefighters, and park guards,[70] and the Delaware River Ports' Council for Emergency Operation urged new steps to avert sabotage at the river's ports.[71]

While sheltering the public was the top priority, evacuation was an option in places like Anchorage, Alaska, which was surrounded by sparsely populated areas. Rations for more than 100,000 meals already had been stored in nineteen "safe-haven" areas in rural Alaska.[72] Jacksonville, Florida, residents could follow planned routes to safer Georgia towns,[73] but in New Orleans, where only ten minutes' warning was expected if missiles were fired from Cuba, the civil defense director said, "Evacuation is out. We have no place to go."[74] Suburban growth limited potential evacuations. St. Paul, Minnesota, officials considered evacuation but realized that any plan to empty the city depended upon first evacuating suburbs, which were not under city control.[75]

Often, existing civil defense issues seemed answerable if governments had faced them earlier. The marking and stocking of shelters easily could have been accomplished if Congress had allocated adequate money and the federal bureaucracy had made that a high priority; however, neither had occurred. Therefore, individuals felt very much on their own. The government, which suddenly seemed to believe public shelters would be beneficial, offered little help—and little hope.

HOME SURVIVAL TACTICS

In October 1962, the possibility of nuclear war suddenly threatened to color everything, even life in what had been a safe haven—the American home. Cold War culture had stressed the importance of a strong nuclear family in combating the Communist threat; however, family ties offered little protection from nuclear war. While some Americans clung fiercely to

Seeking solace in a time of danger, members of Miami's large Cuban refugee community gather at a special Mass on 23 October 1962. Around the country, many churches remained open twenty-four hours a day during the crisis and others held special prayer services. © Bettmann/CORBIS.

daily routines, bittersweet vignettes revealed an air of fatalism gripping many of them. In Virginia, when a mother asked her son why he had devoted an evening to carrying firewood to his back porch, he replied matter-of-factly that he wanted to stay warm while the family took cover from the fall-out.[76] In Minneapolis, a husband departed for work telling his wife, "Well, I'll call you if I hear anything. If there shouldn't be a chance to . . . well, it's been wonderful."[77] The end seemed near. "People have thought in the past it would never happen to them, but now we appear to be on the brink of a shooting war," said county judge Noel Cason in Midland, Texas.[78]

When JFK unveiled the threat of war, he spoke of months of sacrifice ahead, but most Americans measured this crisis in days, hours, and minutes—until the first ship reached the blockade, until the enemy shot down a U.S. plane, until Khrushchev decided whether this gamble was worth a war. As many families realized that the government was not going to save them and might inadvertently be the instrument of their deaths, they increasingly felt that they must rely on themselves. Solutions that required months or weeks to complete, such as building a shelter, held little appeal to those who feared they may be living their last hours. In many places, calls to shelter firms rose,[79] and a New Orleans dealer reported selling two cylindrical shelters that would hold eight to ten people each.[80] Most shelter merchants reported no spike in sales, however.[81]

Instead, while they realized that they would not be protected from the worst effects of nuclear war, many people sought to turn their sanctuaries into bunkers. If an attack occurred, instructions were simple: tune the radio to Conelrad for government announcements and take shelter in a basement or in the middle of a building or, if caught outside, find cover in a culvert or ditch.[82] Col. Aurel Clark, chief administrative officer of the Illinois Department of Civil Defense, said his advice was even simpler—"Take cover and pray."[83] Some had to act. A Miami man worked eight hours to transform an old septic tank into a shelter for seven relatives and friends,[84] and an Ohio father traced a route to fresh water in Canada, stocked his basement with food and blankets, and purchased rifle shells to use against neighbors who might try to invade his family's refuge.[85] At 2 A.M. on 24 October, Memphis police spotted a man holding a pick and standing over a manhole as he tried to determine whether his family could take refuge under the city's streets.[86]

Sadly, many shelter owners realized that when faced with the prospect of Armageddon, Americans would covet their neighbors' shelters. Panic could turn to violence in a matter of moments. By midweek, a Valley Forge, Pennsylvania, man reported that he was fielding only half-joking requests for space in a $16,000 shelter that he had built by hand six years earlier.[87] In Homestead, Florida, a neighbor asked shelter owner Wally Keirstead whether there would be room for his family in Keirstead's shelter. When Keirstead replied that it would house only three, the neighbor said, "Wally, I think you'd rather be in there with me than on the outside looking in."[88]

In some areas, solutions were hard to find. As the mayor of Tampa explained, "We're like New Orleans here. No cellars. Water seeps in."[89] In Washington, where traffic was congested, many people probably would be in their cars when an attack occurred. Consequently, officials urged commuters to keep food and water in their cars and advised citizens to prepare to take food, water, medicines, blankets, and battery-operated radios to public shelters.[90]

Shelter space, both public and private, was inadequate, so the people and the government did what they could in the short term to provide some kind of protection for millions of Americans. Unfortunately, if war came, what could be done would be too little—and too late.

SUPPLY AND DEMAND

As the crisis unfolded, Americans began stocking up for war. Some leaders consciously avoided urging people to fill their cabinets because they wanted to avoid panic, but others stressed the need to prepare. For instance, New Jersey governor Richard J. Hughes urged citizens to stock water, canned food, blankets, and old clothes in a windowless corner of a basement, and he stressed that people could live "for long periods of time without food" if they had a sealed water supply.[91] In some cities, civil defense directors also advised residents to keep their gas tanks full.[92]

Recalling World War II shortages of staples such as bread, Puerto Ricans immediately voiced concerns about maintaining food supplies,[93] and Los Angeles residents flooded into supermarkets after the city's civil defense director suggested that Kennedy would close retail stores if war began. One woman bought twenty cases of bottled water;[94] others were less practical. "I know a woman who bought 40 jars of instant coffee," one woman reported. "I asked her, 'If there really is an H-bomb attack, what are you going to use for water?' She'd never thought of that."[95] A spokesman for Vons' Shopping Bag Grocery Co. reported, "Calls have been received from all stores, particularly for staples and canned goods, which are going by the case."[96]

Miami shoppers, goaded by the Dade County manager's advice that everyone should maintain a two-week supply of food, rushed to stores,[97] and some merchants said sales rose 20 percent.[98] Those seeking to avoid a panic were not helped by the county manager's additional plea for people not to drive at night so that all roads would be clear for military use. Rumors spread in Jacksonville that there were troops all over Miami and that food and services were in short supply.[99]

A Washington supermarket reported heavy buying of canned goods, and bottled water was specially displayed to lure buyers. One woman bought two bottles of water and a case of canned fruit punch because she might shelter twenty-five children in her basement.[100] In Fort Worth, the civil defense director responded to a rush on stores, saying, "The idea is to survive—not to get fat."[101]

Strangely, panic buying overwhelmed some cities and did not occur to any significant degree in other locales. In San Francisco, Columbus, Boston, and Chicago there were no reports of such activity. However, in Austin, shoppers bought one store's entire stock of $2 bulk containers of canned

Box boys at a Los Angeles supermarket struggle to handle a rush in buying after a local civil defense official suggested on 24 October that all families should have at least a two-week supply of food. Rushes on supermarkets and gun stores occurred in several American cities. © Bettmann/CORBIS.

foods and a shopping center allowed customers to buy $100 lots of canned goods. Cashing in on a golden opportunity, a Baton Rouge store offered a list of shelter necessities in one advertisement.[102]

Any housewife who may have feared looking foolish by buying survival supplies could have taken heart in knowing that the high and mighty acted similarly during the crisis. The dean of the Washington Cathedral ordered flooding of a large area of the cathedral's basement "to provide potable water in an emergency," and Secretary of Agriculture Orville Freeman stored 8,400 pounds of processed cheddar cheese and a stockpile of wafers in the department's basement.[103]

Food and water were not the only items in demand. While Bakersfield, California, customers stocked up on sugar, coffee, and chocolate, items scarce during World War II, sales in rifles, shotguns, handguns, and shells more than doubled.[104] Dallas residents also made guns a hot commodity,[105] and sporting goods stores in St. Petersburg, Florida, experienced a jump in sales of handguns and high-powered rifles.[106] Charlottesville, Virginia, gun dealers reported brisk sales, and one Richmond dealer explained that Virginians were not arming themselves against Russians; their anticipated targets were American city dwellers who might seek shelter in rural areas.[107]

A New Orleans shop sold its entire stock of transistor radios.[108] Batteries were hot items in the Texas cities of Beaumont and Houston,[109] and three Houston water distilleries reported a run on distilled water.[110] Columbia, South Carolina, tire dealers said they had served several customers seeking new tires, although they already had good tires, and hardware stores profited from growing demand for portable stoves, exhaust fans, and chemical toilets.[111] Car dealers in Denton, Texas, experienced abnormally heavy demand for new cars,[112] and in Anchorage, a pharmacist reported many shoppers getting prescriptions refilled earlier than usual.[113] At the same time, two New York banks noted clear declines in deposits despite steady increases in previous weeks.[114]

In response to the flurry of food buying and notwithstanding his own decision to hoard cheese, Secretary Freeman assured Americans that food stocks were more than adequate.[115] In Colorado, the agriculture commissioner advised citizens that even if war hit, fresh food supplies would be delivered to the stricken areas immediately—an assertion he could not possibly support.[116] A 1962 analysis of American food supplies showed that retail food stores held a 15.5-day supply of food for every person in the continental United States, assuming that 2,000 calories a day was an adequate diet.[117] And smokers did not have to worry about nicotine deprivation because the tobacco industry had a two-year supply of leaf tobacco.[118] Poultry offered the best hope of continued meat production because the fowl demonstrated resistance to radiation,[119] and a government evaluation noted that most farm commodities were in good supply except wool, hides, and dried fruits.[120]

In quiet talks, the federal government had begun addressing postwar problems such as supplying food to devastated areas. Early in the week, Kennedy met with Department of Agriculture officials to develop distribution plans to bolster survival chances for humans and meat animals.[121] At that time, eighty-one federal warehouses held enough shelter supplies to feed 4 million people[122]—about 2 percent of the population. Although some states had pushed to mobilize peacetime rationing registration earlier in 1962, that step had not been taken;[123] therefore, the government now hastened plans to ration food, oil, and other essentials.[124] By week's end, the administration had begun to distribute "reproduction proofs," which local printers could use to print rationing forms.[125]

The Agricultural Marketing Service's recommendations, finalized about three weeks after the crisis's end, included wartime steps for freezing sales of all food, orders for food distribution companies to report their inventories, plans for requisitioning food supplies, and outlines of rationing measures.[126] In February 1963, a more detailed report planned for each registered family to get a bag of foodstuffs as its first ration[127] and outlined guidelines for rationing gasoline,[128] as well as for freezes on rents and salaries at pre-attack levels.[129] In reality, the president had no power to control wages or prices, but by 25 October, a consultant was writing orders to be implemented if the crisis worsened.[130] Recently declassified papers show that the administration considered asking Congress for authority, but some in the Office of Emergency Planning believed "the president can take emergency actions which are necessary to the survival of the nation without a statutory base."[131]

At the same time, the Department of the Treasury prepared for a postwar world by mapping out emergency monetary programs.[132] During the crisis, Treasury officials considered steps to avoid panic sales of stock or runs on banks.[133] This planning was aimed at avoiding prewar panic and preparing for a postwar economy that "would be fragmented, with some target areas destroyed, others pinned down at least temporarily by heavy fallout, and still others, if prepared, physically able to function in restricted degree." Even in locations that were able to function, "the solvency and operations of our surviving banking and monetary system and institutions would be gravely jeopardized" because local economies depended on the national economy to survive.[134] The Post Office Department started inventorying postwar population registration forms that had been pre-positioned in 39,000 post offices,[135] and the Department of the Interior prepared to activate the Emergency Petroleum and Gas Agency and the Emergency Solid Fuels Administration.[136]

Another big challenge after nuclear war would be providing medical care. The Department of Health, Education, and Welfare's responsibilities included notifying the public about the need for medical self-help measures; contacting volunteer welfare organizations for assistance; establishing procedures for requisitioning shelter, food, and clothing; recommending an embargo on medical supplies set for export; and arranging for narcotics shipments with the help of the Federal Bureau of Investigation and the Bureau of Narcotics.[137] Unfortunately, the Office of Emergency Planning had reached only 20 percent of its goal in distribution of emergency hospital beds.[138] To tackle the shortcomings in medical preparedness, Maryland officials planned a system for dispersing medical personnel throughout the state and for providing special training for doctors, nurses, dentists, veterinarians, and ambulance personnel.[139] In the Los Angeles area, medical sources distributed a book listing 8,000 doctors and their specialties to all civil defense offices,[140] while Dallas and other cities attempted to deal with the possible destruction of city hospitals by preparing 200-bed emergency hospitals that could be dismantled and stored in areas surrounding cities.[141] As stopgap measures, the OEP allotted money for 26,000 first-aid kits to be distributed by 1 December and the administration entered talks with the American Red Cross to expand its blood collection capacity.[142]

Again, the crisis revealed the lack of government readiness to provide the population's basic survival needs. The realization that the government could not distribute basic supplies for those who might survive an onslaught of nuclear weapons led some civilians to embrace panic responses, clearing retailers' shelves of water, food, guns, and radios. Erratic responses of civilians across the nation suggest that local leaders' attitudes played a dramatic role in the emotional responses of their constituents. Many were left to wonder: if the government knew the threat of nuclear war was so great, why were the nation's leaders so unprepared to protect, feed, and care for their constituents?

CRISIS MENTALITY

How worried were most Americans, and how much thought did they give to civil defense? Clearly, some entered a state of near-panic and desperately sought civil defense answers while others remained calm and unbothered, either because they did not expect war or because they thought any preparations would be futile. Surveys conducted in late 1961 and 1962, mostly before the missile crisis, showed that roughly a third of the population believed a general nuclear war was likely,[143] and if that war began, 70 percent thought that bombs and missiles would rain down on their own communities.[144] Faced with the prospect of surviving when friends and family members did not, 30 percent said they would prefer to die.[145] Almost 60 percent believed that family shelter owners would have to fight to keep neighbors out if war began, and 64 percent said that living in a shelter for a long time would drive many people insane.[146] Many, in fact, wondered whether the leisure-conscious, gadget-seeking Americans of the 1960s could accept the austerity of shelter life.

The prospects were grim, but the threat was not great enough to make most Americans lose their heads. Several years before, Eisenhower's civil defense chief Val Peterson had estimated that 83 percent of American men and 55 percent of American women could be made "reasonably panic resistant"

Extra security measures greet tourists at the White House on 23 October. While the nation was not in a state of war, the government was on alert for potential security breaches by innocent-looking civilians. Robert Knudsen photo, John F. Kennedy Library.

with proper civil defense training,[147] and without much civil defense training at all, it appears that most Americans did avoid surrendering to panic during the crisis, although some nervousness was undeniable. An Office of Civil Defense study conducted nine months after the crisis found that more than 40 percent of American adults said they took some civil defense measures during the week-long standoff. Precautions included conducting family discussions about what to do if war broke out when family members were separated, deciding where the family would seek shelter, preparing a fallout shelter space in the home or thinking about construction of a shelter, considering evacuation, and contacting local civil defense authorities.[148] The number who admitted considering civil defense actions may be artificially low because most of us are braver, calmer, and smarter in retrospect than we are in reality, and knowing that the crisis ended peacefully probably affected respondents' recollections about their own mental states.[149] Also, that study suggested that many who did not address civil defense were simply in a state of denial about the danger the crisis presented.[150]

Many Americans had been in denial about civil defense throughout the Cold War. One person who faced up to his denial in 1961 was the Reverend Jack Mendelsohn, a Unitarian minister in Boston. From the pulpit, he said,

"I myself now accept the probability of a nuclear holocaust, the literal cremation of hundreds of millions of people, including myself and my family, within the next five or ten years." And yet, he admitted, "I have made no move to transplant my family to some non-strategic part of the world, somewhere in the Southern Hemisphere let's say. This does not mean, however, that I am not fleeing. It means only that I am fleeing through psychological mechanisms of denial. I am ignoring and dismissing what is simply too painful for me to perceive." He said he simply could not accept the hopelessness of nuclear war, and many of those who did not "panic" during the missile crisis were, like Mendelsohn, in denial.[151]

Lou Oschmann was a navy corpsman in Lakehurst, New Jersey, when the crisis occurred. When he was given a couple of days off, he

> wanted to get away from the military facility, and I wanted not to have to think about it because it weighed so heavily that it was like if you have terminal cancer or something, there are times when you don't think about it, but it stays with you—the whole day. So I took the bus to New York City, which probably would have been a major target, too. I just didn't care: I wanted to escape. I went to museums and spent my days in New York City. I went to a couple of bars. I figured that if I'm going to die in a few days, I might as well be doing something I enjoy—and it made me feel better.

Despite his efforts to hide, "I couldn't even plan for more than a day or two . . . because I didn't know whether I was going to be around that long. I had this sense of just living for the moment . . . one day or one hour."[152]

Forty-year-old Clois Williams, a single African American mother making ends meet by cleaning the homes of white families in the town of Hickory, North Carolina, had little time to worry about foreign affairs, but she couldn't ignore the tension that surrounded her during the crisis. She remembers one day with great clarity; the day after Kennedy's speech, she awoke knowing that her daughter, Katherleen, thirteen, was nervous because her school planned an attack drill. She went to her job, and her employer

> had me take her vacuum cleaner downstairs and look in all the cracks and get rid of the spider webs so the basement could be their fallout shelter. And to tell you the truth, that dark basement scared me more than Khrushchev. I thought cleaning out the basement was silly, because if you're scared, what difference does it make if it's clean? Then, when I got home,

I found out that Katherleen had run home from school scared to death. When she got home, no one was there, so she ran back to find her 5-year-old cousin and bring him home. That night, because of all the running and excitement, she had an asthma attack. The younger folks were just scared.[153]

During and after the crisis, many citizens let Kennedy know they were worried. They sent telegrams advising him that local civil defense programs were poorer than he might think. A Peoria man urged JFK to start rapid construction of public shelters,[154] and a Massachusetts man asked him to relocate food stockpiles in scattered locations across the country.[155] One Californian spoke for many when he declared, "One is shocked that you would bring us to the precipice of . . . [war] knowing fully that should hostilities develop millions of Americans might needlessly lose their lives that otherwise might be spared had you got the civilian defense program 'moving.'"[156]

Inadequate federal funding just added to the problems of local and state governments, which shouldered part of civil defense's cost. In Philadelphia, for instance, officials noted that a hydrogen bomb hitting the city could cause damage not just outside the city limits but also beyond Pennsylvania's borders in New Jersey and Delaware, a reality that complicated state and local efforts and encouraged a feeling of futility.[157] The federal government outlined by our Founding Fathers simply was not designed to protect the population from a massive and catastrophic national threat, particularly without a national consensus on the feasibility of that protection.

As it struggled with organizational and funding shortcomings, the administration faced an increasingly skeptical public. Women Strike for Peace, one of the early 1960s' most prominent pacifist organizations, declared during 1962, "In a nuclear age, shelters do not provide protection and . . . most civil defense measures are woefully inadequate."[158] Many Americans—Cold Warriors as well as pacifists—agreed. What Americans had not truly faced before was whether the risk of nuclear war was worthwhile, given that little protection truly existed.

From documents, news reports, correspondence, and oral history interviews, it is possible to reconstruct glimpses of American life during the crisis. What emerges from these glimpses is not a cohesive portrait of unified action but a collection of individual responses to the threat of nuclear war. It is difficult to generalize about how Americans responded because, for the most part, there is no record of those who ignored the threat or felt any action would be futile. Clearly, the crisis created anxiety and panic among many Americans. Individual citizens as well as individual governments responded in unique ways. The public thirst for information and governmental attempts to prepare for the worst represented understandable efforts to take control of a situation entirely beyond the control of citizens and local governments. Ignoring the crisis was yet another means of asserting control by not allowing events to intrude on daily life.

During that week, many Americans recognized the reality of nuclear war's threat at the same time they acknowledged the unreality of civil defense plans, with inadequate funding, insufficient shelters, a lack of stocked shelters, and no clear evidence that adequate food production could be carried out after the soil had been contaminated with radiation.[159] In short, for the first time, many were willing to reject government reassurances and assert that the emperor wore no clothes. Despite all the drills and civil defense propaganda of the Eisenhower and Kennedy administrations, the nation was not prepared, even seventeen years after the first atomic weapon had been detonated. It is not surprising that public interest in civil defense declined after this period. More like science fiction than fact, the civil defense preparations of this period reflected the kind of frantic guesswork on which they were constructed. No one—not even the most exalted and educated "experts"—really knew what to expect in a nuclear war using such powerful weapons. Hiroshima and Nagasaki were little more than reference points, given the power of nuclear weapons in 1962.

Like people who search the night sky for signs of spaceships from other worlds, civil defense planners recognized that a potential problem might be looming in the darkness but had little idea what to do when it landed on their doorstep. Before the crisis, millions had hidden from the facts, unwilling to face head-on the possibility that contrary to the American penchant for living in the future, nuclear war and the drive to eradicate "the other" threatened to preempt that future. Now it was clear to many. War was not merely a means of eliminating "the other"; it was a dead end for American hopes as well. Civil defense offered no rescue, just false promises of security in a world shaped by insecurity. Within a few years, air-raid drills and fallout shelters would be remnants of a foolish past.

the looking glass

Some of our Government's public relations officials have espoused the desirability of having the Government speak "with one voice" to all news media in matters of national or international policy. The press has responded with one voice, loud and clear, in objecting and protesting what appear as some radically different concepts of getting the news to the citizens of our Nation. —Gene Robb, publisher, *Albany Times-Union*, 19 March 1963

A free press is never in greater danger than in times of war, when the national interest may conflict or seem to conflict with the people's right to know. And the dangers seem as real, whether the war is hot or cold. In many ways, the Cold War of the early 1960s presented more hazards to the media than a declared and definable shooting war because the threat of warfare hung like a phantom over everything with no clear beginning or ending point. Though the Cuban Missile Crisis ended with Kennedy glorified as a hero in much of the media, the Kennedy administration's handling of the media during this period generated doubts among journalists about the government's willingness to tell the whole truth. The administration's conduct introduced "news management" to the American vernacular and led to concerns that undoubtedly colored the media's attitudes toward the White House over the tumultuous years to come.

It is easy to recognize government officials' struggle to balance the obligations to support freedom of the press and to safeguard national security at this time. While officials sometimes used excessive power to quiet the press, they were not alone in the debate over national priorities: journalists wrestled with the same issues because the immense threat of nuclear war made it difficult for reporters and editors to define a truly objective role for themselves. Many believed that only a razor-thin edge separated the United States from catastrophic war against an implacable enemy. As a result, they too readily acted as a government tool at times and often accepted restrictions on their freedoms based on the belief that national security—and survival—sometimes deserved higher consideration than First Amendment rights.

Throughout its short tenure, the Kennedy administration demonstrated great deftness at manipulating the press, and in a surprising number of cases, journalists willingly followed where the White House led. When rumors arose that Kennedy's marriage to Jacqueline Bouvier was not his first, few reporters pursued the story. Most journalists ignored reports of Kennedy's marital infidelities, and even after seeing the ailing Kennedy struggle with poor health and back injuries, reporters continued to accept and proliferate the administration's portrait of a vigorous, healthy leader. In 1961, editors suppressed or watered down reports about the Central Intelligence Agency's plans to land Cuban refugees at the Bay of Pigs, and when the doomed assault occurred, journalists initially assumed a U.S. victory because of the administration's confidence.

Many politicians surround themselves with "spin masters" who can convey their message to the media convincingly, but John F. Kennedy himself had a keen understanding of the press and its workings. Through the influence of his father, Kennedy received scattered assignments as a special correspondent between his World War II tour of duty in the navy and his election to the House of Representatives in 1946. And over the years, he showed an affinity for members of the press, developing close friendships with some of the reporters who had covered him. Among his closest friends were Charles Bartlett of the *Chattanooga Times*, syndicated columnist Joseph Alsop, and Ben Bradlee of *Newsweek*. In addition, Kennedy was what today might be called a "news junkie." As CBS correspondent George Herman reported in 1961, "The president's thirst for newspapers and magazines is unquenchable at any hour of day or night."[1]

Some journalists, such as the *New York Times*'s James Reston, saw danger in Kennedy's closeness to the media: "There's an interesting thing here in the sense that for the first time in a long time the men who are now writing on the national scene—that is to say, writing syndicated columns, writing over the entire nation—are older than the man who happens to be president of the United States and for that reason, perhaps, he pays more attention to us than he should."[2] Reston saw this as a double-edged sword that cut badly in both directions: Kennedy was too responsive to journalists' opinions, and because he made journalists feel important, they became too susceptible to his charms. Acknowledging his own attendance at White House events, Reston said, "That's quite different from J. Alsop going around and telling him how to run the country, and getting into a sort of exchange of information and then pretty soon he's got you in his pocket because this guy can charm the birds out of the trees."[3]

Herman, too, felt the president's closeness to the press was a liability.

> It stemmed from a dangerous excess of esteem which should not be. The newsman's job is not to be charmed, not to be inside the president's social circle, not to meet him at dinner. The newsman's job, as I see it and as I was brought up to see it, is always to be skeptical, always to look at the people in power and think to yourself, "What are they doing wrong? Why are they doing this? In what way does the American people, do my readers, need protection from this man if, in fact, they do at all?" And I think there was a small abdication of this responsibility in the first year or two of Kennedy.[4]

Syndicated columnist Joseph Kraft, on the other hand, thought friendships linking the White House and the press were perfectly natural. "My view is that this is bound to happen or it's going to happen more and more and the healthy relationship is a kind of in and out relationship where some portion of the press corps will have these relationships and another portion will be left out. I don't think that you pass a self-denying ordinance for the whole press corps."[5]

Administration officials prided themselves on good relations with the media, with one claiming that "no president of the United States has enjoyed a more favorable relationship with the American press than does President Kennedy."[6] In retrospect, Edwin Bayley, who served the Kennedy administration in a variety of press relations roles, concluded, "The Kennedys were . . . very effective in buttering up the press, as is only intelligent. I think they made a lot of friends there although I don't recall anybody else taking sides like that."[7] Using secrecy, "planting" questions at news conferences,[8] and wooing journalists with special attention, President Kennedy sometimes was able to make the press function as a public relations arm of the White House.[9] Kennedy was the first to master the new medium, television, through live news conferences.

In the years leading up to the crisis, the media had made Kennedy its star through magazine spreads spotlighting his ever-photogenic family, articles about his heroic World War II exploits, televised appearances that showed off the irreverent and self-deprecating Kennedy wit, and favorable commentary, often written by journalists who fell within Kennedy's coterie of friends. During the crisis, the danger of war emboldened administration officials to test that relationship with the media by restricting journalists' access to news sources. At the crisis's end, the thrill of apparent victory led administration spokesmen to boast too freely about their success in duping the media and their right to do so. As a result, even Kennedy loyalists began to see beyond the star's dazzling persona and look more closely at what was happening behind the curtain.

COLD WAR DRAMA

With the Cold War as a backdrop, Kennedy administration officials found it relatively easy to cast journalists in the role of friendly colleagues rather than adversarial inquisitors. American journalists, like most Americans, feared the Soviet Union and the possibility that many American freedoms, including freedom of the press, might be jeopardized by a Soviet decision to launch nuclear war. The administration's need to keep secrets from the Soviet Union provided an excellent rationalization for hiding the truth from the media and the public. No one—not even the fiercest defender of freedom of information—would have argued that the media should have full access to national security documents; therefore, most disputes about access to information sprang from disagreements over the degree of openness, not from debate over the need for secrecy.

As a result, in this crisis and in others that had come before, reporters often were acquiescent players in the administration's efforts to lower a veil of secrecy around government activity. As I. F. *Stone's Weekly* reported after the crisis, such manipulation "has been facilitated by the readiness of the press corps to be the willing conduit of all kinds of official misinformation and mischief as dished out in the capital's fifty-seven varieties of off-the-record-but-please-use-it press conferences."[10] However, in October 1962, the administration went a step beyond the commonsensical national security catechism of secrecy. When government spokesmen expressed Kennedy's desire to have the government speak with "one voice," that declaration seemed eerily like the practices of totalitarian regimes or of a democratic government in the midst of world war.

After the crisis began with the sighting of Soviet missiles in 14 October reconnaissance photos of Cuba, the administration was unsure how to respond. To ferret out the options without revealing awareness of the missiles, Kennedy and his advisers sought total secrecy. As the Ex Comm commenced meeting surreptitiously, even Press Secretary Pierre Salinger remained in the dark. On the day of the missiles' discovery, officials told 500 journalists in a background briefing that the United States had no intention of

Many journalists photograph President Kennedy as he delivers his dramatic address to the nation on 22 October. Some reporters feared that a misstep might lead to disaster, so they generally accepted the Kennedy administration's statements without question. Robert Knudsen photo, John F. Kennedy Library.

using military force against Cuba. Although the government certainly had planned a long list of sabotage operations in Cuba, no assault was imminent. Nevertheless, journalists later would pinpoint that as the moment when the administration started prevaricating about the missile crisis.[11]

While the secret Ex Comm meetings proceeded, Kennedy continued to follow his previously announced schedule for several days. Then, he cut short a campaign trip, claiming to be ill, and returned to Washington on Saturday, 20 October, to see the latest reconnaissance photos and confer with his advisers. The White House maintained the ruse of a Kennedy illness after his return, telling reporters that he was "considerably better" the following day.[12] After a final meeting with his team on Sunday, 21 October, Kennedy mobilized plans to inform U.S. allies and congressional leaders before revealing the discovery of the missiles and announcing his response in an address to the nation on Monday night. Having the time to deliberate without publicity affected the outcome of the Ex Comm meetings. Robert Kennedy later wrote: "If our deliberations had been publicized, if we had had to make a decision in twenty-four hours, I believe the course that we ultimately would have taken would have been quite different and filled with far greater risks."[13] With emotions running high in the early Ex Comm meetings, most of Kennedy's advisers and the president himself initially favored direct military action against Cuba. If a quick decision had been necessary, U.S. air raids or an invasion might have sparked a larger war.

As the White House prepared to handle the crisis in a public forum, the president asked government spokesmen to review steps taken at the start of the Korean War "in regard to putting holds on the press, if any. Or whether, what the technique was, whether it was done voluntarily, or what they did. Because I think we might have to think about the same sort of thing."[14]

By Sunday, however, the secret was in danger of discovery: noticeable military preparations had begun for the naval blockade and a possible invasion. Over the weekend, the *Virginia News Pilot*, the Associated Press, the *New York Herald Tribune*, the *Washington Post*, CBS News, and the *New York Times* all had asked for an explanation.[15] Washington insiders knew something was brewing, too, but the administration did an unusually effective job of keeping its secret.[16] Almost inevitably, reporters broke through the administration's wall of silence, and the White House learned that Reston and Max Frankel were preparing an article for Monday's *New York Times* that would speculate about trouble in Cuba and suggest that Soviet nuclear weapons were in place there.[17] Before any story could be published, Kennedy himself called *Times* publisher Orvil Dryfoos and *Washington Post* publisher Philip Graham to ask that both newspapers steer clear of the story until he could address the nation. Speaking to Reston, Kennedy warned that publication of the news could enable Khrushchev to give the United States an ultimatum before Kennedy had taken his stand.[18] Although Kennedy had admitted to Dryfoos just a month earlier that the Bay of Pigs disaster might have been avoided if the *Times* had reported fully what it knew in advance,[19] Dryfoos and Graham both complied with Kennedy's plea in this crisis.[20] Other newspapers picked up hints of military activity, and, instead of rushing what they knew into print, they sought government guidance on how to proceed. A State Department memo reported that "Florida papers want to play it on front page tomorrow and have inquired of Department for guidance." The memo called it "real scare stuff."[21]

Most newspapers handled the unraveling secret by publishing vague reports that a crisis air hung over Washington, and none stole Kennedy's opportunity to jolt the Soviet Union with the discovery of the missiles and the tough U.S. response. Salinger announced the president's planned 7 P.M. address at his midday news briefing, and when Kennedy spoke, more than 50 million Americans saw the speech on television.[22] In the address's aftermath, the American people and newspaper editorial pages united behind his leadership, with even the Republican *New York Herald Tribune* declaring, "The people of the United States must and will unite behind the president in the course which Soviet aggression has made inevitable. They can hope, with him, that Premier Khrushchev will abandon a dangerous provocation that his own government declared was useless for their security."[23] While some editorials questioned Kennedy's failure to act sooner, most offered blanket support. The Associated Press compiled excerpts from editorials published nationwide and summarized them by reporting that "the nation's newspapers editorially stood firm behind President John F. Kennedy's decision to quarantine arms shipments to Cuba."[24]

This nearly unanimous support is noteworthy because Kennedy's policy in Cuba had long been a target of vocal anti-Communist politicians and journalists who felt that he had not been aggressive enough about ousting Castro. In the weeks leading up to identification of missiles on the island, conservative Democrats, Republicans, and some journalists criticized Kennedy for not responding immediately to the buildup of Soviet forces and conventional weapons in Cuba. However, identifying Soviet soldiers as "technicians," Kennedy had replied that the influx of Soviet manpower and weaponry in Cuba was defensive and posed no threat to the United States. His toughest critics did not agree. "Mr. Kennedy has abandoned that principle of the Monroe Doctrine which declared that after the year 1823 the United States would not countenance any colonization by a European power or extension of its system in any country in this hemisphere," David Lawrence wrote in *U.S. News & World Report* in September 1962. "Mr. Kennedy chooses now to narrow the Doctrine to cover only 'offensive' action taken by one American state against another with the aid of a European power."[25] Despite this criticism, much of which sprang from Republican senator Kenneth Keating's assertions that Soviet missiles were in Cuba, there was little frank criticism of Kennedy or the blockade in the media during the crisis.[26]

Most members of the media played the role Kennedy had assigned to them without complaint. Sharing his concern about nuclear war, they served as a conduit of Cold War dogma and proliferators of selectively disclosed information. Through editorial endorsements, they embraced the notion that Americans must set aside lingering questions and unite to face a frightening enemy. Then they focused on covering one of the biggest news stories of the decade.

THE PROSPECT OF WAR

After absorbing the shock of learning that their nation was near war, the media focused on serving a public with an insatiable appetite for news. "Throughout the nation," *Newsweek* reported, "Americans hung by their radios and TV sets, and pressed up to television store windows. Transistor radios popped up on streets, in trains, even in theaters. There was the gnawing apprehension everywhere that this time might really be it."[27]

The relatively new medium of television news took advantage of its ability to provide instant coverage and to quench the nation's thirst for up-to-the-minute reports. Television networks then had small reporting staffs, relied heavily on newspaper and wire service reporting for content, and offered only fifteen-minute nightly news broadcasts; however, by interrupting regularly scheduled programming, offering live coverage of United Nations Security Council debate, and producing special reports, the networks could keep the public informed about breaking developments. The National Broadcasting Company interrupted regular programming with news bulletins more than sixty-five times between Monday and Friday of the crisis week and broadcast at least four news specials; the Columbia Broadcasting System broke into regular programming thirty times for news bulletins and produced news specials on five nights. Figures are not available on the American Broadcasting Company's performance, but it, too, offered bulletins and wrap-ups.[28]

"Since the night of Oct. 22," *TV Guide* proudly proclaimed, "television has most emphatically been more than just a handy device to relax the tired breadwinner, soothe the harried housewife or keep the kids out of their hair."[29] Nevertheless, there were gaps in TV coverage. While the networks did interrupt scheduled entertainment programming and preempt shows such as *Stump the Stars*, continuous coverage of events, like the United Nations debate, ended at 7:30 P.M., when the prime-time entertainment schedule began. Only educational television stations in New York and Boston provided full, uninterrupted coverage.[30] *Variety* told its readers that radio still outdistanced television in news reporting, often with virtually

Television played a crucial role in spreading news about the crisis. Cuban refugees gather in a New York hotel to hear the presidential address. In the speech, Kennedy announced that the Soviet Union had placed nuclear missiles in Cuba, and he revealed plans for a naval blockade of the island. © Bettmann/CORBIS.

continuous and comprehensive coverage. According to the show business publication, the networks considered providing continuous television coverage but feared that reporters struggling to fill dead air might lapse into dangerous speculation at a time when the jittery nation was susceptible to panic.[31]

Humorist and talk show host Jack Paar was among those whose hunger for news was not satiated by spotty TV coverage. As the first Soviet ship neared the blockade, Paar "rushed home to throw on the set, couldn't wait till it would warm up, wondering whether I'd see Frank McGee or Walter Cronkite or one of those voices that could be doom, and it warmed up, and in comes [the situation comedy] *My Little Margie*. I flipped to the next channel and there was Joyce Brothers giving advice to the lovelorn and on the third channel was a lady telling you how to make a tuna fish cake. So it was really very reassuring that these are signs everything is going to be all right in the world."[32]

This unsatisfied need for the latest news showed television's potential and probably facilitated network decisions to begin expanding newscasts from fifteen to thirty minutes less than a year later. Because missiles could strike with just minutes' warning, waiting hours for the next available newspaper became unacceptable. Similarly, the American and Soviet governments recognized the advantages of using broadcast media as a means of exchanging messages: although the crisis occurred at the dawn of the space age, communication between governments was slow. The United States and the Soviet Union routinely exchanged communiqués via cables, with a single cable taking as long as seven hours to reach its destination.[33] By the crisis's end, each country decided to communicate by giving statements to its own national media.[34]

While newspapers lacked the ability to provide instant information, they attempted to provide more thorough coverage. Editors filled front pages with accounts of nervous waiting along the blockade line, activation of troops in the United States, strategic meetings at the White House, drama in the United Nations, civil defense measures in the schools, and tension in Moscow. Newspapers devoted much space to pursuing every angle of the story, with the *New York Times* offering sixty-four columns—eight full pages—of coverage on 24 October alone. As the *New Republic* reported, Kennedy "knocked an election off the front page in its final weeks and produced ulcers in 998 reporters on the Washington scene."[35] Responding to civil defense questions, newspapers reported a lack of civil defense preparedness, accelerated efforts to correct that problem, and panic buying of "survival" goods in many cities. Some articles attempted to dig beneath the surface by examining the missiles' real effect on American national security, analyzing the showdown's potential influence on the upcoming off-year elections, and gauging the crisis's business impact, from tourism to oil and gas regulation.

What readers and journalists did not know at that time was that the CIA could disseminate news through the Associated Press and United Press International wire services without editors realizing that they were releasing fabrications created by the intelligence agency. Documents declassified in 2001 revealed this CIA tactic was used during the Bay of Pigs invasion, probably through the employment of agents in the wire services' foreign bureaus, and it seems unlikely such an asset would have been squandered during the missile crisis.[36]

To varying degrees, the media tried to address the cataclysm that might await America. Scripps-Howard newspapers somewhat gruesomely told readers how many minutes it would take a missile to travel from Cuba to key

U.S. cities.[37] The *Detroit Free Press* described what its readers could expect to find outside their windows if a nuclear weapon hit the metropolitan area,[38] while the *Washington Star* drew the obvious conclusion that full-scale war might delay the U.S. mission to land on the moon.[39] As journalists groped for future-oriented approaches to a story with an unknown and possibly "future-less" outcome, they probably heightened readers' fears.

Throughout much of the reporting during this crisis week, journalists impressed their audiences with the monumental nature of the crisis: "One Week May Alter All Future" was the headline on an Associated Press article published in the *Tulsa World*.[40] This fondness for drama led some people to accuse the media of overplaying the week's events to sell newspapers and grab viewers, and clearly, any news event represents a business opportunity to print and broadcast journalists alike. To avoid appearing to hype the story, television executives at CBS and ABC warned their employees to be careful. "I am sure that it is superfluous and even presumptuous of me to remind you that whatever the competitive temptations, this is no time for contrived drama or for doom-laden or hyperthyroid portents," CBS News president Dick Salant told his division.[41] Nevertheless, much of the media characterized the crisis in terms of high drama. For example, television anchorman Walter Cronkite reported on 23 October that "the world was given at least a fifteen-hour moratorium tonight" because activation of the quarantine had been delayed to the following day,[42] and two days later, Cronkite stated that "the world seems to have veered off, at least for the moment, the collision course toward global annihilation."[43] On NBC's *Huntley-Brinkley Report*, Chet Huntley set a sober tone by calling Kennedy's speech "the toughest and the most grim speech by a president since December 1941 when President Roosevelt spoke to the Congress and the nation about the day of infamy . . . the attack on Pearl Harbor."[44]

In a crisis that extends beyond the nation's boundaries, print and broadcast journalists face the difficult challenge of chronicling what is happening in other nations that are often unfriendly to U.S. journalists. Reporting on the crisis's effects in the Soviet Union and Cuba was problematic. American journalists in Moscow could pass on a few details about government activities in the Soviet capital, although the populace's awareness of the crisis and response to it were more difficult to gauge, given the vagueness of Soviet media accounts. Telling the Cuban side of the story was even tougher because restrictions on journalists in the island nation discouraged or displaced American journalists, leaving even the *New York Times* without a reporter on the island.[45] To get some insight on the Cuban side of the crisis,

CBS monitored events there by having a plane fly high above the Caribbean to pick up Cuban television signals.[46]

Despite the temptation to interpret the crisis as a potential tragedy of operatic proportions, most coverage merely matched the events' importance. Almost unfailingly, reporters accepted information provided by government spokesmen, often throwing cold water on rumors rather than promoting them. For instance, there were reports of Texans slipping across the border to the safer ground of Mexico, but the *Laredo Times* buried that scuttlebutt in the middle of an article on the high demand for survival supplies. The newspaper introduced the rumor to its readers in negative form: "A report that there has been a movement of citizens from this side across the border to Mexico was discounted by officials at the bridge."[47] While occasionally falling victim to a desire to overdramatize the dangerous crisis, journalists, for the most part, avoided reporting that might create panic and devoted a great deal of time and news space to disproving rumors, which were prevalent at that time. Media leaders took pride in this "responsible" approach to covering an important national news event.

RESTRAINTS ON THE FREE PRESS

As the delicate process of diplomatic exchanges and the complicated task of mobilizing troops for a possible invasion of Cuba occurred simultaneously, the administration attempted to guarantee that the journalistic community's zeal for news did not endanger national security. After some deliberation, the administration announced that it would no longer issue releases on deployment of forces, estimates of U.S. capacity to knock out targets, intelligence speculation on enemy strength, details of troop movements, levels of military alert, information on aircraft sites, emergency dispersal plans for planes or troops, and U.S. vulnerability. In addition, it asked newspaper and magazine editors as well as TV and radio news directors not to report on any of those topics even if reporters obtained information from other sources, a request that many members of the media labeled as a dangerous plea for self-censorship.[48]

The White House also tried somewhat unsuccessfully to channel all communication through its own press office instead of allowing release of information by State Department and Pentagon sources.[49] In addition, the Department of Defense and Department of State instituted a policy ordering all personnel to file daily reports on their interviews or telephone conversations with reporters or to have a public information representative sit in on each interview, thus narrowing reporters' opportunities to pick up information through informal contacts.[50]

The administration maintained partial secrecy on diplomatic, as well as military, moves. When the president's brother, Robert, met behind closed doors with Soviet ambassador Anatoly Dobrynin and ultimately offered a secret swap of missiles in Turkey for missiles in Cuba, many details of the exchanges were unknown, even to some Ex Comm members. In addition, officials chose not to reveal immediately that a U-2 accidentally had strayed into Soviet airspace on 27 October because they feared limiting Khrushchev's options, according to Salinger.[51]

Going beyond mere restrictions on news releases,[52] the administration also barred reporters from U.S. ships in the naval blockade, thus allowing the White House to issue military reports on a schedule that best suited its goals. A *Miami Herald* reporter attempted to get a close look at the blockade by chartering a twin-engine seaplane and discovered the military was serious about its restrictions—so serious that a U.S. destroyer set its sights on his plane, forcing his retreat to Florida.[53] The American Newspaper Publishers Association and the American Society of Newspaper Editors later asserted that not allowing reporters on the ships gave the public a false image of how the quarantine functioned. Some ships, particularly those from Scandinavian countries, ignored the blockade and proceeded on their way; therefore, the organizations alleged, the administration's claim of an airtight blockade was misleading.[54]

In some quarters, there were charges that the administration had gone beyond safeguarding secrets and had provided distorted information. Some journalists asserted that the administration had exaggerated the range of Soviet missiles in Cuba to bolster Latin American support for Kennedy's actions. While earlier administration estimates had described the range of a medium-range missile as 400 to 700 nautical miles, the administration credited them with a range of 1,000 miles during the crisis. Similarly, the range of intermediate-range missiles, previously set at 1,130 to 1,300 nautical miles, rose to 2,200 miles.[55] Some analysts also suggested that the administration had overstated the advantage that missiles in Cuba would give the Soviet Union.[56]

In addition, the administration attempted to influence even the tone of media coverage. When the first Soviet ships turned around short of the blockade line and sailed back toward the Soviet Union, the White House sought to avoid allowing an undue air of celebration to permeate the coverage because officials did not want to antagonize a potentially mellowing Khrushchev.[57]

Controlling the story became increasingly difficult as a widening circle of officials received briefings on the details—a lesson learned when Rep. James Van Zandt, a Pennsylvania Republican, walked out of a congressional briefing and immediately held a news conference to reveal that a Soviet tanker had been allowed to pass through the blockade.[58] Kennedy was irate that Van Zandt had released the information forty-five minutes before the Pentagon had planned an announcement, and reporters were unhappy about receiving such vital details from someone so far removed from the action. Similarly, through a diplomatic snafu, British officials released photos of the missile sites to their nation's media, though the White House had decided against giving the photos to the American press. With the British press boldly displaying the photos, the White House released them in the United States.[59]

Even with restrictions on the media, another leak caused headaches for Kennedy, forcing him to deny reports that officials believed a 26 October letter from Khrushchev was the product of an agitated or overwrought man. To avert future breaches, Kennedy tightened secrecy more, ordering on 2 November that no aerial reconnaissance photos of Cuba be released even within the government until he had seen them and decided who should have access to them.[60]

In spite of almost universal dismay over restrictions imposed by the administration, most journalists obeyed the rules and did not seek to acquire information on the restricted list. The *Los Angeles Times* even cut short a series of articles on submarines that had started before the crisis began,[61] and NBC canceled a potentially provocative documentary on tunnels built by East Germans attempting to crawl to safety beneath the Berlin Wall.[62] At least one prominent journalist—*Atlanta Constitution* editor Ralph McGill— approved of the administration's tight-lipped approach. "I do want to say that I think a policy of secrecy has been one of the more valuable ingredients of all that has been done," he told Kennedy in a telegram. "I hope this policy can continue and that you can enlist responsible leaders in Congress to join in appeals to the various information media to cooperate."[63] McGill, who favored appointing a panel to set Cold War press guidelines, thought openly seeking to give the government a single voice was wrong, but he also felt the *New York Times* had jeopardized national security by reporting who had visited Kennedy during the week.[64]

Other journalists found the administration's restrictions difficult to swallow. Given the White House's friendly relationship with much of the press corps, many journalists responded with disbelief to the restrictions. Because the *New York Times* and the *Washington Post* already had proven their willingness to put the nation's well-being above the newspapers' needs by withholding news of the missiles' discovery at Kennedy's request, journalists saw the broad-ranging restrictions as unreasonable. Although most moderated their complaints until the crisis had ended, attitudes toward the White House changed. "When Kennedy tried to tighten controls at the State Department and Pentagon," according to CBS's George Herman, "reporters said, 'But we love him. How can he do this to us?' And I think there was this enormous and unprecedented backlash inside the press because they had been so charmed by him."[65]

To minimize complaints, the administration demonstrated its usual efficiency by anticipating reporters' questions. It even produced a twenty-eight-page Pentagon pamphlet with answers to likely questions, such as whether right-wing groups had pressured Kennedy to act in Cuba and whether Kennedy was trying to start World War III.[66] A big part of Kennedy's plan for winning over the press was to recognize the big players and attempt to bring them onto his team. Despite his long-held belief that *Time* had been unfair to him, Kennedy himself gave a briefing to *Time* publisher Henry Luce and managing editor Otto Fuerbringer. The administration courted other influential journalists, such as Walter Lippmann and Reston, in private briefings.[67]

In addition to helping his own cause, Kennedy wanted to make sure these influential writers had access to correct information that reflected his viewpoint because he realized that Soviet officials read U.S. journalism for evidence of trial balloons released by the White House. And as Marianne Means of Hearst newspapers said, "The Russians read the *New York Times*; it's important that the story be accurate in a crisis. They don't read the *San Antonio Light*."[68] When Lippmann suggested that the United States give up its missiles in Turkey in exchange for the removal of Soviet missiles in Cuba, Kennedy could anticipate that Soviets would believe Lippmann was speaking for the White House. In fact, Lippmann told Ambassador Dobrynin that he "caught it hot" after recommending a missile swap and advised the ambassador that because of pressure from conservatives, the administration could not afford to make such a trade to resolve the Cuban crisis.[69] After Soviet ambassador to the United Nations Valerian Zorin quoted from Lippmann's column, angry readers bombarded the columnist with scathing letters, often arguing that his proposal represented evidence that freedom of the press should be curbed.[70] Keeping the swap secret protected Kennedy's image and did nothing for Lippmann's.

CROSSING THE LINE

As the crisis unfolded and wavered in the narrow space that separates war and peace, some reporters found themselves in the unusual position of serving as information conduits between the U.S. and Soviet governments — another deterrent to the quest for objectivity. If journalists act as informal envoys between nations, it is impossible for them to maintain their role as observers.

The case that has become the most widely publicized over the years involved John Scali of the American Broadcasting Company. On Friday, 26 October, he received a phone call from Alexander Fomin, counselor of the Soviet embassy in the United States — a man with whom he had shared lunch on several occasions. The tone of desperation in his source's voice led Scali to meet the man right away for lunch. When he reached the restaurant, Scali found the air of suspense heightened by his companion's refusal to talk while a waiter was nearby, but after they placed their order, Fomin reportedly told Scali, "War seems about to break out. Something must be done to save the situation."[71]

According to Scali, the Soviet official then asked whether the United States would agree not to invade Cuba in exchange for a promise to dismantle the missiles. Scali agreed to approach the State Department to find out. When he later indicated American willingness to make a deal and the Soviets failed to act immediately, Scali regretted his decision to leave the sidelines and become a player in the crisis. Subsequently, he explained that he "thought that . . . [I] had allowed myself to be used in a skillful and treacherous Soviet delaying action . . . meant to stall to give the Soviet military in Cuba time to arm the missiles and to get them operational so that they then would have the option either of threatening to fire them at the United States or indeed going ahead."[72]

Two years later, in spotlighting Scali's once-secret role, ABC News expressed pride in his patriotism but added, "[I]n the future, except in the direst emergencies, we hope governments will find direct channels and we will keep Scali's scoops exclusive . . . on our network."[73] In the late 1980s and early 1990s, when American, Russian, and Cuban participants in the crisis opened a dialogue about what had transpired, Fomin and Scali differed somewhat in recollections of their exchanges,[74] but Scali's choice to take a central role in the crisis was undeniable.[75]

Recent revelations have shown that other American journalists served as unofficial information sources to the Soviet government. Based on what two American reporters had told him, Dobrynin cabled the Soviet Foreign Ministry on 25 October to warn Soviet leaders that the U.S. government had decided to invade Cuba over the next two days and that the U.S. armed services were in "maximum battle readiness including readiness to repulse nuclear attack."[76] Another intelligence officer used *New York Herald Tribune* reporter Warren Rogers as an unwitting source of invasion details.[77] And Frank Holeman of the *New York Daily News* served as a secret connection between the Department of Justice and Soviet intelligence agent Georgi Bolshakov.[78] In addition, Soviet intelligence drew on one intermediary who apparently surreptitiously gathered information from Walter Lippmann.[79]

Because this side of the media's role in the missile crisis did not come to light until years later, it did not galvanize the media to establish new rules on reporters' activities as information couriers between governments. However, it offers additional evidence that reporters had difficulty separating their duties and those of the government when nuclear war was a threat.

TALES OF HEROIC VICTORY

Despite frustration with the administration's restrictions, most journalists viewed the crisis in strictly American terms. For many reporters and editors, the crisis was an issue of "us vs. them" and "right vs. wrong." There was no room for the distancing necessary to protect journalistic objectivity. It was "our" crisis and ultimately "our" victory in the minds of many journalists.

This passage from a 28 October Elie Abel report televised on NBC demonstrates the media's lack of distance as well as its flair for the dramatic: "Khrushchev has offered to remove his offensive weapons from Cuba; if he does we'll lift the quarantine and there will be no invasion. What's in it for the Russians? No more than what's in it for all mankind—the avoidance of an armed showdown which could easily have burned this world to a crisp."[80] In a similar vein, another NBC report declared that "the Voice of America today begins what it calls a crash radio barrage to get our side of the Cuban story to people behind the Iron Curtain."[81]

On almost every issue, journalists were quick to accept and proliferate the U.S. point of view. This was most clear in acceptance of the contention that American missiles in Turkey were fundamentally different from Soviet missiles in Cuba. "The two are drastically different," Howard K. Smith argued on ABC. "Equating the two is like saying a policeman and a gangster are the same because they both carry guns."[82] As Daniel C. Hallin discovered in his study of the media's role in Vietnam, the professionalization of journalism meant that in the early 1960s, news stories dealt strictly with facts and on matters of national security during the Cold War, "official facts" represented objective truth.[83]

Clearly, in times of crisis, there can be a fine line between news and propaganda. Voice of America turned its attention toward pure propaganda, recruiting radio stations in the Southeast to cancel regular programming and to beam the U.S. message into Cuba at night during the "national emergency." And there was discussion of making a TV broadcast to Cuba using an airplane-based TV transmitter.[84] Meanwhile, Castro transmitted a message of his own into the Southeast: "Radio Free Dixie" urged African Americans to intensify pressure for equality.[85]

In its own way, the media played a role in America's propaganda campaign. At the crisis's end, the press could hardly contain its admiration for the young president who had gone eyeball to eyeball with an unpredictable and dangerous enemy. *Life* reported, "The American spirit rose in strength and resolution to the call of the president,"[86] and *Time* declared, "Thus, President John Kennedy appeared to have won in his courageous confrontation with Soviet Russia."[87]

Newsweek noted that the president had recently quoted verses from Domingo Ortega at a State Department event.

Bullfight critics ranked in rows
Crowd the enormous Plaza full;
But only one man is there who knows
And he's the man who fights the bull[88]

Then, the magazine added its own analysis of the man who had fought this bull: "If the president's blockade of Cuba had once and for all stilled the GOP charges of inaction over 'the Cuba mess,' his total victory in the head-on clash with Khrushchev marked his greatest political triumph."[89] Despite Kennedy's stated goal to avoid language that labeled him as a winner and Khrushchev as a loser, the media voiced jubilation, often referring to "Khrushchev's apparent capitulation."

There were quibbles by columnists, mostly about Kennedy's failure to act sooner, but few journalistic accounts failed to report an American victory in a just battle. Among the handful of dissenters was the liberal *New Republic*, which reported gravely, "When one looks back on the events leading up to the president's blockade order it is apparent that unnecessary risks were taken and that the Soviet Union was very nearly backed into a corner from which there was no face-saving escape."[90] The *Nation* agreed, saying Kennedy's "action seems out of relation to the provocation or the occasion—and noticeably so in the way in which, through skillful planning, strict security and artful public relations the stage was set, the interest built up and the decision announced."[91] Some journalists even found reason to praise Khrushchev. "This is no maniac of the Hitler type, looking for a chance to send the world up in a big bonfire," reported William Randolph Hearst Jr. "He is as cunning and calculating a shrewdie as our country has ever had to deal with."[92]

All in all, most in the press agreed: the Cuban Missile Crisis had been a triumph for Kennedy. That result was, in part, a legacy of the administration's skill at news management, and visible preparations for war also colored journalists' perceptions. To guarantee dispersal of news during a war, some reporters had been designated to go to government bunkers, and limited broadcast facilities existed in some bunkers. In addition, the White House had taken steps to set up an Office of Censorship. The Office of Emergency Planning had emergency relocation space set aside for the censors,[93] and on 24 October, Kennedy attempted to recruit former Eisenhower press secretary James Hagerty to head that office. At the time, Hagerty was a vice president of the American Broadcasting Company, and Kennedy's letter indicates that he thought luring Hagerty back into government might be difficult.[94] Also that week, officials of the Office of Emergency Planning met for three days with *Houston Chronicle* editor William P. Steven, as a possible deputy to Hagerty or perhaps a backup for the chief's job; however, subsequent reports show that Steven thought the chief of censorship operations should be intimately familiar with the inner workings of Washington and the officials with whom he would have to work, qualities that he lacked.[95] In addition, the administration made plans to summon to Washington the fifteen-member Censorship Advisory Board, a relic of World War II. Because of the anticipated brevity of all-out nuclear war, Salinger thought the need for censorship in wartime would be quite limited.[96] The finite nature of war made restrictions less likely than in an open-ended crisis such as this one.

Faced with the possibility of nuclear annihilation, Americans, including the journalistic community, felt great relief at the end of the crisis, and it is therefore not surprising that this tense week added to the Kennedy myth that would fully flower a year later when an assassin took his life.

THE PUPPET MASTERS

After the crisis, the government's public information operation dived head-first into hot water. Pentagon spokesman Arthur Sylvester created an uproar by calling the press a weapon in the administration's Cold War armament, and he defended secrecy, suggesting that an administration facing the threat of nuclear war had a right to lie. Sylvester put it plainly, saying the handling of the news is "one of the power factors in our quiver. This precise handling of the release of news can influence developments in the kind of situation in which military, political, and psychological factors are so closely related."[97]

Sylvester's remarks set off alarm bells in newsrooms across the country. His claims suggested that the administration would not flinch at fictionalizing events. In a telegram to Kennedy, Lee Hills, president of the American Society of Newspaper Editors, called Sylvester's remarks "a deep shock to responsible newspaper editors."[98] The *Washington Star* recognized that something fundamental had changed, saying "Mr. Sylvester may have overlooked one likely result of 'the methods we used.' The result that Mr. Sylvester and his superiors, from this time on, are suspect." A few weeks later, Kennedy himself defended his administration's handling of the crisis's earliest stage by keeping the missiles' existence secret. "I have no apologies for that. I don't think that there's any doubt it would have been a great mistake and possibly a disaster if this news had dribbled out when we were unsure of the extent of the Soviet buildup in Cuba, and when we were unsure of our response and when we had not consulted with any of our allies, who might have been involved in great difficulties as a result of our action."[99] In truth, disgruntlement over that initial secrecy was small compared with outrage over Sylvester's remarks, which were not out of line with attitudes within the administration. On 22 October, the day of Kennedy's address, White House military aide Chester V. Clifton reflected that mind-set in a quickly scribbled note that said, "Is there a plan to brief and brainwash key press within twelve hours or so?"[100]

Six weeks after the crisis ended, the American Newspaper Publishers Association, the American Society of Newspaper Editors, and the National Editorial Association issued a joint statement, arguing that in times of crisis, uniform censorship is the best way to protect the nation's security and that full reporting of all information not harmful to the military is essential.[101] In the statement, the organizations sought to make clear that self-censorship was not a desirable means of protecting national security because it was entirely subjective and often self-perpetuating.

In 1963, the debate reached Capitol Hill, where Democratic representative John E. Moss of California convened hearings on the topic.[102] Specifically, Kennedy's accusers alleged that his administration had made intentional misstatements, distorted evidence by withholding pertinent facts, suppressed information, intimidated members of the media, leaked news to favored reporters, and pressured or controlled news sources.[103] After two days of hearings, no significant policy changes sprang from the congressional investigation.

Some journalists saw nothing new in the administration's tactics. Hodding Carter III, then editor and publisher of the *Delta Democrat-Times* in Greenville, Mississippi, and later State Department spokesman in the Jimmy Carter administration, said in 1963, "We had news managers long before Mr. Kennedy went to the White House. We've had it in this country long before and we will continue to be plagued, no matter what our thought horizons become."[104]

Others took the middle road. CBS's White House correspondent Robert Pierpoint said, "There are times when the administration, the Kennedy administration, has the right not to tell anybody anything in the outside world, but I think that those times are very, very rare. And I really don't think they ever have a right to lie."[105] Along those same lines, many reporters voiced the opinion that an honest refusal to comment was preferable to a lie. A third group agreed with the *New York Times*'s Arthur Krock when he wrote that the administration had instituted a policy of news management "more cynically and boldly" than any previous peacetime administration.[106] "Efforts to manage the news—at all levels of government—will continue," the Associated Press Managing Editors' Freedom of Information Committee reported. "When such a tactic is detected, we must protest. But we must depend on skilled and vigorous reporters, backed up by fearless editors, as the major weapon for ripping aside the curtains of secrecy that are used to hide legitimate information. Sound reporting can accomplish more than sounding off."[107]

Newspaper magnate John S. Knight agreed, voicing concern about the press's laxity in pinning down answers and putting the pieces of the puzzle together on their own. He condemned the administration for the subterfuge used to cover up the crisis in the days before Kennedy's speech; however, he expressed greatest alarm over the media's willingness to be spoon-fed information by the White House.[108]

When we look back more than forty years, the press corps of that era does seem surprisingly willing to accept the administration's version of events without much question. Although Keating had asserted that offensive weapons were in Cuba weeks before, reporters readily accepted Kennedy's explanation that Keating had been wrong at the time and that the missile construction had begun after the White House denied Keating's charges. In addition, few reporters pressed for information on why reconnaissance flights had not spotted the missiles sooner.

Reporters also failed to take Kennedy's opponents seriously. Most articles about peace protests described signs carried on the picket line, but few reporters took the time to get direct quotations from protesters or to explain their position. Most strikingly, while some journalists noted that Kennedy's deft handling of the crisis might help Democrats in upcoming congressional elections, few questioned his motives directly. Columnist Drew Pearson was one exception, writing, "In the end what really tipped the scales were political factors, including a report from Vice-President Johnson that Cuba was causing great damage to the Democrats in the election campaign and that the public was getting the impression that Kennedy was indecisive."[109]

In the months after the crisis, reporters voiced more skepticism about whether administration officials had been aware of the missiles in early October when administration spokesmen heaped scorn on Keating's assertions. In addition, because Fidel Castro would not allow on-site inspections of the missile sites, reporters peppered administration spokesmen with questions about how the White House could be so sure no Soviet nuclear weapons remained in Cuba, with the Hearst newspapers promoting rumors that missiles remained, perhaps hidden in caves.[110] The earlier failure to locate the nuclear missiles until construction was well under way tainted intelligence assurances after the crisis that Soviet weapons had, in fact, been withdrawn.[111]

Another postcrisis rumor received widespread attention in the media and demonstrated that journalists' willingness to disseminate unproven allegations seemed to grow as the threat of nuclear war receded. This report, most prominently displayed by Scripps-Howard newspapers, stated that high-altitude Soviet reconnaissance planes had flown over Florida during the crisis. The administration denied those reports, but the rumor was perpetuated by reporters now less likely to accept the administration's word.[112]

Following the crisis, the Kennedy administration faced a more skeptical press, and its successors would feel the onslaught of attacks by reporters who believed the White House was quite capable of following Sylvester's premise and lying. The Johnson administration's misleading statements on Vietnam and the Nixon administration's outright lies about Watergate added to hostility between reporters and the White House. Since then, White House occupants have found that the trust of the media is a very hard prize to win, except in times of war.

MIGHTIER THAN THE SWORD

As Arthur Sylvester had stated, the press could be a weapon in the Cold War; it also could be a political weapon used by one politician to stab an adversary in the back. Johnson apparently feared that his role in the crisis might be misrepresented to hurt him, perhaps under the direction of his nemesis, Robert Kennedy. Johnson asked an aide to analyze one missile crisis account to judge its fairness[113] and later helped to rewrite history by getting out the word that he had taken a vocal and tough stand, an assertion not supported by the Ex Comm tapes released years after his death.[114] However, LBJ was not the real target of character assassination after the crisis.

United Nations ambassador Adlai Stevenson, who had failed to choose Kennedy as his running mate in 1956 and who had stood as an obstacle to Kennedy's presidential nomination in 1960, paid a high price for speaking freely in meetings with Kennedy and the Ex Comm. And the dagger Stevenson felt protruding from his back may have been wielded by the president himself. According to an article coauthored by one of Kennedy's closest friends, Stevenson argued for a negotiated settlement rather than a military showdown, and he suggested the possibility of trading U.S. missiles in Turkey, Italy, or Britain for Soviet missiles in Cuba. In the *Saturday Evening Post* account written by Stewart Alsop and Kennedy confidante Charles Bartlett, one unnamed White House official said, "Adlai wanted a Munich," reflecting antagonism toward Stevenson, as well as the continuing habit of leaders to see the Cold War in terms of World War II. The article, which was accompanied by an unflattering full-page photo of Stevenson, supposedly provided a day-by-day account of what happened in the White House as the crisis progressed. The piece also painted Dean Rusk as unwilling to take a firm stand, but probably its most significant achievement was introduction of the terms "hawks" and "doves" to the nation's political vernacular. While Alsop and Bartlett quoted Stevenson supporters as saying that he backed a trade only after neutralization of the missiles, the authors treated that assertion skeptically. Although Stevenson actually was a small player in the overall article, headlines and positioning spotlighted his statements as the biggest revelation in the account.[115]

Appearing on NBC's *Today*, Stevenson told the viewing audience, "It seems

United Nations ambassador Adlai Stevenson became the victim of political sabotage via the press's poison pen. Here, Soviet deputy foreign minister Valerian A. Zorin, left, and Stevenson, right, listen as Cuba's Mario García-Incháustegui, center, speaks at an emergency session of the United Nations Security Council on 23 October 1962. AP/Wide World Photos.

to me a remarkable story in one respect. As to me, it is wrong in literally every detail." He added, "What the article doesn't say is that I opposed equally emphatically an invasion of Cuba at the risk of world nuclear war until the peace-keeping machinery of the United Nations had been used."[116] Columnist Drew Pearson characterized the article as a ploy by "a public relations administration."[117] The president seemed to feel the reaction of the thin-skinned Stevenson gave the article more attention than it deserved. Stevenson considered resignation but told a friend, "If I quit now it will look like Kennedy dumped me. Or it will look as if there were a split in the party or in policy." Later, the State Department's George Ball said, "After the Cuban Missile Crisis, Adlai was only going through the motions," knowing he would never have a strong voice in foreign policy.[118]

Several Ex Comm members privately condemned the article, citing errors and warning that this kind of reporting could lead presidential advisers to keep their mouths shut rather than participating in an honest exchange of ideas;[119] however, the president pointedly refused to issue a statement that the article was wrong about Stevenson. Kennedy, who had been approached directly by the writers[120] about the article and had given the writers access to both officials and records,[121] later wrote Stevenson, saying "how greatly we have admired your performance at the United Nations" and expressing embarrassment about the article's "obvious inaccuracies."[122]

At a subsequent news conference, Kennedy refused to discuss what positions Stevenson had taken behind closed doors,[123] and speculation quickly turned to the theory that JFK may have fed the story to the writers. "No other president has maintained such close personal contacts with newsmen. Aware of the Kennedy method of the indirect nudge, the planted hint, the push by newspaper column, students of the Administration follow the work of Kennedy's favorite columnists as faithfully as Kremlinologists plod through *Pravda*'s prose," *Time* reported as it suggested Kennedy wanted to oust Stevenson from the United Nations.[124] If Kennedy was not the source, it clearly came from someone else in the Ex Comm, possibly at Kennedy's behest.

The article sparked efforts to identify the leak's source, with some observers suggesting that other reporters were lashing out because of jealousy about Bartlett's special relationship with the president.[125] Indeed, during the most dangerous days of the crisis, when most journalists faced great restrictions, Kennedy had called Bartlett after receiving a bellicose Khrushchev cable and told him, "You'll be interested to know I got a cable from our friend, and he said those ships are coming through. They are coming through tomorrow."[126] After the Stevenson article, the *New Republic* saw damage everywhere. "More than Stevenson has been hurt. The press, the president, the processes of deliberation within government have been damaged," Gilbert A. Harrison wrote.[127] Arthur Krock, who had known Kennedy for years and had helped transform Kennedy's senior thesis at Harvard into his first book, *Why England Slept*, saw the situation this way: "The deduction unanimously made from these circumstances was . . . that the administration's policy of managing the news was not to assure the 'free flow of information' . . . but to harness the flow in the volume suitable to immediate purposes, select the channels of its transmission, and for reasons known only to himself tap even the reservoir of the council that Mr. Kennedy had proclaimed impregnably sealed in the interest of national security."[128]

Records show Stevenson proposing that removal of missiles from Turkey could be used as a bargaining chip,[129] but they also show Kennedy making exactly that deal in secret—a fact missing from the *Saturday Evening Post* article and from all accounts until several years after Kennedy's death. It was probably with a sense of irony that JFK told reporters in a 12 December 1962 news conference, "It is a matter that, as I say, I think can much better be left to history when the whole record will be spread out in great detail."[130] Although at least one report identified National Security adviser McGeorge Bundy[131] as the leak, a former *Saturday Evening Post* editor contended years later that JFK had revealed Stevenson's stand.[132] Alsop also acknowledged later that Kennedy had read the article before publication and proposed only a few changes.[133]

Such stark evidence of press manipulation to achieve a political goal concerned some journalists, but the Stevenson story was just a sample of partnerships between the government and the press. Another clear example springs from coverage of Cuban news in the Miami area. During the crisis, an editor at a Miami newspaper confided to a *Newsweek* reporter that he routinely passed along information from the local Cuban community to the Central Intelligence Agency. The CIA reciprocated by determining each tip's veracity and telling the editor which stories were safe to print.[134] Some journalists saw no conflict in arrangements such as these.

A TOOL IN THE MASTER'S HANDS

Most of the American press acted as a docile servant to the Kennedy administration during the Cuban Missile Crisis, but the crisis itself and the statements of officials afterward nourished the seeds of inherent press skepticism toward the government and heightened fears about government manipulation of the media. As the *Omaha World-Herald* wrote in 1965, "Since the Cuban Missile Crisis of 1962, when the administration manipulated the news and claimed the right to do so, no American can be sure whether his government is giving him the whole story."[135] Kennedy did not live long enough to see that skepticism blossom; however, several of his successors have watched their careers come apart in press reports that sprang from the assumption that the government could not be trusted. In particular, Johnson and Nixon, both of whom developed a near-paranoia about the media, saw their administrations collapse as the press revealed their misdeeds. Bill Clinton similarly found himself the subject of almost endless investigations. Given what happened to his successors, it is easy to imagine that a second Kennedy term might have led a less friendly press corps to investigate extramarital affairs, poor health, and U.S. plots to assassinate foreign leaders.

Surprisingly, with the exception of the secret deal to remove U.S. missiles from Turkey and details of Operation Mongoose, the intelligence operation that sought to undermine Castro, few big secrets about the crisis have come to light in more than forty years of conversation and debate. The administration's restrictions on the press shielded no gigantic transgressions. For

Seeking the latest news on the crisis, New Yorkers flood a newsstand on 24 October 1962. They have no way of knowing that the Kennedy administration sees the media as one of its Cold War weapons. © Bettmann/CORBIS.

the most part, the press and the public knew what was happening, although they lacked the kind of detailed information that would have been available if reporters had been allowed on the blockade line. In fact, the public and the press benefited from the simple fact that communicating via broadcast messages was more efficient for the United States and the Soviet Union than using cables. The need for speed immediately put crucial communiqués in the public domain.

Nevertheless, restrictions on coverage, a stated willingness to mislead the press, and even use of the media to sabotage a man's political career[136] raised doubts about the true nature of the press's freedom in the Cold War. A combination of government interference and a sense of journalistic duty to protect the United States from the Soviet Union truly had transformed the press into a weapon—one that the Kennedy administration wielded quite expertly.

Issues of press freedom have not disappeared since the Cuban Missile Crisis. Similar concerns created debate during the short Gulf War of 1991, when the government kept reporters far from the battlefields; however, since the Cuban Missile Crisis, the press has not allowed itself to be exploited so easily by an administration that uses secrecy to fortify its own position. George W. Bush's "war against terrorism" after attacks destroyed the World Trade Center in New York and damaged the Pentagon on 11 September 2001, brought similar rallying behind the government; however, the press more eagerly raised questions and cautioned against rash actions.

Journalists' growing skepticism flourished in a later Cold War atmosphere that seemed less frightening than the early 1960s. Reporters' presence in the marshy battlefields of Vietnam and television's nightly transmission of war footage into American homes contributed to declining support for that war. Freed from the sense that unity might be crucial for survival, reporters no longer felt that questioning policies might be equivalent to treason.

The unsavory side of the Kennedy administration's relations with the press is often forgotten because public adulation of JFK after his assassination glorified his role in the crisis. In the aftermath of Kennedy's sudden death, the press's grievances against him and his administration became lost in grief and dismay. Kennedy's Camelot became a political ideal, but as Richard Nixon almost certainly must have noted, one man's Camelot is not that different from another man's "Imperial Presidency"[137]: a glow of fond recollection obscured the Kennedy administration's flaws, while the harsh spotlight offered no such advantage for his successors.

Later presidents often have felt besieged by reporters unwilling to believe government stands and driven to acquire prestige by uncovering the kind of backstage maneuvering that JFK so skillfully obscured. Such aggressive, in-your-face reporting bolstered opposition to the war in Vietnam, public outrage over Watergate, investigations of the secret Iran-Contra arms-for-hostages deal, and the sex-scandal-induced impeachment of Clinton. So-called honeymoons with the media have become extremely rare and short, and this crisis almost unquestionably contributed to today's fiercely adversarial relationship between the media and the president—a relationship that colors Americans' perceptions of their nation and their culture.

CHAPTER FIVE
politics and strategy

Have you considered the very real possibility that if we allow Cuba to complete installation & operational readiness of missile bases, the next House of Representatives is likely to have a Republican majority? —Treasury secretary Douglas Dillon, note written in Ex Comm meeting

Although the Cuban Missile Crisis seemed perfectly timed to benefit the Democrats in the 1962 election, John F. Kennedy had little control over its timing or its outcome. In many ways, he just played the hand he had been dealt by Khrushchev, by the Republicans, and by the American public. Communism had become the boogeyman in America's nightmares, and Kennedy knew that he must act forcefully, even if a confrontational approach threatened to trigger nuclear war. After raising tensions with his initial response, he chose quiet diplomacy when the outbreak of war seemed imminent, and both approaches matched the American mood. In an abstract sense, Americans were willing to risk a military confrontation to block the spread of Communism and end a threat to the United States; in reality, they were not ready for war.

For months leading up to the crisis, the GOP had sounded a steady drumbeat of complaints about Kennedy's failure to respond to a Soviet military buildup in Cuba. By capitalizing on public fears and outrage, Republicans hoped to gain twenty or more seats in the House of Representatives in 1962. Under pressure to act vigorously, the administration had considered taking aggressive steps even before news of Soviet missiles in Cuba, and when a 14 October U-2 flight captured the missiles on film, Kennedy knew that he must respond with bold action. Exactly how much the upcoming election affected JFK's decision to confront Khrushchev remains a contested issue, as does the crisis's impact on the election. Ultimately, Kennedy's decision to implement a naval blockade reflected the political culture of the early 1960s, which required a firm response to any Soviet threat coupled with wariness about charging headlong into war. Through publicly aggressive and privately prudent strategy, Kennedy served his constituents' interests and safeguarded their physical survival at the same time.

Although his name was not on the ballot, JFK believed the 1962 election's outcome was critical to his success as president and to his legacy. With southern Democrats often joining Republicans to stifle his initiatives, much of his legislative program was at a standstill. Despite a Democratic 64–36 margin in the Senate and a 263–174 majority in the House, Congress approved only 48.4 percent of his legislative measures in 1961 and 44.6 percent in 1962.[1] To win approval of his social agenda, including progressive measures such as the proposed Medicare program, he needed a Congress populated by more Democrats from the East, Midwest, and West. Although his approval ratings were consistently high, he wanted a better record of success in Congress before he faced reelection in 1964. In addition, rapidly unfolding events in the civil rights movement threatened to force Kennedy into taking a stronger stand on expanded rights for African Americans, which could further weaken Democratic solidarity in the next presidential election.

To strengthen his party in Congress, Kennedy had committed to heavy campaigning for congressional and gubernatorial candidates. Polls indicated that turnout would be low, with less than 30 percent of Democrats and 43 percent of Republicans casting ballots. The Democratic Party hoped the popular president, who had provided virtually no coattails to carry Democrats into office in 1960, could bring out the vote for his party's candidates now. He put his prestige on the line by deciding to campaign forcefully in an uphill battle:[2] not since 1934 had a party controlling the White House gained seats in the House in off-year elections, and an August Gallup Poll had shown that twenty-four of thirty-five marginal Democratic seats were in danger.[3]

Kennedy knew that public response to his Cuban policy could weigh heavily against him. Since Castro's rise to power in 1959, the island's fate had proven to be the embodiment of many Americans' fears. When Kennedy ran against Richard Nixon for the presidency in 1960, he had used Cuba's shift to Communism to paint the Eisenhower administration as weak and ineffectual, arguing for more assertive efforts to oust Castro.[4] Less than a year later, after the disastrous failure at the Bay of Pigs, Kennedy felt the same heat that he had applied to Eisenhower. That fiasco contributed to his administration's decision to launch Operation Mongoose and use covert means to destabilize Castro's hold on Cuba. According to one administration memo, "The Secretary of Defense felt it necessary for political reasons that some action be taken with respect to Cuba to insure the president's future."[5] In October 1962, when a U-2 plane photographed missile sites in Cuba, Kennedy faced an opportunity and a perceived obligation to act. The crisis landed in his lap at a time when it could make or break the Democrats' chances at the polls.

Beyond derailing the GOP's biggest campaign issue, the crisis removed the president, vice president, and cabinet members from the campaign trail and made civil defense a hot issue in some states. Public opinion initially backed the blockade. Only 4 percent of those surveyed opposed Kennedy's tough countermove,[6] and telegrams reaching the White House overwhelmingly endorsed his course. Unless the crisis ended badly, the Democrats seemed likely to benefit.

While most Americans backed the quarantine, there were limits to their willingness to fight over Cuba. A Gallup Poll released on 14 October, the day of the U-2 flight, showed that only 24 percent favored sending U.S. troops to Cuba.[7] Three days later, another Gallup Poll indicated that 51 percent believed an invasion of Cuba would trigger all-out war with the Soviet Union.[8] Touching the same theme, *Christianity and Crisis*, a Christian journal, warned in mid-October that "for the United States to use its power to control the internal affairs of Cuba today would backfire so badly that we would probably be in a much worse position afterward than we are now."[9] According to another survey, after the missiles' discovery, 60 percent of Americans accepted the assumption that some shooting would be necessary to end the standoff. Pollster Stanley Lubell said a typical response to the blockade's implementation was: "I'm scared out of my mind, but it had to be done." Slightly fewer than half of Lubell's respondents believed that the United States or the Soviet Union would use nuclear weapons if the crisis led to military conflict.[10]

Across the country, signs of support for Kennedy's confrontational policy arose spontaneously.[11] In Philadelphia, members of the Union League, which had gathered for a concert, voted to support JFK's stand, echoing a league decision in 1915 to endorse Woodrow Wilson's policies in the period leading up to U.S. involvement in World War I.[12] Similarly, the Texas Association of Broadcasters voiced its support for the naval quarantine within hours of Kennedy's announcement.[13] One letter writer asked Vice President Lyndon Johnson to tell the president he was willing "to serve in any capacity to bring the present conflict with Russia to an immediate successful conclusion even if it necessitates riding the first bomber to Moscow."[14]

Still, not everyone backed JFK. On one side, some Republicans thought he had created a crisis for political purposes; on the other, peace activists felt that he had provoked a nuclear showdown unnecessarily. Kennedy did not choose what may have been the safest course: quiet negotiations could have reduced the possibility of a war sparked by a hair-trigger response to some minor infraction. However, peace talks lacked the toughness he wanted to demonstrate, and by warning in September that he would act if Cuba received "offensive weapons," he had limited his own options. When the crisis ended with an apparent U.S. victory, his approval rating rose to 74 percent,[15] up from 62 percent in early October.[16] And while his success did not guarantee Democratic wins, another embarrassing failure in Cuba could have ensured GOP gains.

THE POLITICS OF TOUGHNESS

Looking back more than forty years, both American and Soviet policies seem at times to have been foolhardy. In this crisis, both risked a catastrophic war just to make a show of force. It seems almost as if some form of mass hysteria gripped the United States and its leaders, given the popularity of Kennedy's dangerous course; however, the nation and its leadership were convinced that the Soviet threat had to be met with aggressive action.

While Kennedy and his advisers believed the presence of Soviet missiles in Cuba was an unacceptable risk, they responded with an equally threatening action. The tapes of Ex Comm meetings show that no one in Kennedy's inner circle accepted negotiation as a viable political response to the planting of Soviet missiles in Cuba. The idea, which Adlai Stevenson favored, received little consideration. As the Ex Comm saw it, Khrushchev was a bully and Kennedy's political career would end if he did not boldly challenge that bully.[17] Presidential counsel Ted Sorensen contended that negotiation "was a route which we saw getting us nowhere and just leading us that much closer to the brink of war,"[18] and Robert Kennedy believed his brother would be impeached if he did not respond militarily. Although some members of the Ex Comm believed the missiles in Cuba did not significantly alter the balance of power, the panel's debate primarily centered on whether to institute a blockade or to attack Cuba directly through bombing raids or invasion. The possibility of avoiding confrontation altogether was unimaginable to the men who held the world's future in their hands. They did not actively seek a self-destructive war, but they were willing to play Russian roulette with the nation's future rather than appear weak by actively seeking peace. Later, when the threat of war seemed imminent, they followed a more conservative course by using diplomacy to work out a semisecret deal with Khrushchev.

Thus, as Kennedy revisionists, such as I. F. Stone, Barton J. Bernstein, and James Nathan, have argued, JFK did worsen the situation initially by publicly challenging the Soviet Union and threatening war;[19] however, as more recent historians have noted, he showed restraint in dealing with the downing of a U-2 plane and in bringing the crisis to a peaceful end through backdoor diplomacy. The historical record—now enriched by the Ex Comm tapes, conferences involving participants on all sides, the opening of Soviet archives, and post–Cold War declassifications of U.S. documents— has shown what was then secret: both Kennedy and Khrushchev were willing to negotiate and make concessions to avoid war, although politics required tough stands in public.

Most Americans agreed with the decision to act rather than talk, believing that dealing with Soviet leaders was a waste of time. Many saw Communists as untrustworthy, manipulative, and almost subhuman. Democratic senator Richard Russell of Georgia was in tune with the times when he said: "Working behind the traditional Communist facade of treachery, deceit and falsehood the Soviet Union has transformed Cuba into a powerful military base which threatens the security and freedom of the United States."[20] Americans wanted to give Khrushchev a bloody nose, and if Kennedy could not do it, they probably would find someone who could. His shaky record in Congress and his failure at the Bay of Pigs had made JFK vulnerable, and like many vulnerable creatures, he wanted to project an aggressive image. By setting up the blockade, Kennedy almost literally was drawing a line in the sand and daring the Soviet leader to cross it. The president knew that his strategy did not guarantee a good outcome and easily could have propelled the world into nuclear war. However, he benefited from the opportunity to make secret deals and from Khrushchev's prudence in withdrawing the missiles, thus playing out his role as a cowardly bully who ultimately backs down.

Beyond bowing to the political imperatives of the day, JFK embraced the role of masculine risk-taker. This is evident in his Cold War rhetoric and in his private life. As a Cold Warrior, he did not shy away from daring the Soviet Union to push him too far; as a husband, he jeopardized his career and his marriage in a long series of careless affairs. Late-twentieth-century scholarly interest in gender issues has led to several analyses that draw connections between Cold War foreign policy and an ideology of masculinity.[21] Examining Kennedy specifically, Robert D. Dean has contended that "Kennedy both shared and exploited popular fears that equated a perceived 'crisis' of American masculinity with the decline of American power abroad, using them to frame his presidential campaign and his programs while in office." In the years after the apparent Soviet leap ahead in the space race, U.S. policy-making developed against a backdrop of Cold War anxieties about a decline in American manhood, according to Dean,[22] who believes Kennedy and his aides acquired a "warrior" philosophy through all-male aristocratic boarding schools, Ivy League colleges, and elite military service. Dean suggests that Kennedy identified the strength of male bodies with the strength of the state, despite his own weakened, sickly condition.[23] After the GOP held the White House for eight years, "Kennedy and his allies in the liberal establishment deployed a rhetoric of polarized opposites against political opponents: manly strength and feminized weakness, youth and age, stoic austerity and debilitating luxury," Dean argues.[24]

Dean is not alone in counterposing Kennedy's own frailties and his gospel of masculinity. In Nigel Hamilton's JFK: Reckless Youth, Henry James Jr., a Kennedy friend, asserts that JFK's adventurous sex life may have been an overcompensation for feelings of femininity.[25] In The Kennedy Obsession, John Hellmann suggests that the frequently hospitalized Kennedy assumed a mantle of sexual bravado in adolescence to obscure his shortcomings.[26] Reinforcing his image, Kennedy wrote two Sports Illustrated articles, one as president-elect and one as president, in which he tied male strength to national power. "If we are to retain this freedom . . . then we must also be willing to work for the physical toughness on which the courage and intelligence and skill of man so largely depend," he wrote.[27]

Kennedy's choice of the New Frontier to define his administration interwove these ideals. Frontier mythology celebrates the heroics of male individuals taming a continent and forging a nation—and Kennedy often emphasized the contributions that a single individual could make to the future of his nation. As Kennedy and Khrushchev squared off in the crisis, an almost unavoidable metaphor is the scene of two gunfighters facing each other and the prospect of death at high noon. It is a masculine image that glorifies risking life itself just to win the war of the moment.

Whether Kennedy saw himself as a pioneer gunfighter or a chivalric knight, he felt that a showdown over Soviet missiles in Cuba was unavoidable. Whether the crisis threatened his masculinity or just his political career, he knew that he had to demonstrate American toughness. To understand the crisis's political impact, it is essential to recognize the cultural forces that motivated and reacted to his actions, and to accept the perceived inevitability of confrontation.

Unintentionally, Khrushchev turned a potential disaster into a godsend for Kennedy. After months of attacks from conservative Republicans and southern Democrats, the crisis created a situation in which counteraction seemed imperative, even for those who rejected right-wing depictions of Castro's regime as a Communist "invasion" of the Western Hemisphere. By acting against Soviet aggression, Kennedy could expect support across a broad political spectrum.

To many Americans, it did not matter that Castro was Cuban or that Cuba was a sovereign nation. Instead of seeing the sole Communist regime in the Americas as an aberration on an impoverished island, many convinced themselves that Cuba embodied a huge threat even before the missiles arrived. When reporters for the *Austin American* interviewed readers during the crisis, "those interviewed seemed to take for granted the right of the U.S. to declare a blockade on Cuba."[28] Castro's regime was an affront to many Americans. As Eisenhower's secretary of state, Christian A. Herter, had declared in 1960, "Any Communist regime established in any of the American republics would in effect constitute foreign intervention in the Americas."[29]

Many Americans saw no obvious parallels between U.S. missiles in Europe and Soviet missiles in Cuba. The rationalization was simple: the United States had placed missiles in Great Britain, Italy, and Turkey to *defend* against Communist aggression. And although invasion of Cuba had been a hot topic in U.S. politics since Castro's revolution, Americans were unwilling or unable to consider the possibility that Cuba or the Soviet Union might view the United States as an equally aggressive threat to Cuba.[30] After all, they reasoned, the United States just wanted to *free* Cuba. Clearly, Castro was not an elected leader. However, U.S. missiles in Europe did represent a threat to the Soviets and the United States embodied a danger to Castro's regime.

Nevertheless, the *Manion Forum*, a conservative publication, reported on 14 September 1962: "Our bungling, pro-Communist stupidity of the last five years is now paying off in bitter, bitter coin."[31] Two weeks later, the same publication declared dramatically, "On three sides, we are surrounded, fenced in by Communist military power—east, west and now south, in Cuba."[32] U.S. superiority in nuclear weaponry and the small size of Cuba were easy to overlook when many Americans were drowning in fear of Communist world domination.

Voters, like Kennedy, were wary of U.S. intervention in Cuba before discovery of the missiles; however, given news of this new threat, most felt JFK's action was appropriate, probably because it followed the pattern of brinkmanship exercised by his predecessor, Eisenhower. Khrushchev, too, had revealed his willingness to play the game of "I Dare You" with his histrionic promises to "bury" the West. However, both Kennedy and Khrushchev realized the game was not as simple as it appeared. During the Cuban Missile Crisis, Kennedy always attempted to leave a means of graceful retreat for Khrushchev, and the Soviet leader acted with the understanding that dramatic moves on his part might lead to increasing pressure on the young president for an American military response. While playing a public and highly masculine game of chicken, both men remained totally aware of the possible repercussions if the game went too far.

LEADING THE CHARGE

For months, the voices of doom had besieged the administration, predicting that Cuba would become a dangerous Soviet base. The White House ridiculed them, belittled them, and tried to ignore them, but the issue would not go away. In the fall of 1962, New York's Senator Kenneth Keating, a Republican, had maintained a crusade on the issue. He first had sounded the alarm in August[33] after the State Department reported fifteen Communist bloc cargo ships heading for Cuba.[34] On 31 August he announced that 1,200 Soviet troops had arrived on the island, and he insisted these were uniformed servicemen, not harmless "technicians," as the administration had claimed.[35] On the same day, he warned in a press release that the Soviets might be constructing "elaborate and sensitive devices" in Cuba to monitor and control missiles from Cape Canaveral.[36]

In all, Keating made ten Senate speeches and fourteen public statements on Cuba between 31 August and 12 October. He also devoted much of his weekly television and radio interview show in New York and his biweekly television forum in New York City and Buffalo to the subject. Keating's release of so many different allegations allowed the administration to dismiss specific charges, characterizing them as misinterpretations and exaggerations, but Keating made himself impossible to overlook. During September, Kennedy asserted that the only Soviet missiles in Cuba were ground-to-air missiles with a range of fifteen miles. "These new shipments do not constitute a serious threat to any other part of this hemisphere," the president told the nation.[37]

When Keating first specifically mentioned nuclear missiles on 10 October, he claimed that there were at least a half-dozen launching sites for

Senator Kenneth Keating, R-N.Y., led pre-crisis Republican attacks on the Kennedy administration. In late summer and early fall, he condemned Kennedy's failure to stop a Soviet arms buildup in Cuba, but during the crisis, he, like most Republicans, supported the president's strategy. *U.S. News & World Report* photo.

intermediate-range tactical missiles,"[38] but he underestimated their numbers and the time needed for them to become operational.[39] Reports of Soviet missiles in Cuba were not new. In fact, plans for intermediate-range missile sites had been reported by two columnists for the *Miami News*[40] as early as March 1962, a month before Khrushchev's decision to deploy the missiles. In June 1962, South Carolina's conservative L. Mendel Rivers of the House Armed Services Committee wrote to CIA director John McCone: "I am informed that four IRBM missile bases are ready in Cuba."[41] Despite these reports, Kennedy's team discounted the possibility. As Assistant Secretary of Defense Paul Nitze argued in a briefing paper for a September television interview, "Putting offensive missiles in Cuba would be a drastic change in Soviet policy of not putting nuclear weapons in the hands of satellites who might irresponsibly touch off a war. I should imagine the Soviets would think long and hard about the consequences of taking such a step in Cuba."[42]

As the election approached, Republicans stepped up the heat on the Cuban issue because of an obvious increase in arriving Soviet materiel and personnel. Senator Homer E. Capehart, a Republican from Indiana, demanded an invasion of Cuba in response to the reported presence of Soviet combat troops,[43] and a 13 September White House memo written by Kennedy's National Security adviser McGeorge Bundy reported that "the Congressional head of steam on this is the most serious that we have had." Bundy pointed out the risk of appearing weak and indecisive, and he concluded that "one way to avoid this hazard is to act by naval or military force in the Cuban area."[44] While still seeking to minimize the buildup's importance, Kennedy publicly made it clear he would take action if offensive weapons were placed in Cuba.

Presidential reassurances aside, the issue continued to generate heat. Members of Congress and newspaper editors polled in September rated Cuba as an important election issue more often than any other topic.[45] Newspaper publisher William Randolph Hearst Jr. reported that "Democratic Congressmen who had to face their constituents on the hustings in this election yelled 'Help!' as they found how sore the voters were over the inaction in Washington."[46] On the day of Kennedy's speech announcing the blockade, the Republican Congressional Committee issued its newsletter, which reported that the three Republican chairmen "agreed with neutral observers that Cuba was the No. 1 issue of the 1962 campaign."[47]

Adding an impetus for action, Congress passed a joint resolution on 3 October urging steps to prevent Cuba from exporting revolution and to guarantee that the Soviet Union did not use Cuban soil to create a military threat to the United States.[48] In an article written before the crisis became public and published while it was under way, Charles H. Percy, 1960 Republican Platform Committee chairman, condemned U.S. policy toward Cuba, "where the failure of the administration's policy is manifest and overwhelmingly clear."[49]

Just days before the crisis began, the president went on the offensive against one accuser, Indiana's Capehart. Campaigning for the senator's challenger, Democrat Birch Bayh, Kennedy criticized the incumbent's "19th Century voting record" and proclaimed that "those self-appointed generals and admirals who want to send someone else's sons to war, and who consistently voted against the instruments of peace ought to be kept at home by the voters and replaced by someone who has some understanding of what the 20th Century is all about."[50]

For the most part, however, Kennedy shied away from Cuba as a campaign issue. As *Time* reported, "Cuba might as well have been on another planet," based on how often Kennedy mentioned the island as he campaigned. The White House argued that domestic issues were most important in winning votes for congressional and gubernatorial candidates, but *Time* bemoaned Kennedy's decision to run from the issue of Cuba, saying that it was unlikely voters would hear "from their president about the issues that seem to concern them most."[51]

When Kennedy and his closest aides learned that nuclear missiles were in Cuba, they were living within this political pressure cooker. The crisis created new dangers that made the heat of a campaign seem tepid by comparison. And yet the campaign was a part of their lives and their careers that could not be entirely cast off, even in a time of international crisis.

GOVERNMENT VS. POLITICS

The approach of off-year congressional elections undoubtedly weighed heavily in the minds of Ex Comm members as they gathered to map out a Cuban strategy. Nevertheless, tapes of the meetings show surprisingly little time or conversation devoted to analyzing the political impact of the crisis. In sometimes twice-daily meetings, participants made passing references to the Republican Party and to potential negative reactions, but there was little coherent discussion of how the crisis might figure into party tactics. Ironically, one of the few direct comments about the danger of GOP gains came from Secretary of the Treasury C. Douglas Dillon, a Republican and a contributor to Richard Nixon's 1960 campaign against Kennedy.[52] In a note handwritten during one of the early Ex Comm sessions, Dillon expressed concern that inaction on Cuba might lead to an adversarial GOP majority in Congress, thus paralyzing U.S. foreign policy.[53]

In public, the administration attempted to avoid tying the crisis to politics. Once the crisis became public, both President Kennedy and Vice President Lyndon Johnson canceled remaining campaign appearances.[54] And the White House asked cabinet members to refrain from campaigning. Even former Democratic president Harry S. Truman followed Kennedy's lead by canceling appearances, and he urged Republicans to cast aside partisan divisiveness at this time of crisis.[55]

Refraining from politicking may have helped the Democrats by suggesting to Americans that this administration cared more about the business of government than political one-upmanship. In addition, the crisis drew attention to the advantages of having a youthful team in the White House, with newspaper articles noting that Kennedy's lights burned late into the night and that several key administration officials literally lived in their offices until the crisis ended.

With the imminent threat of nuclear war, patriotism became intertwined with support for the Democratic president and the government in general. For instance, the Kings County (New York) Trust Company gave its customers pins of American flags. Here, John J. Lynch, president of the bank, pins a flag on Nancy Meringolo of Bath Beach. *New York World-Telegram and Sun*, Library of Congress.

And while members of Congress were not subject to White House restrictions, the crisis disrupted many campaigns. First, Kennedy called congressional leaders back to Washington for a last-minute briefing before his address to the nation. (As did the members of the Ex Comm, those leaders initially saw an attack on Cuba as the best option, and they were unhappy that Kennedy already had committed to a blockade they felt an obligation to support.) Two days later, congressional leaders received another briefing, and when released to return to campaigning, all agreed to remain available to return to Washington on eight hours' notice if Kennedy called.

The White House's scheduling of five regional briefings for elected officials further interfered with campaigns. In Charlotte, North Carolina, for instance, incumbents' campaigns screeched to a halt when officials rushed to Atlanta for a briefing given to officials from Georgia, Florida, South Carolina, Alabama, Virginia, Tennessee, Kentucky, and Mississippi.[56] Attending briefings probably boosted incumbents' reelection chances by providing an opportunity to represent their constituents in a crisis; however, canceling campaign appearances carried a cost, too. Wisconsin governor Gaylord A. Nelson, who was in a tight Senate race, feared the missile crisis might irreparably damage his campaign for two reasons: first, Kennedy eliminated a scheduled stop in the state; second, the president had bolstered the incumbent Republican senator Alexander Wiley's standing by involving him in special briefings for sixteen congressional leaders.[57]

While most candidates vocally supported the quarantine, one reportedly was under strict orders not to mention Cuba at all. Thirty-year-old Edward Kennedy, seeking election to his brother's former Senate seat, received directions from Sorensen not to discuss Cuba in his campaign appearances. Apparently, the White House feared Khrushchev might interpret the political novice's off-the-cuff comments as White House policy.[58]

After Khrushchev agreed to dismantle the missiles, the White House continued to project a sense of distance from the campaign, but the Democratic National Committee produced drafts of "fairly tough speeches" on Cuba for candidates across the country to use during the last week of the campaign to promote their president, as well as their own candidacies.[59]

While candidates spread the party line, Kennedy used silence to his advantage. His understanding of the crisis's political power was clear in his decision to keep secret his promise to remove U.S. nuclear missiles from Turkey.[60] Officials had considered removing the outdated missiles from Turkey months before,[61] but any sign of a swap could have debilitated Kennedy's reputation as a Cold Warrior and the Democrats' chances of holding their own in the election. In this case, silence was more than a virtue; it was a political necessity.

THE LOYAL OPPOSITION

For Republicans, it was challenging to maintain the precarious balance between patriotic support of the nation's leader and political attack on the same man. As the United States' most visible Democrat, Kennedy represented an inviting target, but Republicans who failed to stand behind a Democratic president in a time of international crisis risked alienating voters. Months of GOP carping about JFK's Cuban policy made the situation all the more ticklish. "The Republican dream," liberal columnist Max Lerner had written before the crisis emerged into public view, "is that its party leaders and candidates will be able to attack the Kennedy administration on Berlin and especially on Cuba without having to think up a program of

New York governor Nelson Rockefeller, a potential Republican presidential contender, talks to reporters after a meeting between President Kennedy and the Governors' Civil Defense Committee on 27 October 1962. AP/Wide World Photos.

actions different from the president's on either issue. They know that the country is aroused over Cuba. They also know, however, that the country is against intervention or blockade which could lead to war."[62] Thanks to the Cuban Missile Crisis, the hope of fulfilling that Republican dream vanished. Until or unless Kennedy faltered, Republicans who attacked the president were tiptoeing through a minefield.

Two days after Kennedy's address to the nation, Jacob Javits, a liberal Republican senator from New York, showed impatience with Kennedy critics on the Right, calling for an end to "niggling criticism" of the president "in this moment of grave national emergency."[63] When proponents of Barry Goldwater's budding campaign for the presidency in 1964 refused to cease attacks on the White House, columnist Ralph McGill condemned them, saying that "they shrilled like cheap fifes of tin as they cried for war and blood and for loosing the dogs of war."[64]

Still, some members of the GOP voiced skepticism. Rep. Thomas B. Curtis of Missouri called the showdown "phony and contrived for election purposes."[65] Bob Wilson, chairman of the Republican Congressional Committee, said GOP chances for major gains in this election had been "Cubanized"[66] and alleged that the missiles had been in Cuba "for months."[67] Wilson's committee asserted, "The New Frontier pattern of seeking an 'accommodation' everywhere else in the world had been so sharp for so long that few could believe it could change so suddenly," adding that "the New Frontier's kid-gloves policy toward Cuba for the past twenty-one months just did not jibe with the president's tough words on Cuba" during the crisis.[68] In Atlanta, one anti-Kennedy picket carried a sign that spoke for many skeptics: "Are we risking nuclear annihilation so that the Democratic Party can win an election?"[69] To help struggling Republicans, the party's national research division prepared a primer on the GOP's view of Eisenhower's successes and Kennedy's failures in Cuba. The report also listed twenty-six Republicans in Congress who had recommended a blockade in the months before Kennedy deployed his "quarantine."[70]

Nevertheless, the nation's top Republicans were careful to demonstrate solidarity. Former presidents Herbert Hoover and Eisenhower urged Americans to unite behind Kennedy. As the nation's most popular Republican and Kennedy's immediate predecessor, Eisenhower found himself in the most difficult position. The crisis demanded collegiality, but relations between Eisenhower and Kennedy remained somewhat prickly because much of Kennedy's 1960 campaign had been powered by criticism of Eisenhower's foreign policy.[71] After the failure of the Bay of Pigs operation, Kennedy had told Eisenhower, "No one knows how tough this job is until after he has been in it a few months," and Eisenhower had retorted, "Mr. President, if you will forgive me, I think that I mentioned that to you three months ago."[72]

In 1962, before the missile crisis became a campaign issue, Eisenhower had reminded voters that during his eight years in the White House, "no walls were built, no threatening foreign bases were established."[73] Then the crisis abruptly transformed the former president into a Kennedy adviser. He received several briefings during the crisis and privately encouraged the president to maintain a hard line, even after Kennedy reached a deal with Khrushchev. To resist letting the Soviet Union believe that political divisions weakened the United States, Eisenhower now pledged that "whatever the government decided to do, they would have my support."[74] Nevertheless, he refused to set aside all of his complaints about the administration, saying that "a united America need not and should not degenerate into a conformist, a silenced America."[75]

When Khrushchev offered to withdraw the missiles, Eisenhower and Kennedy conferred by telephone and the retired general warned Kennedy that "our government should be very careful about defining exactly what was meant by its promises." He contended that it would be a mistake to give the Soviet Union an ironclad promise not to invade Cuba[76] and favored delaying such guarantees until the United States could confirm that the missiles had been removed.[77] And when some of Eisenhower's acquaintances expressed concern that Kennedy had conceded too much to resolve the crisis, Eisenhower quietly consulted with the CIA's McCone.[78]

With the crisis apparently resolved, Eisenhower returned to more partisan campaigning and found himself in a state of dismay. While he asserted that Republicans deserved much of the credit for the military strength that enabled the nation to achieve Soviet withdrawal of the missiles,[79] Eisenhower felt that "some people are forgetting the events leading up to the latest crisis and now see the president as a knight in shining armor chasing Khrushchev back to his lair in the Kremlin." Although voters recalled Kennedy's Bay of Pigs failure, Eisenhower believed the administration's decision to stop campaigning let the more positive, new image predominate.[80]

Like Eisenhower, two potential Kennedy opponents in the 1964 election —former vice president Richard Nixon,[81] then embattled in a race for California's governorship, and New York governor Nelson Rockefeller—publicly backed Kennedy's actions.[82] Rockefeller even chose one of JFK's favorite words to describe his speech, saying, "The president has spoken with vigor."[83]

In the wake of the crisis, Rockefeller could expect a new boost to his own presidential hopes: his role as head of the Governor's Civil Defense Committee put him in the spotlight as civil defense agencies struggled to improve their readiness. Within days of the missiles' discovery, federal officials met with Rockefeller and his committee, and Assistant Secretary of Defense for Civil Defense Steuart Pittman sensed that the New York governor was seeking a bigger, more visible role in implementing the national civil defense program.[84] Rockefeller also moved forcefully to bring New York's civil defense plans to a maximum state of preparedness.

Rockefeller was not running in 1962, but Nixon's race against California governor Edmund G. Brown was one of the most prominent contests in the off-year election—and the crisis offered no built-in advantage for Nixon. In fact, as Rockefeller's deputy on the governor's committee, Brown had the advantage of being able to play the role of a hardworking public servant too busy to campaign. Despite his reputation for petty retribution, Nixon grudgingly had stepped forward to offer support to Kennedy, who had claimed the

White House in a razor-thin victory over the then-vice president in 1960; however, in so doing, Nixon made it clear that he believed the action was overdue. "As one who has urged that stronger action be taken in Cuba, I fully support the action the president has taken today," he said after Kennedy's 22 October speech.[85]

Two days later, with Brown off the campaign trail, Nixon felt it necessary to defend his continued stumping. "It would be a distortion of our system and not in the best interests of California to declare a moratorium on political debate because of the desire of all Americans to support the president's Cuba policy," he told voters.[86] In fact, Nixon contended, the crisis showed the importance of electing a governor with his foreign policy credentials because California could not afford "a provincial administration."[87] While Nixon harangued Brown, the governor canceled appearances so that he could attend to the business of state, but he continued his campaign "in a limited way." Brown called on voters to show courage, and he publicly asked Nixon to cease campaign tactics that reflected badly on his patriotism or loyalty.[88] In at least one way, however, the crisis seemed to work against Brown: Kennedy canceled his campaign swing through California.

As events unfolded, Nixon increasingly abandoned his statesmanlike pose and returned more forcefully to his combative style, particularly on the issue of civil defense. Los Angeles experienced rushes on supermarkets during the crisis, so Nixon logically assumed lack of governmental preparedness would be a compelling issue among the state's voters. On 28 October, he issued a statement pointing out the inadequacy of California's civil defense plans and proposing a seven-point program to accelerate civil defense preparations without succumbing to panic.[89] When the Democrats for Nixon Committee sponsored a television forum for the candidate to express his views the following day, Nixon accused Brown of negligence in properly preparing the state for war, although the Eisenhower administration in which he served had done no better.[90] Noting other problems in the state such as smog and overcrowded classrooms, he again attacked Brown's civil defense efforts two days later and urged California voters not to let the international crisis obscure the shortcomings in Brown's service.[91] The following day, he drew the public's attention to a 20 percent reduction in civil defense funding under Brown and accused the incumbent of "shocking attempts to hoodwink the people of California into a false sense of security."[92] On 3 November he dramatically assailed Brown again, citing inadequacies in the state's emergency communication center and the state's failure to develop a plan for emergency distribution of a 2-million-bushel stockpile of wheat. The director of the California Disaster Office should not be allowed to "play Russian rou-lette with the lives of 17 million people in the event of enemy attack," Nixon told California voters.[93]

While Nixon campaigned, Keating quietly continued his own offensive. Vindicated by the missiles' discovery, Keating did not flinch when admin-istration officials argued that the nuclear weapons had not been in Cuba when he had made his allegations.[94] Instead, he asked Secretary of Com-merce Luther Hodges for detailed information on U.S. steps to curb trade with Cuba.[95] Keating was not among Republicans who bemoaned the crisis's potential election boost for Democrats. He said, "If the price the Republi-cans must pay for the president's action is the loss of some Congressional seats or some votes, I think it's a pretty small price."[96] Not everyone believed Keating's motives were pure. Journalist Drew Pearson alleged that Keating's attacks on JFK had been engineered by fellow New Yorker Rockefeller to give him an issue to use against Kennedy in a potential 1964 Kennedy-Rockefeller battle for the presidency. Keating denied that allegation.[97]

As the crisis sharpened attention on civil defense and foreign policy, an epidemic of political sniping was inevitable. In Alaska, Republican guber-natorial candidate Mike Stepovich denounced the state's civil defense pro-gram, saying that it was "so horribly disorganized for the past four years it could not even produce an accurate inventory of the equipment it pos-sesses." The state's civil defense director condemned the candidate's deci-sion to use such a serious issue as an opportunity for political potshots.[98] In Pennsylvania, the race between former Philadelphia mayor Richardson Dil-worth and wealthy Rep. William W. Scranton turned nasty when Dilworth declared Scranton unfit to head the state "in this time of crisis."[99] And in New York City, television station WPIX received 300 complaint calls when the Socialist Workers Party candidate for Senate attacked the U.S. stand on Cuba.[100]

When Khrushchev agreed to withdraw the missiles, political analysts concluded that Kennedy's handling of the crisis would help Democratic con-gressional candidates more than it hurt them. For instance, Fletcher Knebel reported in his "Potomac Fever" column in the *Washington Post*: "Some Re-publicans are frustrated by Khrushchev's backdown. They had been claim-ing Kennedy did too little too late—and already they were poised to accuse him of doing too much too quickly."[101]

With the party's big issue stolen by Kennedy, the Republicans downsized their ambitions for the 1962 election. Stopping short of incendiary criticism of the president, they helped to show the Soviet Union a united front, which could not have bolstered Khrushchev's resolve.

THE RESULTS AND BEYOND

In the aftermath of the crisis, the 1962 election drew more voters than any nonpresidential election in history, with nearly 54 million Americans participating at the polls.[102] That turnout was up 5.8 million from 1958.[103] Bucking the trend toward big losses for the party in power, the Democrats won twenty-five of the thirty-nine Senate races in 1962 for a net gain of four seats, and the Republicans acquired only two additional seats in the House. *Congressional Quarterly* concluded that although Kennedy made a net gain of ten "hard-core" supporters, the overall results would neither enhance nor deter his chances of legislative success in the House.[104]

Less than a week after the conservative *National Review* had predicted that many "Democratic heads will roll,"[105] with Republicans accumulating at least twenty more seats in the House,[106] Democrats won 52.1 percent of the overall vote, compared to 56.3 percent in 1958, when Republicans held the White House. Democrats were victorious in twenty of thirty-five gubernatorial races, but Republicans gained 150 seats in state legislatures across the country.

Despite Nixon's feverish efforts, Brown won the California race, 3,037,109 to 2,740,351. The crisis was not the key issue. Brown was popular, and Nixon had fierce California enemies who recalled his efforts to label opponents as Communist sympathizers in the witch-hunt days of the late 1940s and early 1950s, when he represented the state in the House and Senate. In addition, he had created party turmoil by entering the contest somewhat late—in September 1961—after two lesser-known Republicans had declared their candidacies.[107] One candidate, conservative businessman Joe Shell, drew support from flourishing Goldwater Republicans in southern California and got 33 percent of the primary vote, shattering Republican solidarity.[108] Stephen Ambrose noted that Nixon was also handicapped by having a new staff, by having to contend with allegations that his brother had improperly accepted a loan from billionaire Howard Hughes, and by really not wanting to be governor. His loss led to the "last news conference," in which he told reporters they would not have him "to kick around anymore."[109]

The California Poll, conducted by the University of California State Data Program in cooperation with the Field Research Corporation, found that the crisis had little impact on voters. The survey, which gauged public opinion after Khrushchev agreed to withdraw the missiles, found that most of those polled said the crisis had no significant effect on their choice for governor.[110] Of course, Nixon might have been able to change more voters' minds in the absence of a crisis, and years later, Brown speculated that for Nixon, it "would have been better to have been quiet for a week himself."[111] In the governor's races in Alaska and Pennsylvania, too, those candidates who had made the crisis an issue lost. Voters also ousted Indiana senator Capehart.

While many observers focused their attention on the crisis's impact, the most meaningful 1962 election results revealed the beginning of a shift in power bases as the Republicans showed growing strength in the once solidly Democratic South. Five new GOP congressmen joined seven Republican incumbents from the South.[112] Republican congressional candidates drew more than three times as many votes as they had attracted in 1958.[113] Kennedy's decision to enforce integration of the University of Mississippi in the fall of 1962 probably contributed to this change, but it enhanced the Democrats' standing in northern industrial states at the same time.[114]

Disagreement persists about the crisis's role in the results. Democratic gains may have been almost inevitable because the 1960 election represented the first time in the twentieth century in which a party regained control of the White House while failing to raise its strength in Congress. Rather than providing coattails to carry Democratic lawmakers into office, Kennedy ran 5 percentage points behind the Democratic candidates for House seats. It has been estimated that Kennedy's Catholicism cut 2 million voters from the traditional Democratic voter pool. The expected return of those voters in 1962 virtually guaranteed Democratic gains, analyst Angus Campbell argued before voters went to the polls.[115] Historians Thomas G. Paterson and William J. Brophy found in an in-depth study that the crisis's impact was "indiscriminate" and that Democrats were bound to do well in 1962 anyway.[116] Local issues and incumbencies were bigger factors. Although Kennedy's ratings jumped after the crisis, his popularity apparently was not transferable: in some states where he became closely tied to candidates, Republicans won.[117]

According to a poll conducted by the Institute for Social Research at the University of Michigan, 21 percent of voters decided whom they backed in congressional elections in the last two weeks of the campaign, during or after the crisis. Among those voters, Democrats had a slight advantage, with 29.4 percent either voting a straight Democratic ticket or favoring the Democrats on a split ticket. Republican results showed 17.9 percent of those last-minute decision makers voting a straight ticket or favoring the Republicans on a split ticket. Still, more than 50 percent of voters who made up their minds during that time period split their ticket and could not say that they favored one party over the other, which suggests that the crisis was not an overwhelmingly motivating device in moving voters into the Democratic column.[118]

After the election, political pressure over Cuba endured. Removing the threat of nuclear war provided fertile ground for doubts about the administration's account of how the crisis had unfolded. The newly formed Committee for the Monroe Doctrine responded to Kennedy's vow not to invade Cuba by saying, "The presidential guarantee would appear to amount to a guarantee that Cuba will, without forcible interference by the United States, be permitted to remain as a Communist colony."[119] The like-minded Liberty Lobby reported that it "knew from the start that the 'crisis' was artificial because we were informed by three different sources almost two months ago that there would be some sort of decisive action taken against Cuba before the election!"[120]

Weeks later, Ex Comm records show officials wrestling with ways to reassure Kennedy's constituents after Castro refused on-site inspections to determine whether the weapons had been removed. "The question of offensive weapons still in Cuba goes beyond the [Soviet bombers known as] IL-28s, so far as the public is concerned. It is closely related to persistent public doubts about what else may still remain in Cuba, a set of doubts that is still being confused and nourished by continuing speculation and rumors," an unsigned committee report stated. That report also noted that in light of Keating's early assertions that missiles were in Cuba, there was growing skepticism that the discovery occurred as late as 14 October as a result of an "intelligence gap."[121]

IN RETROSPECT

Unquestionably, the Cuban Missile Crisis had a political dimension, and, ironically, John F. Kennedy is one politician who never was able to reap the benefits of his success at the polls. Among skeptics, questions about the reality of the crisis and its timing would continue for many years, but the demise of the Cold War has proven most of those suspicions to be unfounded.

The opening of Soviet archives and revelations from Soviet leaders of that era have shown that, if anything, the crisis was far more dangerous than the administration suggested. Khrushchev, like Kennedy, saw nuclear war as a viable option. If the United States had invaded Cuba, it would have found 40,000 Soviet soldiers instead of the anticipated 10,000[122] and would have learned that the Soviet Union had armed its forces with tactical nuclear weapons to repel invaders.[123] In addition, declassification of Kennedy's Ex Comm tapes has provided an amazingly detailed view of what happened in the panel's deliberations, and there is nothing to suggest that political motives affected the crisis's timing. Recorded conversations confirm the administration's assertions that a U-2 plane's photographs first located the missiles on 14 October.

The administration did not employ blatant political maneuvering to create a crisis that would boost Kennedy's standing. Nevertheless, it would be wrong to suggest that its handling of the crisis showed no interest in political repercussions. Clearly, politics functioned as a subtext for the Ex Comm's deliberations. The nation's system of government motivates elected officials to respond to what they see as the public will. The White House knew that Democrats might suffer if the administration failed to act on Cuba. Without a crisis to discourage Republican finger-pointing, the GOP probably would have made gains. On an unspoken level, knowledge of those realities probably contributed to the administration's initial choice of confrontation over formal negotiation and led to Kennedy's concerted efforts to conceal the deal to dismantle weapons in Turkey. Formal high-level negotiations might have stretched beyond the election and news of a missile swap may have made the administration's position look weak.

As a politician and as a leader, JFK did not perform as he did for purely personal gain: he represented the wishes of his constituents and pursued the course that he believed to be appropriate. He played the role assigned to him by the public in 1962 and followed a script written over the preceding years of the Cold War. To survive politically, he had to walk a tightrope between war and peace because Americans did not trust negotiations in response to a Soviet show of force. At the same time, as polls on possible invasion of Cuba showed, Americans were reluctant to shed blood. It is ironic that the public would back a confrontational approach that threatened to explode into nuclear war while favoring a more cautious approach to the engagement of U.S. soldiers. This provides evidence of a continuing "disconnect" between Cold War dogma and the United States' unwillingness to face the dangers of nuclear war.

Cold War leaders faced the challenge of achieving military superiority without the inevitable loss of life that comes on the battlefield. To achieve success, leaders had to triumph in the drama of the public arena rather than on the front lines. Kennedy showed the wisdom to pair his tough public stance with reasonable concessions behind closed doors. Given U.S. expectations, public concessions to Khrushchev would have been risky, but given the danger of imminent war, private concessions were vital. Making the missile deal sealed the peace; keeping it secret preserved JFK's career. With no public hint of appeasement, he and his party emerged as winners.

children of the cold war

The Cuban Missile Crisis threatened imminent nuclear war. And the only answer they could come up with was sending kids running home from school, and timing them. — Ellen Bartlett, *Boston Globe*, 22 October 1988

In the early 1960s, fallout shelters, air-raid sirens, and mushroom clouds were as much a part of everyday life for young Americans as their prized 45s and portable radios. Learning about the atomic bomb's power at the same time that they mastered tying their shoes, baby boomers entered a world that offered greater opportunities and more devastating threats than the world their parents had known as children. Though members of the older generation had experienced depression and world war, they had not faced the prospect of war at home or the possibility of human extinction. While baby boomers enjoyed relative prosperity, the existence of a future was no longer a foregone conclusion. Hence the common joke among youngsters: "What are you going to be *if* you grow up?"[1] Though it was a joke, it said something about that generation's worldview. Living with the possibility that adults might eliminate their chance to grow up, youths were preconditioned to question the wisdom of the older generation's choices. The questioning and cynicism began early and quietly, but it contributed to the shouts that would rock America later in the decade.

Young people in the "space age" understood nuclear war's grotesque potential for destruction, but adult authority figures asked them to accept an idea less plausible than many ghost stories — that ducking under their desks and covering their heads offered some hope of escaping the most powerful weapon ever created.[2] Many knew the truth: they could depend on the survival of nothing and they could not believe what adults told them about nuclear war. As children, they could not make the judgment that many adults were "in denial." Nuclear war was a nightmarish ghoul that threatened their nation, their families, and their very lives, and yet it possessed an unreality equaling any cautionary fairy tale. Adults could kill all of the children, and adults could mislead all of the children. The truth and the future were both unknowns, owned by adults and potentially stolen from a generation of children.

Nuclear war had found its way into children's lives quickly: within days of the Hiroshima and Nagasaki attacks, some children had incorporated atomic bombs into their war scrimmages, according to a *New Yorker* report in August 1945.[3] By the end of the 1950s, 60 percent of U.S. children reported having nightmares about nuclear war.[4] Television, which was metamorphosing from an entertaining diversion to a real power in U.S. homes, brought the threat of annihilation and other harsh realities into the nation's living rooms. As a result, children could not enjoy the innocence once common in protective homes, sociologist Maria Winn concluded.[5] Instead, the bitter truth gained a foothold in every home.

As Kennedy faced this crisis, children were not far from his mind. "You know if it weren't for the children, it would be easier to say you could press that button," Kennedy said, as longtime chum Dave Powers recalled years later. "I'm talking about all of the children in America and all of the children all over the world who could suffer and die if I made the wrong decision."[6] Kennedy took a break from crucial Ex Comm meetings to carve a pumpkin and help four-year-old Caroline and her toddler brother John Jr. prepare for Halloween.[7] Like many parents, he sought to protect his children in a time of crisis by performing routine activities; however, Halloween goblins could not compete with nuclear war in a contest to frighten children.

"The Cuban Crisis . . . was perhaps the first vivid threat to peace and security which this generation of schoolchildren could recall. It filled them with worry and with gratitude for the man who had averted the threat of war," wrote Roberta S. Sigel of Wayne State University in response to a Detroit survey done after Kennedy's murder. The results showed that among 1,349 elementary and secondary school students, almost all cited the crisis as part of his legacy.[8]

Kennedy's mail demonstrated children's fears. "I am 9 years old. I don't like the plans you are planning. I am too young to die," wrote a boy in 1961.[9] In their letters, youngsters told JFK that they felt the nearness of war, and they expressed their dread of devastation, hunger, and a possible Communist takeover. They also asked him to explain why war was necessary. One girl told Kennedy that she believed God was "on the USA side."[10] An eleven-year-old boy asked, "What will be left of this wonderful world in ten years if someone presses the button?"[11]

The anti-Communist rhetoric that reverberated through American culture during the Kennedy era conditioned children to be afraid of the Soviet Union and to believe that it was capable of unthinkable evil, great ruthlessness, and dishonorable cowardice. Many readily available sources of information, including newspapers and schoolteachers, referred to Communists as "Reds," a dehumanizing term that fit nicely into slogans—just as "Japs" had in the 1940s. Even magazines that promoted good citizenship, such as the Boy Scouts of America's *Boys' Life*, labeled Communists simply as Reds with no effort to understand or explain what that epithet implied.[12] Schoolyard chatter added other epithets, such as Commies and pinkos.

Adults, who seldom examined the true nature of Communism that existed beyond these stereotypes, almost never encouraged children to reach a deeper understanding of the nation's adversary. As evil as Communism seemed, many adults feared its potential allure to young people. Some parents used the "Communist" label to apply to anyone who was different, and children accepted that terminology, transforming the world into a dangerous place, with agents of subversion lurking around every corner. As a professor of education noted in 1951, "Primary school children believe that Communists are bad men that want to kill us." Then, wrote Howard A. Lane of New York University, "they hear father infer that the neighbor who raises questions about the local civilian defense program is probably a Communist!"[13]

Comic books joined the Cold War, too, by painting an ugly portrait of Communism's potential and nuclear weaponry's power. The Christian Anti-Communism Crusade offered children a simplistic vision of the Soviet Union through a comic book titled *Two Faces*. "When Khrushchev acts like a madman he is simply applying a form of Communist 'science.' As world Communist Leader, he is committed to use every possible means to change the face of the earth," one character contended. *Two Faces* also depicted slave labor in the Soviet Union as well as firing squads that eliminated the sick and the weak.[14] Often, adults stacked these publications in church vestibules, apparently giving anti-Communism God's seal of approval. The *Red Iceberg* attempted to show young readers that Communism was far more dangerous than it appeared. Projecting Communism into the lives of even the youngest pupils, the book portrayed teachers, libraries, scientists, magazine and newspaper editors, radio and TV stations, and African Americans as prime targets of Communist infiltration.[15] Besides making venomous attacks on Khrushchev, the comic book argued that Communism had corrupted young protesters who demonstrated against the excesses of the House Un-American Activities Committee.[16]

In the 1961–62 school year, *Treasure Chest of Fun and Fact,* a comic and game book that had close ties to the Catholic Church,[17] devoted part of each issue to an anti-Communist message. Every month, the series "Godless Communism" related a skewed version of Soviet history. Describing how Communism rose to power in Russia through the violence and bloodshed of revolution, this history failed to note that the United States' sovereignty also was the product of a bloody revolutionary war. One issue in the series provided a nightmarish vision of life in the United States under Communism—an existence in which newspapers would be closed, teachers would be replaced by mindless ideologues, and the sanctity of the American family would be violated by a government only interested in warm bodies to fill factory jobs.[18] A later offering in "Godless Communism" declared that Bolsheviks were "the sinful roots created by Lenin to grow the sinful seed planted by Karl Marx, [and] such evil roots could grow nothing but evil fruit."[19]

At the same time, *The Hulk* and *Spider-Man,* both of which debuted in 1962, showed the eerie and mysterious force of nuclear energy through the eyes of cartoonist Stan Lee. *The Hulk* chronicled the adventures of a scientist, David Banner, whose exposure to radiation made him at times become a superstrong hulk, while Spider-Man was a student who developed superpowers after being bitten by a spider that had been subjected to high doses of radiation.[20]

Comic books also advised children about the necessity for civil defense through melodramatic storylines and puzzles based on the terminology of preparedness programs.[21] As a further step to integrate fear of Communism into children's daily lives, the Children's Crusade Against Communism produced bubble gum trading cards in the 1950s with anti-Communist themes. Cards manufactured under the title *Fighting the Red Menace* carried stark images of war scenes and titles such as "Putting out Atomic Fire" and "Negro GI's Hold the Line."

Older children and adolescents developing a taste for satire could learn about Communism through *Mad* magazine. Khrushchev's short stature and bald head created the perfect image to pop up on *Mad*'s pages. For instance, a December 1961 spoof showed him greeting a young girl, saying, "And we will bury you, too . . . my little Capitalist Dollink!"[22] An April 1962 spread titled "Nuclear Jitters" showed a man constructing a fallout shelter and marking it with a "No Trespassing" sign. A journalist snaps a photo of

Young Americans often saw Communists as successors to World War II Nazis, as seen in this June 1962 tongue-in-cheek *Mad* magazine portrayal. Although both Nazi Germany and the Soviet Union were totalitarian regimes that offered little freedom for their citizens, their political beliefs actually were quite different. From MAD Magazine #71. © 1962 E.C. Publications, Inc. All rights reserved. Used with permission.

the man at night, and he dies of fright, believing the flash to be the first sign of a nuclear blast.[23] In June 1962, *Mad* addressed the issue of Americans' aversion to learning about the Soviet Union with "A Mad Guide to Russia, also Known as the U.S.S.R. (Undermining, Sabotaging, & Sabre-Rattling)," a primer that enumerated the Soviet population as American stereotypes might: "1 million workers, 49 million soldiers, 50 million secret police, and 99 million spies."[24]

Children's television, too, gave youngsters a vision of Communism through humorous yet wicked characters, such as Boris Badenov and Natasha Fatale, the evil but incompetent spies on the *Bullwinkle Show*. These Communists were sly, untrustworthy, and gutless—and easily outwitted by an effeminate flying squirrel and his loyal friend, a numbskull in moose's clothing.

Finding humor in nuclear science was more difficult than poking fun at Communists. To make the topic less threatening, Walt Disney's blossoming child-entertainment enterprise produced a book in 1956 and a film in 1957 titled *Our Friend the Atom*. The story began with a fable that equated the splitting of the atom with the escape of a genie from its bottle. The atom, like the genie, represented a force capable of wondrous good—and terrible destruction. The book predicted that soon atomic-powered planes would fly at twice the speed of sound, and it stated that by the end of the twentieth century, the atom would have all but eliminated the need for coal or oil.[25] However, even the world according to Disney could not avoid addressing the atom's potential as a weapon: it labeled atomic science as "a frightful terror which everyone knows exists, a sinister threat, mystery and secrecy. It's a perfect tale of horror."[26]

One common classroom tool in the early 1960s was *My Weekly Reader*, a news magazine for children. At that time, when the elementary school population was 32.4 million, it had a readership of 13 million. In some ways, *My Weekly Reader* was a propaganda tool promoting the American way of life. In 1960, it introduced its readers to Castro by praising his enemies and saying, "Castro is afraid of this opposition. To keep the masses behind him, he started a 'hate-America' campaign. He spread rumors that the U.S. planned to invade Cuba."[27] (At that time, the United States was helping Cuban exiles plan an invasion of Cuba.) In the weeks before the missile crisis, *My Weekly Reader* told its nine- to eleven-year-old audience, "The U.S. fears that the Soviet Union may use Cuba as a base for spreading Communism to other countries in the Americas."[28] By depicting Communism as monolithic and evil, *My Weekly Reader* reiterated Cold War dogma. Older students who read *Senior Scholastic* after the crisis learned that "Communism is a world-wide threat—not just a threat to the Western hemisphere."[29]

The Cold War and nuclear war clearly had found a place in children's lives, with some teachers challenging students to macabre tasks such as mapping the circle of destruction from a 50- or a 100-megaton bomb.[30] In many places anti-Communism and civil defense became completely intertwined. Colorado's "civil defense" education plan, drawn up in the early 1950s, included studying the meaning of democracy, singing patriotic songs, learning basic first-aid skills, and understanding the concept of mutual self-protection.[31] The traditionally patriotic Boy Scouts of America made an emergency preparedness program one of its top priorities in 1961–62.[32] However, in the Milwaukee schools, a curriculum guide in 1957 urged honest communication with students: "Without unduly alarming or creating fear, teachers can bring pupils to understand that no physical barriers exist today to make the Milwaukee Metropolitan Area immune to attack in the event of another world conflict."[33]

Historian JoAnne Brown has argued that the federal government toned down civil defense literature from 1951 through 1965 to remove the fearsome images that might keep children and adults awake at night;[34] however, this sanitized view may have been more frightening than a realistic description because it made the reality of nuclear war unspeakable. Children wanted to believe what adults told them, but they could not believe cold descriptions of civil defense procedures that avoided the real likelihood that millions would die in a nuclear war.

One prospect of civil defense was particularly unsettling—the likelihood that families might be separated. As Anna Freud wrote about children during World War II, "The shock of being separated from their mothers . . . is much greater than the one a child receives when the house in which he lives together with his parents is destroyed by bombing."[35] Most American children would have been terrified by an extreme measure, which was outlined by an editor at *Scientific American* in 1962 and published in the *Nation*. James R. Newman proposed sending children from the United States to the Southern Hemisphere, where they probably, but not certainly, would be safe from the perils of nuclear war. Such a massive relocation project would cost $25 billion, which was less than the United States eventually would pay for a massive fallout shelter program, Newman argued. "With the children gone, without the distractions and temptations of their cries and complaints, we could give ourselves over completely to the serious business in hand," he wrote.[36]

Freud, with Dorothy Burlingham, wrote that young children were likely to be most disturbed by the fear of war. In *War and Children*, their ground-breaking analysis of children's responses to air raids during the Battle of Britain in World War II, they revealed that small children, who usually have active imaginations, experience fears that are different from and more intense than those expressed by older children.[37] Along the same lines, several studies conducted in the early 1960s showed that anxiety over nuclear war decreased with age. A study of 4,000 Philadelphia children, ages ten to nineteen, asked the participants what they viewed as the nation's top problems, and the results demonstrated that concern with international issues declined as children moved through their teen years. While about half of ten-year-olds cited Russia and war as the major issue facing the nation, less than 30 percent of nineteen-year-olds cited that as the biggest challenge.[38] In another study of 602 Washington state high school students, the threat of war "greatly affected" only about 4 percent, with students' greatest fears involving their personal lives.[39] An additional study found that as youths aged, opposition to the idea of fallout shelters as safe havens grew.[40] Thus, as fear of nuclear war declined, the need for civil defense as a magical reprieve declined.

A key factor in children's perceptions of the Cold War was mother love.

A January 1962 study conducted by Louis Harris and Associates showed that mothers of children under the age of ten exhibited more concern about Communist advances than the average American. Ninety-two percent thought that Communism was gaining ground, compared with 84 percent of the total population. In addition, 62 percent believed that war with the Soviet Union was inevitable unless there was a dramatic change in the Soviet system; only 57 percent of the general population agreed.[41] Since many middle-class women in the early 1960s were housewives, it seems likely that spending much of the day with their small children exposed youngsters to these attitudes.

Not surprisingly, teachers and parents started noticing new themes in children's artwork during this era. Mushroom clouds began appearing with unsettling frequency,[42] and during the missile crisis, one *Miami Herald* columnist wrote about a six-year-old girl who drew two pictures in sequence— one showing a nuclear explosion, the other illustrating her own death. Even very young children were subject to crisis-driven tensions: one mother was startled when her four-year-old son added to his prayers a plea for the safety of "our soldiers and sailors."[43]

For this generation, war became part of the family. Unlike all of the wars since the Civil War, nuclear war would be fought at home. One mother reported that when her family heard an explosion, her husband ran to check the furnace while her twelve-year-old son went to the window, looked out, and said, "No mushroom cloud." Then the child smiled and returned to his homework.[44] "We grew up having air raid drills, so it was in our mental DNA," said film executive Michael Fuchs, who was a senior in high school during the missile crisis. "I remember many times hearing noises that would make me say, 'Could that be . . . ?'"[45]

Coping with the constant threat of war unavoidably affected young people's lives. While growing up in an era of mass communication opened their minds to ideas from many sources beyond parents and teachers, facing annihilation ushered in other unthinkable thoughts, such as the concept that adults might choose the wrong wars to fight. Later, an eruption of youths' quiet doubts into the public arena would bring open rebellion of one generation against another.

DRESS REHEARSALS FOR WAR

Beginning in the 1950–51 school year, air-raid drills in schools taught children in New York, Los Angeles, Chicago, Detroit, Milwaukee, Fort Worth, and San Francisco to duck beneath their desks when they heard civil defense sirens. An animated film featuring Burt the Turtle, who took cover inside his shell, taught even the youngest children these safety measures. "Surprise drills" in which teachers abruptly stopped teaching and yelled, "Drop!" began in Los Angeles within the same time period, as did "sneak attack drills" in New York.[46] By the mid-1950s, development of the more powerful hydrogen bomb made duck-and-cover drills more clearly inadequate. As a result, some schools prepared their own shelter areas and performed drills in which children ran to these dark places to take refuge from a faceless monster called nuclear war. To many youths, these events seemed like little more than charades in which adults tried to mislead children and make them feel safe in a world plagued by dangers too horrible to face.

As technology improved, some schools focused on getting children to their homes before a missile could strike. This objective necessitated another kind of drill in which students tried to run home within fifteen minutes —the predicted advance warning time of a missile attack from the Soviet Union. Those children who did not make it home within the allotted time period could assume that they would not die with their families. One writer described the atmosphere: "Kids were reminded constantly by civil defense drills that any day, while they were sitting at their desks or playing kickball in the schoolyard, their world could be destroyed by a country thousands of miles away."[47]

What to do with children in the event of an attack became an issue of controversy in which school systems chose divergent paths. Whereas Los Angeles planned to send students home, Philadelphia decided that children should stay at school unless there was significant warning, a decision that created challenges for educators. Most basic was the simple fact that some old schools could be expected to collapse after a blast—and they would offer little protection from fallout.[48] In addition, Philadelphia's plan called for designating all public and private elementary schools as mass care centers, which meant that in addition to caring for terrified children, the schools' staffs would aid wounded and homeless adults who would flood into the schools.[49]

A January 1962 poll of educators showed that 69 percent of them thought there was at least a 5 percent chance of nuclear war by 1982, and most felt that the schools should prepare students for that possibility.[50] A month later, another survey found that 68 percent believed evacuating students was best.[51] In March 1962, *Scholastic Teacher* randomly chose school superintendents and asked about civil defense and nuclear war curriculum issues. Of the forty responding, most had vague plans. One administrator explained

Students at Philadelphia's Cathedral Parochial School take part in a simulated 1957 evacuation of schoolchildren from the city's center to the suburbs. Taking a bus to the suburbs to escape nuclear war seemed an unlikely solution with only minutes' warning between an attack from the Soviet Union and destruction in the United States, but schools persisted in these drills. *Philadelphia Bulletin* photo, Temple University Libraries, Urban Archives, Philadelphia, Pennsylvania.

Schoolchildren in Topeka, Kansas, practice for nuclear war in 1960. About 31,000 students take cover when sirens announce a civil defense drill. There was little hope that ducking under a desk would save anyone in a nuclear attack, particularly with more powerful hydrogen bombs, but children all over the nation routinely followed this drill. © Bettmann/CORBIS.

his lack of coherent action: "There is so much controversy that we have done nothing."[52]

School drills drew some protests. New York's Civil Defense Protest Committee argued that "our children are oriented to war in kindergarten through drills and posters. Radio and television are constantly greeting young ears with the message of war."[53] The group contended that drills created unnecessary psychological pressures on schoolchildren.[54] Urging an end to all drills, the committee said, "Children now are taught to accept and 'believe in' a neurotic world run riot with fear and stupidity. Our school system is preparing children for mass burial rather than kindling within them the spark that exists in all mankind for a world at peace."[55]

In their helplessness to overcome the threat reflected by drills, many youths felt they knew the future: "It was extinction, and it was just a matter of time," according to one child. Psychologist Sibylle K. Escalona argued that "growing up in a social environment that tolerates and ignores the risk of total destruction by means of voluntary human action tends to foster those patterns of personality functioning that can lead to a sense of powerlessness and cynical resignation." In the early 1960s, Escalona and other psychologists asked 350 youths to imagine the world in ten years. There was no mention of war in the questionnaire, but 70 percent spontaneously mentioned the bomb as a sculptor of their fates.[56]

Another psychological study sought to measure youngsters' anxiety about nuclear war by asking parents whether children talked spontaneously about war. In a paper presented at the 1963 meeting of the American Psychological Society, M. E. Allerhand reported that 70 percent of the 200 couples in his May 1962 study reported that their children talked about war, and 35 percent noted emotional reactions to the threat of war. Still, 60 percent of parents believed they would have no trouble controlling their children's behavior in a shelter, which Allerhand classified as "the denial of reality." Also, his results showed that children learned about nuclear war from television or radio five times as often as they drew information from either parent. Fewer than half of the parents said they had discussed nuclear war with their children.[57] Just as most children acquired the facts of life from sources other than their parents, they learned the facts of death from others, too.

Years after the crisis, Michael J. Carey interviewed more than forty people who had been children at the time of civil defense drills and asked for their impressions. What he found was that bright children, even when quite young, recognized that "duck and cover" drills were a pointless exercise. "Talk of survival seemed like a cruel hoax from the beginning," he concluded.[58] And yet adult authority figures all the way up to the president advocated civil defense that seemed patently unworkable.[59]

College students' feelings about nuclear war understandably differed from those of younger students. A 1954 study done in a time of relative peace but immediately after announcement of the hydrogen bomb's development found that 80 percent of 200 Brooklyn College students believed that another world war was likely and 65 percent thought the hydrogen bomb would be used. Just over 60 percent believed that they would survive.[60]

In 1961, researchers asked 180 students at the University of Wisconsin to describe their feelings about nuclear war and civil defense. Interestingly, that study found that 59 percent believed there was a danger of nuclear war. However, only 6 percent said they worried about nuclear war often; 33 percent, occasionally; 35 percent, rarely; and 26 percent, never. Eighty-four percent felt the nation's civil defense protection was inadequate and voiced helplessness.[61]

It is difficult to quantify nuclear war's impact on young lives. It was a part of life for all those maturing after 1945, shaping their fears and their visions of the future. Born in 1938, Lou Oschmann often worried about the Cold War as a teen in the 1950s. "Nuclear war was something that was always on my mind or in the back of my mind. It was very difficult for me to plan for the future knowing that I could be annihilated at any moment." Growing up in Philadelphia, he developed a fear of reading the newspaper and watching the news. "I went through cycles where I would be fascinated by what was going on. Then I would get depressed from knowing so much that I wouldn't read it for weeks at a time because I was afraid that it would get worse. I would become like an ostrich sometimes and try to stay away from it."[62]

FACING THE CRISIS

Through vignettes and newspaper accounts, it is possible to acquire a sketchy vision of young people's responses to the possibility of nuclear war against the Soviet Union during the crisis, and some scientific studies provide finer details in a picture impossible to capture fully. Children lead much of their lives away from adults who might observe their behavior. Also, with time, memories flatten and fade, making it impossible to draw an accurate picture of one's own childhood. Therefore, much of that life remains a secret even forty years later. All we can hope to attain are glimpses of young people's experiences and the crisis's effect on their lives.

During the crisis, Frazier Cheston, president of the National Association for Mental Health, urged parents to speak with their children about the showdown to explain the reasons for risking mass destruction. "It is possible for the adult to paint a picture of freedom and right versus slavery and wrong, and to point out no effort is too great to protect the way of freedom," he said.[63] In Boston, parents received different advice. "Tell the children to do their homework and forget it," recommended Dr. Harry C. Solomon, Massachusetts commissioner of mental health. "Since the dawn of history there has been crises. The only way to prepare to meet a crisis is to do your daily work," Solomon argued, while another doctor told parents to "turn off the television. Television today is a long parade of what might happen anticipating anxiety."[64] Individual schools made choices about whether the crisis should be a topic for classroom discussion. In some schools, teachers avoided the issue, while others devoted entire days to it.[65]

Barbara Barnett grew up as a military dependent. Her father, a marine who had fought in World War II and Korea, was based in Okinawa when the crisis occurred, and nine-year-old Barbara lived with her mother and three younger brothers in a mobile home on her grandparents' North Carolina farm just a few miles from Camp Lejeune. "The thing I remember most was being scared because I kept thinking there was going to be a war and the second thing was we will be blown up," she said. "I remember asking my mother whether there was going to be a war. She said, 'Oh no,' but I had the feeling that was just another way of saying, 'Sit down and be quiet.'" While her mother tried to ease her fears, Barnett recalls, her fourth-grade teacher "told us that there probably was going to be a war and that the Russians were going to attack us and that we were probably going to be hit because we were near a military base."

Civil defense drills gave Barnett little hope for survival. "At school, we had drills where we were supposed to pretend the bomb had gone off, and we'd get under our desks. Then we'd see how fast we could get to the bus. If war came, we were supposed to get on the buses after hearing air-raid sirens. My biggest worry was what if I couldn't get home in time. I was afraid of being separated from my parents." Since her father was in the military, "war was not an abstract thing because I had heard my father talk about World War II, and he was in Korea . . . so war was very real—like Daddy going to work every day. I feared that my father would fight and die, and I would never see him again." Looking back, Barnett said, "the thing that strikes me about this is how ludicrous it was—to put us on a school bus. . . . I guess we had to know why we were doing these drills, but telling a child that there's going to be a war is a pretty scary thing."[66]

Bill Dingfelder celebrated his tenth birthday in Tampa, Florida, during the crisis, and he associates that birthday with the military buildup in his area. "I remember clearly many planes in the air from MacDill Air Force Base in Tampa, even more than usual. I also remember having air-raid drills where we would duck under our desks. . . . I remember seeing President Kennedy on TV talking about the crisis, and also a general sense of anxiety in the air." Dingfelder recalls seeing newspaper photos of the missile installations in Cuba, "and of course, I remember some talk about building fallout shelters, but not in my family: my parents thought that if there was nuclear war, such shelters wouldn't make much difference in the long run."[67]

Bill Scicchitano, a sixth-grader in Philadelphia at the time, remembers that his parochial school principal spoke to the children over the school's intercom system and warned that there was a possibility of war with the Soviet Union. She urged the pupils to pray for peace. "I think everybody painted the Russians, you know, as the infidels," he said. "They were the evil empire. They were going to bomb us any minute, and . . . there was sort of a hysteria about them."[68]

Inside and outside of school, children displayed differing responses to events unfolding on the international stage. A fifth-grader in Atlanta's Wadsworth Elementary School passed a note to a boy sitting near her. "Are you scared?" it asked. The boy responded with a note saying, "No." The girl handed him another note. It read: "I am."[69] A Massachusetts girl wrote to a friend, "Can you imagine not seeing another Christmas, Thanksgiving, Easter, birthday, dance, or even Halloween? . . . We're just too young to die."[70] In Washington, a father received a worried telephone call from his fourteen-year-old son at a New Hampshire preparatory school; the boy asked his father in a shaky voice, "Dad, should I come home?" His father replied, "Peter, you try hard to do your job well, and I'll try to do my job well. And I think we'll be all right."[71] At an air force base school near Rapid City, South Dakota, a teacher joked with his seventh graders, "If the Russians attack during my history test, I'm going to be really upset."[72] One girl hid under her bed when searchlights lit up her neighborhood: she assumed missiles were coming, but in reality, the lights were a sign that life was proceeding in its mundane way, with the grand opening of a supermarket.[73] In Miami, a high school sophomore told the *Miami Herald* she hoped "that if a bomb comes, I'm not around to see what happens afterward."[74]

For some, recollections remain haunting. At the elite Hotchkiss School in Connecticut, administrators called boys to the chapel to pray for peace. "A vivid memory of our sixteenth year—along with proms, high school sports and our first driver's license—was the prospect of instant obliteration," wrote political scientist Michael Mandelbaum and Strobe Talbott, who would grow up to edit Khrushchev's memoirs and act as deputy secretary of state in the Clinton administration.[75] A woman, who was a fourteen-year-old in Rochester, New York, recalled simply that it was "scary as hell."[76] What another man remembered most clearly was that Miami's Catholic schoolchildren "lined up at the confessionals and attended special Masses."[77]

Not all youths were frightened, however. Marion Sharp, then a Las Vegas teenager, recalls that she largely ignored the crisis. She remembers there was extra activity at the Nevada Test Site, where nuclear weapons were tested; however, she said, "I'm not a big newspaper reader. So, you know, just if it was big in the news was I really aware of it." When asked whether nuclear war scared her, she replied, "I was in high school. I wasn't afraid of anything."[78]

Some teens and young adults found an opportunity in the prospect of nuclear annihilation. In his memoir, *Too Good to Be Forgotten*, literary agent David Obst described his frantic efforts to lose his virginity by asking the object of his affections "whether she wanted to live without ever having made love." Ironically, the then-sixteen-year-old's chosen site for this aborted rendezvous was a neighboring family's fallout shelter.[79] A woman who was a sophomore at West Chester University remembers being called to an assembly at which officials warned young women not to give up their virtue because of end-of-the-world pleas.[80]

Among school administrators, the crisis generated new civil defense concerns.[81] In Washington, the need to stock school shelters sparked a plea for parental donations of nine dollars per pupil,[82] and there was bad news in New Orleans, where only eight schools qualified as shelters.[83] Administrators in Carlisle, Pennsylvania, looked at the idea of installing radio remote-control alarms at each school,[84] and Dallas's school system considered buying Conelrad radio receivers to hasten civil defense notification.[85] In the Richmond area, where schools had required a civil defense drill every two months, the Henrico County school board decided that was no longer sufficient.[86] Several systems scheduled additional air-raid drills as tensions rose, and in the face of existing inadequacies, Maryland's Prince George's County began contemplating construction of underground schools that could double as fallout shelters.[87] Still, for most children, there was no refuge. One woman recalls air-raid drills she experienced as a six-year-old in Shelburne, Vermont, in October 1962. "When the siren went off," she said, "we were to get up from our desks, stand at attention, wait for a signal from the teacher. We were to walk single file from the classroom, get on a school bus. . . . The bus would take us to a disembarking point. From there we were to run home as fast as we could."[88]

At the time of the crisis, many school systems hustled to formulate or re-formulate answers to the biggest question facing them: whether children should be sent home or kept in school if an attack seemed imminent. In Wichita, all schools would be evacuated and children would be sent home;[89] in Houma, Louisiana, all children would remain in school;[90] in Jacksonville, Florida, some schools would shelter children while others would evacu-ate, depending on agreements between parents and administrators;[91] in Los Angeles[92] and Harrisburg,[93] the strategy would depend on whether school officials believed they had an hour of warning or just minutes. Some princi-pals faced greater dilemmas, summed up by a later publication for admin-istrators. It said that "where facilities are inadequate, [the principal] must decide which children will be given a chance for their lives—and which will not!"[94]

For the students and faculty of an elementary school in Los Angeles County, the chilling closeness of war turned into a nightmare on 30 Octo-ber two days after Khrushchev announced withdrawal of the missiles. At the Miraleste Elementary School, the civil defense alarm, tested every day at 9:30, suddenly sounded at 8:40. It warned officials of a yellow alert, which meant that a nuclear attack was likely within an hour. A secretary checked with phone company workers, who assured her the line was func-tioning properly. At 8:42, the principal ordered evacuation. Confused and frightened, many small children burst into tears. Older youngsters tried to quiet upset kindergartners and fielded their unanswerable questions: "Are we going to live any longer? Are we going to be safe?" Nervous teachers divided the children into ten groups, and each group left on foot with the goal of escorting each child to his or her home. One six-year-old boy did not make the walk home. He remained alone at school with administrators be-cause his home was not within walking distance. At 8:52 A.M., the phone company finally acknowledged that a malfunction had set off the alarm by mistake. Teachers retrieved the children, and school began again with a lot less innocence than it had possessed just an hour earlier.[95]

These snapshots of young people's responses to the crisis can be placed in greater context by several scholarly efforts to clarify students' attitudes. During the crisis, Milton Schwebel, a professor of education at New York University, sought to augment research already done on young people's re-sponses to the threat of nuclear war. In late 1961 and early 1962, Schwebel had interviewed 2,200 public and private school students in three different regions to determine their attitudes. He found that 45 percent of junior high school students expected war to break out, while 46 percent disagreed. Surprisingly, Schwebel learned that below average students were more likely to be worried about war than bright ones. Students attributed their fears to ongoing international tensions, pervasive human greed, the possibility of someone accidentally triggering war, and the belief that fighting is inevitable among humans. Forty-eight percent of the junior high school students expressed support for fallout shelter construction, and 40 percent opposed it. Among high school students, nearly 70 percent opposed shelters and only 21 percent favored them. Students supporting shelters argued that they were "better than nothing," while opponents called them "stupid, a farce, a money-making proposition," and "like building your own tomb."[96]

When the crisis occurred, Schwebel again polled 300 junior high and high school students. At that time, when world leaders believed war was close, 69 percent of the students surveyed thought that war was unlikely. Schwebel concluded that this optimism reflected teens' primary mechanism for dealing with the crisis: denial. Many answers carried this theme: "If I allowed myself to think about it, I'd be miserable." And perhaps they were right. One student who admitted fears wondered, "If I live, dare I bear children?"[97] Schwebel found that responses showed an awareness of the Cold War's inherent dangers; however, he asserted, "most did not clearly visualize their own death." Students more often referred to fears about family members dying. These findings again showed that smart students were less likely to voice fright, and Schwebel inferred that the students most aware of war's danger "may be less able to face the possibility to admit or to comprehend that human beings could turn the nightmare into reality."[98]

A study conducted by Jiri Nehnevajsa and Morris I. Berkowitz during the crisis asked 194 Pittsburgh-area high school and college students to rate the level of international anxiety and found that students ranked the tensions between 9 and 10, a significant rise over a 6 rating in previous surveys from 1959 through early 1962.[99] In addition, high school students believed that a major war was the crisis's most likely outcome, whereas college students remained somewhat more optimistic.[100] "Of all those students who regard a war as likely, only a negligible number think that the war will end in anything less than total destruction of both social systems," the study concluded.[101] Most subjects characterized civil defense systems as weak or nonexistent.[102]

Many adults had no idea how to help children cope with the threat of nuclear war. Some foundered: "Already my sick children are getting sicker because their parents are saying things in front of them that they shouldn't," said a Miami child psychologist.[103] For many parents, the crisis confirmed that they had brought children into a dangerous world. Some accepted that reality with fatalism, assuming they had no control over their fates. Some went to great expense to offer even a modicum of safety for their families. Still others simply discounted the possibility of nuclear war and honestly could convey that belief to their youngsters. Saddest of all were the parents driven to desperation, such as mothers in Anchorage, Alaska, and elsewhere who sought out local engravers to have dog tags made so that their children's bodies could be identified after an attack.[104] An Alabama historian recalled his response to receiving his dog tags as a child: "I always felt the dog tags were given to you so that if your body was almost utterly destroyed by the bomb, there would still be the dog tags."[105] San Francisco and Seattle distributed tags free to public school students, and Philadelphians could buy them in local stores. Strapped for money, the Denver and Detroit schools urged parents to put name tags in their children's clothes.[106]

Clearly, both young people and their parents feared the prospect of war but felt helpless to protect themselves. The myth of civil defense had little more credibility than tales of the Easter Bunny. However, while adults expected children to stop believing in the Easter Bunny at a certain age, they continued trying to sell the story of civil defense even when children had reached high school. Most children found no comfort in this fairy tale.

CRUSADE FOR PEACE

While evidence of the crisis's effects on children is fragmentary, its impact on college campuses is clearer. Some students joined peace protests, but most nervously reported to class and listened to debate about the wisdom of U.S. policy. For young men, the possibility of facing the military draft cast a shadow over these days as their futures in college appeared vulnerable to world events. Rising campus anxieties reflected growing divisions about Cold War policies.

The atmosphere at Harvard was glum, according to observers, and at Florida State University, a college journalist said students were "nearly panicked."[107] Some students at the University of Miami checked out of their dormitories,[108] and at Temple University, a campus meeting centered on whether the university should stage an air-raid drill.[109] Some collegians in New England reportedly loaded their cars and sought refuge in Canada.[110]

Swarthmore College's *Phoenix* chastised JFK for choosing the easy path of

Protesters for and against the U.S. blockade in Cuba march in front of the White House on 27 October 1962. Antiwar groups marched alongside anti-Communists who advocated tougher action against the Soviet Union and Cuba. Robert Knudsen photo, John F. Kennedy Library.

embracing rigidity instead of flexibility, and Cornell University's *Daily Sun* advocated peace talks. The *Daily Tar Heel* at the University of North Carolina in Chapel Hill said, "With his futile attempts to build up armed forces in the Caribbean without letting everybody know why, Kennedy has made another radical break from all traditions that American citizens have come to hold so dear."[111] On Wednesday, 25 October, The *Daily Princetonian*'s lone editorial was a fictional account of armed Cubans seizing control of Soviet missiles and launching a nuclear attack.[112]

Fears of war were common among more than half of the sixty-nine students who filled out questionnaires at the University of Michigan during the crisis. Thirty-seven acknowledged "feeling scared," according to a report by Mark Chesler and Richard Schmuck.[113] Members of the "scared" group tended to be less certain that public opinion could affect the government's course and less supportive of aggressive actions.[114]

Of all student activities, peace protests garnered the most attention, and although peace activists were in the minority and many of them were not college students, the groups' actions are worthy of study because of the ways in which they foreshadowed young people's protests against the war in Vietnam. In the early 1960s, peace groups, which often relied on college students as their foot soldiers, focused primarily on ending nuclear testing in the atmosphere. By drawing attention to the dangers of radioactive fallout, the movement contributed to the self-imposed testing moratorium initiated by the United States and the Soviet Union in 1959. After that success, interest in the peace movement declined, but the renewal of testing in 1961 and 1962 instilled new life in peace activism.[115] A 1962 Rand report showed new concern in the military-industrial complex about pacifists' growing clout: "The Peace Movement is finding new advocates for its ideas while retaining its initial supporters. . . . Its support is spreading among different groups of society . . . it is beginning to influence influential people," and it "has a large potential for generating powerful political influences on military strategies and programs."[116] Like the Vietnam protesters who would follow, demonstrators in the Kennedy era for the most part could be divided into two groups: liberal intellectuals and disgruntled college students of draft age. Complementing these groups were scientists who opposed municipal contributions to civil defense on the grounds that shelters created a false sense of security.

In 1961, however, the peace movement had acquired a new respectability with the birth of Women Strike for Peace during the Berlin crisis, when the United States and the Soviet Union stood toe-to-toe in a confrontation over control of the city.[117] At a time when conservatives often characterized peace activists as "soft on Communism," these neatly dressed middle-aged women in flowered hats and white gloves gave the peace movement a new look. Few could argue with the effort to guarantee their children's health and their futures. Though it had little organizational structure, Women Strike for Peace had mobilized 50,000 women on 1 November 1961 to oppose renewed nuclear testing in the atmosphere and to endorse a U.S. disarmament initiative. The demonstrators, many of whom were housewives, marched in cities across America, sometimes with children at their sides. Carrying signs with slogans such as "Save the Children" and "Testing Damages the Unborn," up to 800 marched in front of the White House.[118]

Because Women Strike for Peace believed that it should advocate respect for the nation's leadership, the group avoided criticizing Kennedy directly. Instead, it clung to his rhetorical embraces of peace and built its stands on that "common ground."[119] When crises arose, this approach paralyzed the group. Wary of drawing attention away from disarmament and alienating Kennedy backers, it had difficulty reacting swiftly. After many phone calls among chapters, most eventually issued statements condemning both Khrushchev's decision to put missiles in Cuba and Kennedy's belligerent response. And a day after Kennedy's speech, mothers marched in New York in an evenhanded protest against Soviet missiles in Cuba and U.S. missiles in Turkey and Italy.[120] Members joined student dissidents at the White House on Saturday, 27 October, and participated in New York City's biggest peace demonstration ever on 28 October. "If we can just live through the present appalling crises constructive peacetime programs will be a most welcome program," leader Dagmar Wilson wrote.[121] A few Women Strike for Peace members considered more radical actions. Participants in a New York meeting discussed chartering a plane to Havana and staging a sit-in on the runway, according to author and member Amy Swerdlow, but the organization never executed the plan. Afterward, the Ann Arbor, Michigan, chapter recommended designating a group of women willing to serve as hostages in international crises as a deterrent to nuclear warfare.[122]

Another major force in the peace movement was the National Committee for a Sane Nuclear Policy, known as SANE. This organization, with leaders such as Socialist Norman Thomas and members both young and old, more nearly fit the stereotype of a liberal, intellectual peace advocacy group. Like Women Strike for Peace, SANE devoted much of its time to opposing atmospheric tests. On Monday, 22 October 1962, the national board of SANE met as Kennedy spoke, and immediately afterward, SANE issued a press release praising his decision to seek diplomatic solutions through the Organization of American States and the United Nations. On Tuesday, SANE urged the Soviet Union to stop arms shipments to Cuba and asked the United States to cancel the blockade and consider giving up U.S. missile installations in Turkey in a swap. On Wednesday, the organization issued a policy statement, which appeared the following day as a full-page *New York Times* advertisement. In it, SANE condemned both sides for unnecessarily heightening the chances of nuclear war.[123] Local SANE units bombarded Kennedy and other officials with telegrams urging a peaceful end to the crisis,[124] while the national director lobbied for peace at the United Nations.[125] On Sunday, 28 October, SANE helped to organize the huge rally in New York City.[126]

Students who had supported SANE by the thousands in earlier years had begun to establish their own movement by 1962.[127] The Student Peace Union and Students for a Democratic Society (SDS) drew their membership more directly from the college population. Student pacifists founded the Student Peace Union in 1959, and by October 1962, its membership totaled about 3,000 college and high school students.[128] The group's constitution capsulized its goals simply: "The Student Peace Union is an organization of young people who believe that war can no longer be successfully used to settle international disputes and that neither human freedom nor the human race itself can endure in a world committed to militarism."[129] When its leaders learned of the blockade, they warned, "Last night President Kennedy announced an action which may be the beginning of the nuclear holocaust all of the arms of both sides were supposedly preventing."[130] In Minneapolis, a crowd of 5,000 booed and threw eggs at peace advocates from the Student Peace Union.[131] In the melee, eggs hit two faculty members.[132] The Student Peace Union also mapped out rallies in Chicago, Columbus, Cleveland, Houston, Seattle, Miami, and Berkeley.[133] The group organized 300 students for a large Los Angeles demonstration[134] and sent busloads of students to Washington to march outside the White House.[135]

Students for a Democratic Society signaled the arrival of the New Left in the organization's *Port Huron Statement* of 1962, which described a generation scarred by atomic fears and "guided by the sense that we may be the last generation in the experiment with living."[136] At the University of Michigan in Ann Arbor during the crisis, about 400 demonstrators organized by SDS passed out leaflets seeking an end to the "game of chicken" and 600 students jeered them, pummeling protesters with eggs and stones.[137]

As antiwar demonstrators marched in cities around the world to protest Soviet and U.S. brinkmanship, peace rallies occurred in every section of the United States, with college professors and students often embodying the core group of protesters. On Wednesday, 24 October, at Indiana University in Bloomington, a fistfight broke out in a confrontation between about fifteen peace demonstrators and hundreds of angry onlookers. Kennedy supporters booed the demonstrators and then surrounded a flag pole and sang the national anthem.[138] Police arrested two protesters.[139] In Atlanta's Hurt Park, about twenty-five activists from two African American colleges voiced opposition to the quarantine and urged the nation to solve the crisis through diplomacy, not warfare. About thirty minutes later, a larger group of Georgia State students marched in favor of Kennedy's quarantine. Organized through a series of phone calls about the first rally, the pro-JFK crowd included one student with a "Better Dead than Red" sign[140] and another with a placard that read "Look what pacifism did for India."[141]

On the following day, SANE leader Thomas led more than 200 pickets demonstrating at Philadelphia's City Hall, where passersby drew those on the picket line into heated arguments.[142] In Pittsburgh, about 300 University of Pittsburgh students jostled and jeered peace activists on Friday.[143] At the University of Chicago, the Student Government Council decided to send Kennedy a resolution deploring U.S. action.[144] A SANE speaker at Cornell University was shouted down by a crowd that included students who had been approached by the Minutemen, a right-wing group that was collecting goods for a guerrilla war if a Communist invasion occurred. When the speaker yelled, "Are you ready for nuclear war?" The crowd responded, "YES!"[145]

On Saturday in Washington, 500 pickets marched at the White House. Police arrested three protesters for disorderly conduct and briefly detained one man, whose sign declared, "Kennedy Is a Traitor."[146] In San Francisco, proponents and opponents of JFK's policy held rallies at opposite ends of Civic Center Plaza. About 2,000 took part, with 75 percent opposing the blockade. One peace activist, who wore white coveralls and had painted his face and hands green, handed out "literature from outer space" condemning mankind's behavior. In the pro-Kennedy rally, one speaker praised members of the two-year-old right-wing group Young Americans for Freedom, saying, "That beatnik element down there doesn't speak for you students of the bay area in any way."[147]

The week's largest protest attracted more than 8,000 pacifists representing about twenty organizations to the area around the United Nations in New York on Sunday. Despite several efforts by anti-Castro demonstrators to disrupt the rally, the event remained peaceful.[148]

While dissension is generally associated with youth, many college students condemned those who dared to question U.S. policy. "It is not easy to understand such extremities by American students in times like these," an editorial in the *Temple University News* asserted. "It is time the members of SPU grew up and faced fact. Nuclear war won't be averted by picketing or issuing statements calling for unilateral steps by one country without proof that the other nation involved will respond in kind."[149] Across the country, at the University of California at Berkeley, the message was roughly the same. An editorial saluted Americans' right to free speech and applauded using that right to debate public policy; however, at the future home of the Free Speech Movement, a *Daily Californian* editorial argued: "When the country is in peril, when it looks as if those guarantees may not be worth a damn tomorrow morning when that country is a 3,000-mile stretch of rubble, why don't you stop talking?"[150] Even the *Village Voice* called the movement "no longer pertinent to what was happening in the world."[151]

In addition to launching counterdemonstrations in some cities, students who favored a hard line against Communism staged demonstrations of their own. At Florida State University, 200 burned an effigy of Castro and chanted, "To Hell with Fidel."[152] And the Young Americans for Freedom, who boasted the support of high-profile right-wingers such as Arizona senator Barry Goldwater, picketed the White House for a tougher response to Khrushchev's gambit.[153]

After the missile crisis, which SDS members Tom Hayden and Dick Flacks characterized as "the week of madness," strengthening the peace movement became an important objective for student activists. "The priority today, as never before, is power," Hayden and Flacks wrote. "Unless we can penetrate the political process, by direct participative means, then it is unlikely that even modest changes in foreign policy will be effected in the near future."[154]

Within the nation's other major protest movement, the civil rights movement, there was skepticism about the government's goals. Martin Luther King Jr. questioned the nation's wholehearted embrace of freedom in other lands. "The justification for risking the annihilation of the human race was always expressed in terms of America's willingness to go to any lengths to preserve freedom," he wrote in his 1964 book, *Why We Can't Wait*. "To the Negro that readiness for heroic measures in the defense of liberty disappeared . . . when the threat was within our own borders and was concerned with the Negro's liberty."[155] Often those most reluctant to give rights to African Americans, he asserted, seemed most willing to risk nuclear war.

Bob McGruder was an African American student at Kent State University in 1962 and an ardent Kennedy fan in those days when civil rights protests offered hope and the Cold War promised only fear. Years later, he recalled formal discussion of the crisis in his political science classes and personal soul-searching among staffers at the campus newspaper, the *Kent Stater*. "In one class, I was required to write a daily journal, and I remember that I devoted one day's entry entirely to the Cuban Missile Crisis, which is evidence of how important it was in our lives. We were all young, idealistic Kennedy lovers at that time. We thought he was different, and at first, we were disappointed that he was engaging in this eyeball-to-eyeball behavior. Suddenly, our young hero was involved in combat with a short, fat guy."

All in all, "it was scary," concluded McGruder, who would go on to become executive editor of the *Detroit Free Press* in the 1990s and one of the first African Americans to hold such a position. "There was lots of talk about fallout shelters, and triangles [denoting public shelters] were appearing on buildings." When Khrushchev backed down and agreed to withdraw the missiles, McGruder and many of his friends felt more than relief. "In the end, even the most idealistic among us gave into the urge to say to ourselves, 'Ha! We showed them!'"[156]

Although the crisis provided a stage for peace advocates and strengthened support for their cause in some quarters, the peace movement faltered in its 1962 efforts to gain political clout by electing representatives. While five peace candidates won seats in Congress, nine lost.[157] "The electorate of the United States is not yet ready to elect peace candidates," the Student Peace Union told its members.[158] If anything, the crisis cut backing for peace candidates, according to SANE's analysis. Two independent peace candidates, who ran primarily to educate the public on peace issues, lost about half of their backing during the crisis.[159] A year later, with the completed U.S.-Soviet agreement to ban atmospheric nuclear tests, peace organizations lost much of their support and entered a period of quiet before the storm over U.S. policy in Vietnam.

Some of the seeds of the peace movement that blossomed in the late 1960s were planted in the demonstrations of the missile crisis period, which, like youth-driven Vietnam protests, reflected the viewpoint of only one segment of college students. In both cases, many of the activists embraced a counterculture evident in fashion choices that defied the popularly accepted styles—beards in 1962 and longer hair in the late 1960s. Among Vietnam War opponents, the rightness of the American decision to support South Vietnam and send U.S. men into the battlefields of Southeast Asia were key issues. At the time of the missile crisis, the threat was more global. Student peace activists in 1962 expressed anger that adults in government seemed to be risking the future of the nation and the world just for the chance to claim victory. Those who spoke out represented the feelings of many people silently paralyzed by fear or cloaked in denial.

conclusion

If anybody is around to write after this, they are going to understand that we made every effort to find peace and every effort to give our adversary room to move. I am not going to push the Russians an inch beyond what is necessary.—John F. Kennedy

For John F. Kennedy, the Cuban Missile Crisis lasted thirteen days, as his brother's memoir famously recounted, but for most Americans, it represented one week of imprisonment in fear, expectation, and/or denial. For the public, the crisis began when Kennedy threatened military action if the Soviet missiles were not withdrawn. The immediacy of the threat was unmatched in the Cold War. Kennedy's speech began a countdown of hours and days until the first Soviet ship reached the blockade; if that ship did not stop, the Ex Comm and much of the American public believed a clash might trigger nuclear war and eradicate the future. For many Americans, the clock was ticking loudly, and like men standing before a firing squad, they waited and wondered whether they would feel anything before the end came.

The *New Yorker* capsulized the effects of that uncertainty in this way: "We waited for something to happen, gauging, minute by minute, in something like pain, our ignorance of what the next minute would bring, and feeling the dead weight of the conviction that no one on earth—not the president, not the Russians—knew what it would bring."[1] Pollster Elmo Roper dispatched a telegram to Vice President Johnson, detailing public sentiments as he saw them. "It is my earnest conviction that the American Public—and for all I know the world public—is in such a state of shock and numbness and resignation to the possibility of the final war that they need the reassurance, directly from the president, that he is ready to embark on some new and gigantic and imaginative effort to ensure the peace of the world."[2] The sense that the crisis might spawn not just war, but "final war," added to the desperation of many. During that week, feelings of doom captured a part of the American heart and then let go as suddenly as they had come.

At the crisis's close, CBS newsman David Schoenbrun described its effects on the American psyche: "A once-favored theory that war was unthinkable in the thermonuclear age has just about been atomized, for a lot of people have been thinking about war in these past few weeks and preparing for it. As the president has been saying, we came right up to the brink and looked down into the abyss. And now this is a grim fact of sudden death that we must live with."[3] Twenty-seven years later, Soviet operative Georgi N. Bolshakov described the crisis's impact, noting that "America for the first time felt the breath of war at its door. War knocked at the door of every American. It was also a psychological turning point in American thinking."[4] To suggest that this crisis represented just one more episode in the Cold War like so many others is to hide from the truth: the threat was real; it was immediate; it was only ninety miles away.

As a people, Americans watched the unfolding crisis warily. Some exhibited panic; some closed their eyes to the danger; others accepted whatever fate had to offer. As a group, they neither lost their heads nor showed tremendous bravery. Instead, each one endured the tensions in his own way. Many put their faith in God, in Kennedy, or in U.S. military might; others saw no hope. Humorist Art Buchwald wrote tellingly: "We weren't a dove or a hawk—we were chicken. It had nothing to do with the issues. We just didn't want to die."[5]

Analysts of John F. Kennedy's leadership style and his lasting hold on the American imagination often have cast the spotlight on his enjoyment of individual competition and his passion for confronting an enemy head to head in a struggle to measure each man's mettle. True to form, Kennedy's initial response to discovery of nuclear missile sites in Cuba was: "He can't do that to me!"[6] He visualized the confrontation as a face-off between Khrushchev and himself, and much of his reasoning in choosing to address the missile threat aggressively sprang from his own competitive spirit. However, while Kennedy may have approached this crisis as a matador armed only with a cape and a sword, most Americans had no weapon whatsoever to use against this enemy; instead, they were more like helpless men stumbling into the annual running of the bulls in Pamplona, rushing to avoid being gored, and hoping fate would spare them.

There are rumors that one Kennedy administration official became so frazzled that he drove his car into a tree at 4 A.M. one day during the crisis.[7] Years later, Robert Kennedy wrote about the pressures on members of the Ex Comm: "Each one of us was being asked to make a recommendation which would affect the future of all mankind. . . . That kind of pressure does strange things to a human being. . . . For some, it brings out characteristics and strengths that perhaps they never knew they had, and for others,

Maintaining his weekly ritual, President Kennedy attended Mass on Sunday, 28 October, after learning that Nikita Khrushchev would withdraw missiles from Cuba. Here, he leaves the church with aide Dave Powers. Abbie Rowe photo, John F. Kennedy Library.

the pressure is too overwhelming."[8] More than 180 million other Americans faced just as big a threat without any power to avert it.

And for many, the crisis brought an unexpected realization of unpreparedness. In the nuclear era, some nations had made genuine efforts to set up civil defense systems that would protect most of the population. The United States never did, and yet, when tensions were at their highest, America's leaders were unwilling to tell the public the truth: minimal civil defense efforts would not save most of the population in a massive nuclear war.

The Cuban Missile Crisis put the spotlight on America's civil defense charade. During the 1961 Berlin crisis, Congress had approved its largest civil defense appropriations ever; however, as concerns about Berlin faded, Congress refused to invest heavily in a system of public shelters. Then, in October 1962, when Americans learned that nuclear war might be days, hours, or minutes away, they realized that what had seemed to be civil defense momentum in 1961 had produced little to protect them in 1962.

Some scholars have asserted that media coverage of civil defense peaked in 1961 and have drawn the conclusion that public interest in civil defense sharply declined after the Berlin crisis. However, while the Berlin crisis sparked many Americans to ask questions about preparation of private shelters, it did not lead millions of Americans to evacuate their homes or to flood into supermarkets buying up survival supplies, as the missile crisis did. The week-long confrontation over Cuba generated a greater sense of urgency. In addition, the *Readers' Guide to Periodical Literature* shows that more articles about civil defense were published in popular periodicals in 1962 than in 1961. There were fifty-seven in 1961, sixty-four in 1962, and only twenty-eight in 1963.[9] The *New York Times* covered the months-long Berlin crisis on a daily basis and generated more than 350 articles about civil defense in 1961, more than 220 articles in 1962, seventy in 1963, and only twenty in 1966.[10] Since the Berlin crisis was considerably longer than the missile crisis and occurred earlier in the year, it is understandable that *New York Times* civil defense articles reached higher totals in 1961 than in 1962, and it is clear that Americans' interest in civil defense plummeted not at the end of 1961 but after the missile crisis had revealed the meaninglessness of a lean-budgeted civil defense program.

Americans did not come out of the Cuban Missile Crisis campaigning for civil defense. A sharp drop in interest was obvious because of declines in media coverage, public drills, and private shelter construction. However, as in so many issues that relate to Americans and civil defense, there is a disconnect between what people said and what they did. A 1964 poll by the University of Pittsburgh showed that 35 percent of Americans said the Cuban Missile Crisis increased their interest in civil defense.[11] Still, it seems apparent that most Americans walked away from the crisis accepting what their leaders had been afraid to say: that a minimal program was pointless and that a more effective program would be very expensive and still would offer no guarantees for many Americans. U.S. leaders had been right in surmising that voters would not rally around another huge and expensive federal bureaucracy that intruded in daily life. As another 1964 study done for the Office of Emergency Planning by the Hudson Institute concluded, the American public "supports the belief that war is a not-inconceivable possibility, supports the idea of shelter or other civil defense programs as a form of protections, but is little inclined to do anything about it. . . . It seems plain that most of the public would accept a cost-less, effort-less civil defense program if it were given to them."[12] In fact, after living with the fear of the missile crisis, most Americans apparently accepted that defenselessness was a part of the nuclear age or they simply prolonged their state of denial about nuclear war and its dangers.

In an era when America would be torn apart by frustrations, disappointments, and suspicions, the Cuban Missile Crisis represents one near-tragic event that raised serious questions about government credibility. During the showdown's nerve-rattling days and even in the relief-filled weeks that followed, civil defense chaos, news management, character assassination, and political maneuvering heightened skepticism about the government's honesty. Even while citizens cheered President Kennedy for his apparently deft handling of the confrontation, uncertainties surfaced about his administration's dedication to the truth. Some historians have claimed the roots of the divisiveness and cynicism that shook the nation in the 1960s and 1970s can be found in the Vietnam War or Watergate. I could assert that the missile crisis was the real fount of that loss of faith, which still permeates American culture; however, to do so would be to embrace a fallacy. The currents of history do not flow from a single source; they are continuously channeled through the twists and turns of human experience. Those who embrace a single cause for enormous changes in the American consciousness miss the point. It is possible to say that the assassination of Rev. Martin Luther King Jr. in 1968 caused rioting in many urban areas, but the sparks that lit those fires had accumulated over hundreds of years. One isolated issue did not redirect American thinking over the last half of the twentieth century. Many events became conduits for new ideas and new doubts.

Because my research shows that this frightening week touched American lives in a dramatic way, I conclude that the Cuban Missile Crisis represents an often overlooked national passage that almost certainly contributed to changes in the American state of mind.

While interest in civil defense waned, Americans embraced a more cautious and flexible foreign policy that endeavored to avoid slipping into nuclear war. Kennedy's American University speech in 1963 laid new groundwork for peaceful coexistence with Communism, and there is little doubt that Barry Goldwater's presidential campaign in 1964 suffered as a result of Americans' perception that he might launch a nuclear war to defeat Communism. The long conventional war in Vietnam was damaging to American society, but there was no widespread voter support for injecting nuclear weaponry into that conflict. While Kennedy's apparently tough stand in the missile crisis may have given him new flexibility by limiting criticism from the Right, the crisis's legacy was much more careful use of nuclear threats on both sides.

As the week's storyline had evolved, Khrushchev's backstage subterfuge and Kennedy's muscular diplomacy seemed to risk everything, but when the curtain came down, little had changed. One American pilot had died, Kennedy had gained prestige, and Khrushchev had lost some of his power base. But no missiles had been fired, no governments overthrown, no cities decimated. Still, like a tragic tableau presented by Arthur Miller or Tennessee Williams, the crisis had the power to haunt the minds of its audience. As Americans walked away from this confrontation, many were changed.

The United States' most potentially deadly crisis, a conflict in which hundreds of millions of people might have died, was relatively short: while the open showdown lasted only a week, there was less than a month between the blockade's establishment and its end.[13] At the same time that Kennedy lifted the quarantine, he canceled the Strategic Air Command alert. A day later, Soviet and Warsaw Pact nations ended their alerts as well. Soviet bombers left Cuba on 6–7 December, and on 12 December, Khrushchev notified the Supreme Soviet that all missiles had been withdrawn.[14]

Following Kennedy's death, authors of the "Camelot" myth, which portrayed the slain leader as a valiant champion of human rights and U.S. strength, placed the crisis at the center of his legacy. Like the trials of Hercules, it became a test of the hero's steely courage and righteousness in accounts by Robert Kennedy and Kennedy loyalists, such as Theodore C. Sorensen and Arthur M. Schlesinger Jr.[15] The crisis evolved into a heroic Kennedy tale, and the confrontation's effects on 185 million other Americans receded from public memory. To a degree, I believe, the crisis became overshadowed by JFK's 1963 assassination. The motorcade, the gunshots, the beating of drums, the riderless horse—these became the most persistent Kennedy moments in public memory. And over the years, historians have failed to examine the people's experiences during the crisis, leaving a gap in our knowledge, which this book intends to fill.

That sense of living on the bull's-eye, which seemed so palpable in October 1962, was revived for many Americans on 11 September 2001, when more than 3,000 people died during terrorist attacks in the United States. Muslim extremists seized four airliners, using two to strike the World Trade Center in New York and one to crash into the Pentagon. The fourth plane crashed in western Pennsylvania, killing the passengers and crew. In the aftermath of those attacks, an aura of helplessness shrouded a nation shocked by such losses and such insecurity; a new "other" became a threat to the bright futures of Americans. That horrifying day and its aftermath represented the only occasion that has provided younger generations with a taste of the precariousness and vulnerability Americans experienced during the missile crisis.

The vulnerability of America's civilian population remains an issue today. In early 2003, the Homeland Security Department of President George W. Bush's administration urged civilians to purchase duct tape and sheets of plastic to protect themselves from terrorist attacks using chemical or biological weapons, a "duct-tape and cover" maneuver that recalls the Cold War era's civil defense pattern of recommending small measures to defeat mighty weapons. In addition, Bush has promised voters an antiballistic missile system to block a limited nuclear attack by terrorists or rogue nations, although his opponents assert that his plan amounts to a fairy tale about a system that never would work.

Despite the threats of terrorism in the early years of the twenty-first century, Americans today are experiencing just a taste of the feelings that pervaded October 1962. A single, horrifying terrorist attack can kill thousands, but if the Cuban Missile Crisis had flared into nuclear war, tens of millions of people would have died, and whereas the 11 September attacks erased two buildings from the American landscape, a flurry of hydrogen bombs could devastate a multitude of cities. For many Americans, the nation's engagement in such a war would have been a death sentence, and the experience of waiting for the executioner to deliver the coup de grâce helped to shape who Americans are today.

notes

ABBREVIATIONS USED IN THE NOTES

AFHRC   Air Force Historical Research Center, Montgomery, Ala.

AWC   Army War College, Carlisle, Pa.

BL   Bancroft Library, Berkeley, Calif.

CA   City Archives, Philadelphia

CUOHP   Columbia University Oral History Project, New York

DDEL   Dwight D. Eisenhower Library, Abiline, Kans.

DDELOHP   Dwight D. Eisenhower Library Oral History Project, Abilene, Kans.

HI   Hoover Institution, Palo Alto, Calif.

HSTL   Harry S. Truman Library, Independence, Mo.

JFKL   John F. Kennedy Library, Boston

JFKLOHP   John F. Kennedy Library Oral History Project, Boston

LBJL   Lyndon Johnson Library, Austin

LOC   Library of Congress, Washington

MA   Municipal Archives, New York

ML   Mugar Library, Boston University

MT&R   Museum of Television & Radio, New York

NA   National Archives, Washington

NAII   National Archives II, College Park, Md.

NSA   National Security Archive, Washington

NYTA   *New York Times* Archives

NYUA   New York University Archives, New York

PC   Peace Collection, Swarthmore College, Swarthmore, Pa.

RA   Rockefeller Archives, Pocantico Hills, N.Y.

RNL   Richard Nixon Library and Birthplace Collections, Yorba Linda, Calif.

RWWL   Robert W. Woodruff Library, Atlanta

SGML   Seeley G. Mudd Library, Princeton

SHSOW   State Historical Society of Wisconsin, Madison

UOR   University of Rochester Rare Books Department, Rochester, N.Y.

USMCHC   United States Marine Corps Historical Center, Washington

YUL   Yale University Library, New Haven, Conn.

CHRONOLOGY

1. Department of Defense, "Department of Defense Operations during the Cuban Crisis," 11, National Security Files, Box 55, Cuba Subjects—Cuban Testimony, Defense and Military Resources Folder, JFKL.

2. Jeffrey C. Kitchen, Memorandum to the Secretary et al., 22 Oct. 1962, Box 147, George Ball Notebook, George Ball Papers, SGML.

3. Blight and Welch, *On the Brink*, 90–91.

4. Gribkov, "View from Moscow and Havana," 45.

5. Wilson oral history interview, 20, JFKLOHP.

6. Paul Weeks, "Crowd Gathers Silently on Street and Listens Intently to President," *Los Angeles Times*, 23 Oct. 1962, A1.

7. "8:25 A.M. Report," WNBC Television, 23 Oct. 1962, National Broadcasting Company Records, Box 266, Oct. 23, 1962, Folder, SHSOW.

8. United Press International, "Former President Applauds Cuba Move," *Wichita Eagle*, 23 Oct. 1962, 7A.

9. "CBS News Extra: U.S. Quarantines Cuba," 22 Oct. 1962, MT&R.

10. George Gallup, "Americans Back Kennedy on Cuba Blockade Decision," *Philadelphia Evening Bulletin*, 24 Oct. 1962, 30.

11. "CBS News Extra: U.S. Quarantines Cuba," 22 Oct. 1962, MT&R.

12. Salinger, *With Kennedy*, 267.

13. Marshall S. Carter, Memo to Special Group, 16 Oct. 1962, Rockefeller Commission Records, Record 1781000210499, NAII.

14. Penkovsky's orders were to alert his American contacts that a Soviet nuclear attack was imminent by calling a phone number and blowing into the phone three times. On 2 November, someone did exactly that, but because the worst of the crisis appeared to be over, the message was not taken seriously. Later, the U.S. government learned that Penkovsky had already been in custody when the message was sent. See Sagan, *Limits of Safety*, 147.

15. Joseph W. Sullivan, "Cuban Crisis Upsets Tourist Industry in Florida and Caribbean," *Wall Street Journal*, 25 Oct. 1962, 1.

16. Jack Heil, "Troops Reach Key West," *Washington Star*, 25 Oct. 1962, A5.

17. "White House Imposes New Security Checks," *New York Times*, 24 Oct. 1962, 22.

18. White House Post Logs, 23 Oct. 1962, Record Group 87, U.S. Secret Service, Appointment Records, JFKL.

19. United Press International, "Kennedy Signs Aid Measure," *Philadelphia Evening Bulletin*, 24 Oct. 1962, 30.

20. Ralph McGill, "Mood Piece from the U.N.," *Atlanta Constitution*, 24 Oct. 1962, 1.

21. "CBS News Special Report," 23 Oct. 1962, MT&R.

22. "'Even the Fruits of Victory Would Be Ashes in Our Mouth'—Kennedy," Social Protest Collection, Box 24, Folder 24–36, BL.

23. United Press International, "Pravda Fails Its Deadline," *Wichita Eagle*, 23 Oct. 1962, 1.

24. Akers oral history interview, 39, JFKLOHP.

25. "News of Blockade Spurs Varied Activities in City," *Cincinnati Enquirer*, 24 Oct. 1962, 19.

26. "Many Veterans in Phila. Area Seek to Enlist," *Philadelphia Inquirer*, 24 Oct. 1962, A7.

27. Bob Pimentel, "The Campus and Cuba," *Daily Californian*, 24 Oct. 1962, 1.

28. "Pan Am, KLM Halt Flights to Cuba after Its Warning," *Wall Street Journal*, 24 Oct. 1962, 18.

29. Blight and Welch, *On the Brink*, 306.

30. Beschloss, *Crisis Years*, 496.

31. "The Air Force Response to the Cuban Crisis 14 October–24 November 1962," January 1963, Document CC02811, NSA.

32. Associated Press, "Polaris Subs Plot Secret Course in Response to Alert," *Washington Star*, 24 Oct. 1962, A9.

33. Department of Defense, "Department of Defense Operations during the Cuban Crisis," 11, National Security Files, Box 55, Cuban Testimony, Defense and Military Resources Folder, JFKL.

34. Robert F. Kennedy, *Thirteen Days*, 68.

35. "Florida Airline Flights Continue," *Washington Star*, 25 Oct. 1962, A5.

36. Sullivan, "Cuban Crisis Upsets Tourist Industry."

37. "The Air Force Response to the Cuban Crisis 14 October–24 November 1962," January 1963, Document CC02811, NSA.

38. Stephen Trumbull and Bob Reno, "Security Lid Tight in Key West," *Miami Herald*, 25 Oct. 1962, 1A.

39. Herald Tribune Service, "Control Programs Are under Study," *Cincinnati Enquirer*, 25 Oct. 1962, 1.

40. "If Shooting Starts, Industry Could Mobilize for Limited War Now Faster Than in Korea," *Wall Street Journal*, 24 Oct. 1962, 1.

41. Fred Olmsted, "Crisis May Hike Car Sales," *Detroit Free Press*, 25 Oct. 1962, 1A.

42. "Presbyterians Urged to Pray in Cuba Crisis," *Philadelphia Evening Bulletin*, 25 Oct. 1962, 3.

43. "Crisis Starts Prayer Chain," *Hartford Courant*, 25 Oct. 1962, 2.

44. "Downtown Service Set," *Birmingham News*, 25 Oct. 1962, 1.

45. "Vice President Lyndon B. Johnson Daily Diary," 24 Oct. 1962, Pre-Presidential Daily Diary, Box 2, October 1962 Folder, Vice Presidential Papers, LBJL.

46. Henry Burris to Lyndon Johnson, Washington, 24 Oct. 1962, Vice Presidential Security File, Box 8, Policy Papers and Background Studies (VI) Folder, LBJL.

47. Letters, 24 Oct. 1962, Vice Presidential Papers, Box 135, Cuba 3 of 8 Folder, LBJL.

48. Robert Goralski, "Situation Report," NBC News, 24 Oct. 1962, National Broadcasting Company Records, Robert Goralski Papers, Box 10, Folder 8, SHSOW.

49. "CBS News Special Report," 25 Oct. 1962, MT&R.

50. Arnold M. Lubasch, "Stevenson Dares Russian to Deny Missiles Charge," *New York Times*, 26 Oct. 1962, 1.

51. Associated Press, "Eisenhower Advocates Sacrifices in Crisis," *Washington Star*, 26 Oct. 1962, A11.

52. "White House Drops All Social Events," *New York Times*, 26 Oct. 1962, 18.

53. Pierre Salinger, News Conference, 25 Oct. 1962, Pierre Salinger Papers, Box 50, Press Briefings/JFK 10/24/62–10/28/62 Folder, JFKL.

54. Kern, Levering, and Levering, *Kennedy Crises*, 129–30.

55. Sergei Khrushchev, *Nikita Khrushchev*, 618.

56. Stephen Trumbull and Bob Reno, "GI's Occupy Hotel, Beach at Key West," *Miami Herald*, 26 Oct. 1962, 13A.

57. United Press International, "Keys Jammed," *Boston Traveler*, 26 Oct. 1962, 2.

58. "Atom-Age Army Can Still Snafu," *Miami Herald*, 26 Oct. 1962, 2A.

59. James Russell, "Crisis Is Blow to Some Firms, Boon to Others," *Miami Herald*, 26 Oct. 1962, 12A.

60. "7:25 A.M. Report," WNBC Television, 26 Oct. 1962, National Broadcasting Company Records, Box 266, WNBC Television Oct. 26, 1962, Folder, SHSOW.

61. "War Restrictions Return as City Responds to Crisis," *Philadelphia Inquirer*, 26 Oct. 1962, 1.

62. Anatoly Dobrynin to the Soviet Foreign Ministry, Washington, 25 Oct. 1962, Cold War International History Project, comp., "Russian Documents on the Cuban Missile Crisis."

63. "Food Buying Rush Continues for 2nd Day," *Los Angeles Times*, 26 Oct. 1962, 1.

64. "Foreigners Leaving Bay Area," *San Francisco Chronicle*, 26 Oct. 1962, 7.

65. J. Edgar Hoover to Robert F. Kennedy, Washington, 27 Oct. 1962, Presidential Office Files, Box 115, Cuban Security 1962 Folder, JFKL.

66. Allyn, Blight, and Welch, eds., *Back to the Brink*, 76.

67. Associated Press, "Kennedy's Lights Burn Late," *Washington Star*, 26 Oct. 1962, A8.

68. May and Zelikow, eds., *Kennedy Tapes*, 478.

69. United Press International, "Photographers Are Barred at Entrance to White House," *New York Times*, 27 Oct.1962, 7.

70. David Braaten, "500 White House Pickets Split Sharply, but Parade," *Washington Star*, 27 Oct. 1962, 7.

71. Beschloss, *Crisis Years*, 514–15.

72. Associated Press, "Republicans Score Timing of Blockade," *New York Times*, 27 Oct. 1962, 7.

73. "Don't Believe It!" *Miami Herald*, 27 Oct. 1962, 1A.

74. "This 'Funny' Crisis," *Miami Herald*, 27 Oct. 1962, 1A.

75. "North Shore Raid Siren Sounds Off," *Florida Times-Union*, 27 Oct. 1962, 25.

76. "Railway Scene in Area Recalls Wartime Era," *Commercial Appeal*, 28 Oct. 1962, 15.

77. "Close Access to Mississippi during Night," *Chicago Tribune*, 27 Oct. 1962, pt. 1, p. 3.

78. United Press International, "N.Y. Wants 49,000 Crisis Firefighters," *Boston Traveler*, 27 Oct. 1962, 3.

79. J. Edgar Hoover to Robert F. Kennedy, Washington, 27 Oct. 1962, Presidential Office Files, Box 115, Cuban Security 1962 Folder, JFKL.

80. "Civil Defense Plan Is Devised for Post Office," *Scranton Tribune*, 26 Oct. 1962, 11.

81. John Handley, "Memories of the Queen Mary: Immensity, Beauty and Comfort," *Chicago Tribune*, 19 Jan. 1986, Travel, 3.

82. Wilson oral history interview, 30, JFKLOHP.

83. Alexander Mozgovoi, "The Cuban Samba of the Quartet of Fox Trots: Soviet Submarines in the Caribbean Crisis of 1962," Military Parade, Moscow, 2000, translated by Svetlana Savranskaya, NSA.

84. Allyn, Blight, and Welch, eds., *Back to the Brink*, 96–97.

85. Smith, "View from Washington," 142.

86. Associated Press and United Press International, "U.S. Calls 14,000 Reserves," *San Francisco Chronicle*, 28 Oct. 1962, 1.

87. Freedman, *Kennedy's Wars*, 219.

88. Blight, *Shattered Crystal Ball*, 99.

89. Blight and Welch, *On the Brink*, 313.

90. Fursenko and Naftali, *"One Hell of a Gamble,"* 284–85.

91. "Telecons 6–12/62," W. Averell Harriman Papers, Box 581, Public Service–Chronological File–Telecons 6–12/62 Folder, LOC.

92. May and Zelikow, eds., *Kennedy Tapes*, 629.

93. Steuart Pittman, "A Report on National Civil Defense Readiness," 27 Oct. 1962, Office of Emergency Planning Records, Microfilm Roll 1, JFKL.

94. "The Age of Desensitization," *Saturday Review*, 27 Oct. 1962, 24.

95. Nikita Khrushchev, *Khrushchev Remembers*, 497–98.

96. Chang and Kornbluh, eds., *Cuban Missile Crisis*, 391.

97. Freedman, *Kennedy's Wars*, 201.

98. May and Zelikow, eds., *Kennedy Tapes*, 682.

99. "Harrison, Congressmen Welcome Cuban Accord," *Richmond Post-Dispatch*, 29 Oct. 1962, 1.

100. *CBS Washington Report*, 28 Oct. 1962, MT&R.

101. Joseph J. McMahon and Frank Toughill, "Air Force Call-up Ends Reservist's Honeymoon," *Philadelphia Evening Bulletin*, 29 Oct. 1962, 1.

102. "Wed Saturday, Called Sunday," *Boston Globe*, 29 Oct. 1962, 1.

103. Emanuel Perlmutter, "Rally Held Here by 8,000 Pacifists," *New York Times*, 29 Oct. 1962, 20.

104. United Press International, "Cuban Crisis Spurs Church Attendance," *Philadelphia Evening Bulletin*, 29 Oct. 1962, 3.

105. "Church Services Reflect Feelings," *Harrisburg Patriot*, 29 Oct. 1962, 1A.

106. Associated Press, "The Prayers on a Church Lawn in Key West," *New York Herald Tribune*, 29 Oct. 1962, 23.

INTRODUCTION

1. Weart, *Nuclear Fear*, 259.

2. Beschloss, *Crisis Years*, 232.

3. This is clearly a conception of the American character as developed by European immigrants to what would become the United States. Another group of early Americans came to the United States on slave ships, probably with no hope for tomorrow and the realization that they no longer owned their lives. Native Americans preceded the Europeans to this land and experienced genocide at their hands. The forward-looking facet of the American character, like many others, is traceable to European roots because white Americans long have represented the dominant culture in the United States. Over the years, this aspect of the American character has, in many cases, been adopted by those whose ancestors interacted with Europeans under much less hopeful circumstances.

4. Campbell, *Writing Security*, 16.

5. Niebuhr, *Children of Light*, 55.

6. McCoy and Ruetten, *Quest and Response*, 264.

7. Engelhardt, *End of Victory Culture*, 53.

8. Mead, *And Keep Your Powder Dry*, 17.

9. "The Image Abroad of U.S. Science and Technology—Draft," 1 July 1960, White House Office, Box 14, President's Committee on Information Activities Abroad Folder, DDEL.

10. "CBS News Special Report," 12 Apr. 1961, MT&R.

11. "Madman, Parts 1 and 2," 20 Oct. 1962 and 27 Oct. 1962, MT&R.

12. Slotkin, *Gunfighter Nation*, 500.

13. Schlesinger, *Paths to the Present*, 18.

14. Sorensen, *Kennedy*, 308.

15. William H. Craig, Memorandum, 24 Jan. 1962, Rockefeller Commission Records, Record 1781000210414, NAII.

16. Marshall S. Carter, Memo to Special Group, 16 Oct. 1962, Rockefeller Commission Records, Record 178100210499, NAII.

17. Central Intelligence Agency, "Operation Mongoose: Main Points to Consider," 26 Oct. 1962, Rockefeller Commission Records, Record 1781000310010, NAII.

18. Fursenko and Naftali, *"One Hell of a Gamble,"* 155.

19. Zaloga, *Target America*, 208. Recently declassified records show that the United States actually photographed thirty-three medium-range missiles on Cuban soil and later counted forty-two on departing Soviet ships. See Central Intelligence Agency, "Chronology of Specific Events Relating to the Military Buildup in Cuba," 24 Nov. 1962, 2, NSA.

20. Central Intelligence Agency, *Secret Cuban Missile Crisis Documents*, 269.

21. Gribkov, "View from Moscow and Havana," 31, 39.

22. Ibid., 36.

23. Blight, Allyn, and Welch, *Cuba on the Brink*, 59–60.

24. Freedman, *Kennedy's Wars*, 166.

25. Blight, Allyn, and Welch, *Cuba on the Brink*, 61. According to General Herbert Powell, U.S. Army invaders would have had similar weapons and permission to use them. See Powell oral history interview, 25, AWC.

26. Freedman, *Kennedy's Wars*, 167.

27. National Resources Defense Council, "Table of US Nuclear Warheads: 1945–1970," *Archive of Nuclear Data* Website, 25 May 2000, <http://www.nrdc.org/nuclear/nudbdatainx.asp>.

28. National Resources Defense Council, "Table of USSR/Russian Nuclear Warheads: 1949–1970," *Archive of Nuclear Data* Website, 25 May 2000, <http://www.nrdc.org/nuclear/nudbdatainx.asp>.

29. Garthoff, *Reflections on the Cuban Missile Crisis*, 142.

30. *Studies in the Employment of Air Power*, vol. 6, ch. 5, p. 388.

31. Ibid., 388–89.

32. Nitze, *From Hiroshima to Glasnost*, 222.

33. Hilty, *Robert Kennedy*, 260, 446.

34. Beschloss, *Crisis Years*, 469.

35. May and Zelikow, eds., *Kennedy Tapes*, 145.

36. Beschloss, *Crisis Years*, 483.

37. Sorensen, *Kennedy*, 702.

38. Acheson oral history interview, 24, JFKL.

39. Wade oral history interview, 328, AFHRC.

40. Department of Defense, "Department of Defense Operations during the Cuban Crisis," 19, National Security Files, Box 55, Cuba Subjects—Cuban Testimony, Defense and Military Resources Folder, JFKL.

41. "Cuba Fact Sheet," 2, National Security Files, Countries, Box 36, Cuba General 10/26/62–10/27/62 Folder, JFKL.

42. Freedman, *Kennedy's Wars*, 175.

43. Department of Defense, "Department of Defense Operations during the Cuban Crisis," 15.

44. Kovacs oral history interview, 2, JFKLOHP.

45. "Urgent to All Base Residents," Edward O'Donnell Papers, Folder 74077-10.V, HI.

CHAPTER ONE

1. "If H-Bomb Comes—What You Can Do about It," *U.S. News & World Report*, 8 Apr. 1955, 126.

2. Horelick, *Cuban Missile Crisis*, 5.

3. Ted Lippman, "Atomic War in 10 Days Possible, Russell Warns," *Atlanta Constitution*, 25 Oct. 1962, 1.

4. Martin J. Sherwin, "The Militarization of Foreign Affairs," *New York Times*, 7 Nov. 1982, sec. 7, p. 7.

5. Transcript of first Executive Committee Meeting, 16 Oct. 1962, Chang and Kornbluh, eds., *Cuban Missile Crisis*, 88.

6. Blight, *Shattered Crystal Ball*, 8.

7. Blight and Welch, *On the Brink*, 188.

8. John F. Kennedy, *Prelude to Leadership*, 7.

9. Nikita Khrushchev, *Khrushchev Speaks*, 362.

10. Hachiya, *Hiroshima Diary*, 8.

11. Arthur W. Mielke, "Hiroshima: Our Guilt and Our Atonement," 20 Apr. 1958, in Butler, ed., *Best Sermons*, 287.

12. James Reston, "Dawn of the Atom Era Perplexes Washington," *New York Times*, 12 Aug. 1945, 12.

13. "A Decision for Mankind," *St. Louis Post-Dispatch*, 7 Aug. 1945.

14. "Operation Alert 1957: Exercise Only," White House Office, Office of the Staff Secretary, Emergency Action Series, Box 5, Operation Alert 1957 (President's Formal Actions) (1) Folder, DDEL.

15. Marc Trachtenberg, "American Thinking on Nuclear War," in Jacobsen, ed., *Strategic Power*, 355.

16. Weart, *Nuclear Fear*, 235.

17. Ibid., 227.

18. Rose, *One Nation Underground*, 166.

19. Ibid., 156.

20. Thomas Powers, "Nuclear Winter and Nuclear Strategy," *Atlantic Monthly*, Nov. 1984, 60.

21. Lewis Mumford, "The Morals of Extermination," *Atlantic Monthly*, Oct. 1959, 43.

22. Philip Nash, "Bear Any Burden? John F. Kennedy and Nuclear Weapons," in Gaddis et al., eds., *Cold War Statesmen Confront the Bomb*, 124.

23. Kennedy also often used Munich as a touchstone. His senior thesis at Harvard and his first book, *Why England Slept*, examined British slowness to prepare for World War II. See Hamilton, *JFK: Reckless Youth*, 318–19.

24. Eisenhower oral history interview, Dulles Oral History Project, 50, CUOHP.

25. Craig, *Destroying the Village*, 69.

26. Trachtenberg, *Constructed Peace*, 162.

27. Stewart Alsop, "Kennedy's Grand Strategy," *Saturday Evening Post*, 31 Mar. 1962, 14.

28. Lippmann, "Address by Walter Lippmann before the Women's National Press Club, January 10, 1962," Vice Presidential Papers, 1962 Subject Files–Public Information Box, District of Columbia 2 of 2 Folder, LBJL.

29. Gallup, *Gallup Poll*, 1758.

30. Presbyterian Church of the United States, *Minutes of the General Assembly and Report of Assembly Agencies*, 198.

31. Sidey, introduction to *Prelude to Leadership*, xliv.

32. Chang and Kornbluh, *Cuban Missile Crisis*, 154.

33. "We Are on the Alert," *Red Star*, 24 Oct. 1962.

34. Blight and Welch, *On the Brink*, 163.

35. In 1961, Khrushchev sought to eliminate the Western presence in Berlin, located deep inside East Germany, and thus to remove an escape route for East German refugees. When the West objected, weeks of bluster followed before he ordered construction of a wall separating East from West Berlin and ending the flood of refugees.

36. Boyer, *Fallout*, 82–83.

37. Weart, *Nuclear Fear*, 213.

38. Minutes of Cabinet Meeting, 6 Mar. 1959, Cabinet Series, Box 13, Cabinet Meeting of March 6, 1959, Folder, DDEL.

39. Aronow, Ervin, and Sidel, eds., *Fallen Sky*, 61.

40. Ibid., 82.

41. Ibid., 101.

42. Martin Mann, "Man's Last Big Blast," *Popular Science*, Sept. 1962, 113.

43. Aronow, Ervin and Sidel, eds., *Fallen Sky*, 103.

44. "Report by the PSAC Panel on Civil Defense," National Security Files, Box 295, Report by the PSAC Panel on Civil Defense Folder, II-1 and II-2, JFKL.

45. Ibid., II-3.

46. Ibid., II-12.

47. Aronow, Ervin, and Sidel, eds., *Fallen Sky*, 129.

48. Kahn, *On Thermonuclear War*, 21.

49. Ibid., 20. This theory remains controversial: A *New York Times* analysis in 1983 concluded that even an exchange of only 100 megatons could cause catastrophic harm to Earth. See "The Winter after the Bomb." *New York Times*, 6 Nov. 1983, sec. 4, p. 20.

50. Orear, Schreiber, Holton, Luria, Salpeter, Morrison, Meselson, and Feld, "An Answer to Teller," *Saturday Evening Post*, 14 Apr. 1962, 69.

51. Ibid., 71.

52. McEnaney, *Civil Defense Begins at Home*, 31.

53. Ibid., 45.

54. "Discussion at the 318th Meeting of the National Security Council, Thursday, April 4, 1957," Papers of the President of the United States (Ann Whitman File), National Security Council Series, Box 8, 318th Meeting Folder, DDEL.

55. "The Postattack Situation," *New Republic*, 15 Jan. 1962, 19–20.

56. "CD Chief Says Nelson Isn't Even Convinced," *Milwaukee Journal*, 13 Nov. 1959, Part 2, 1.

57. Robert B. Meyner, "The Cruel Deception of Civil Defense," *Progressive*, June 1960, 14.

58. Minutes of Cabinet Meeting, 13 July 1956, Cabinet Series, Box 7, Minutes of Cabinet Meeting—Operation Alert Folder, DDEL.

59. McEnaney, *Civil Defense Begins at Home*, 33.

60. Minutes of the Second Plenary Meeting of the Interim Assembly, 17 June 1955, 7, Cabinet Series, Box 5, Special Cabinet Meeting of June 17, 1955 Folder, DDEL.

61. Rose, *One Nation Underground*, 27.

62. Minutes of the Second Plenary Meeting of the Interim Assembly, 1.

63. "If Bombs Do Fall—Who'll Run Things," *U.S. News & World Report*, 16 Oct. 1961, 46–49.

64. "The Human Effects of Nuclear Weapons Development," Papers of the President of the United States (Ann Whitman File), National Security Council Series, Briefing Notes—Box 9, Human Effects of Nuclear Weapons Development (2) Folder, DDEL.

65. Notes on the Expanded Cabinet Meeting held from 2:30 to 3:45 P.M. on Wednesday, 25 July 1956, 2, Cabinet Series, Box 7, Cabinet Meeting of July 25, 1956—Operation Alert Folder, DDEL.

66. Weart, *Nuclear Fear*, 131.

67. Notes on the Expanded Cabinet Meeting held from 2:30 to 3:45 P.M. on Wednesday, 25 July 1956, 8–9.

68. Oakes, *Imaginary War*, 84.

69. "And Back in Washington," *New Republic*, 15 Jan. 1962, 10.

70. Hopkins, "Urban Dispersal in the United States."

71. Wadsworth oral history interview, 61, CUOHP.

72. "Evacuation Called 'Tool' in Red Talks," *Washington Post*, 6 Aug. 1961, B1.

73. "Cabinet Minutes, July 12, 1957," 2, Papers of the President of the United States (Ann Whitman File), Cabinet Series, Box 9, 7/19/57 Folder, DDEL.

74. Diary entry for 24 January 1957, Papers of the President of the United States (Ann Whitman Diary Series), Box 8, January 1957 (1) Folder, DDEL.

75. *Highlights of the U.S. Civil Defense Program*, 4.

76. Bruce Watson and William L. Bird Jr., "We Couldn't Run, So We Hoped We Could Hide," *Smithsonian*, Apr. 1994, 46.

77. *Family Fallout Shelter*, 4–5.

78. Rose, *One Nation Underground*, 31.

79. *By, for, and about Women in Civil Defense.*

80. *What You Should Know about Radioactive Fallout,* 10–11.

81. Javits, "Construction of Civil Defense Shelters," 5889.

82. Kennedy, "Radio and Television Report to the American People on the Berlin Crisis," *Public Papers of the Presidents: John F. Kennedy, 1961,* 302.

83. Weart, *Nuclear Fear,* 255.

84. "A New Urgency, Big Things to Do—and What You Must Learn," *Life,* 15 Sept. 1961, 96.

85. "The Devious Arithmetic of Civil Defense," *Progressive,* February 1962, 18.

86. Watson and Bird, "We Couldn't Run, So We Hoped We Could Hide," 46.

87. "Civil Defense: Who'd Survive," *Newsweek,* 7 Aug. 1961, 48.

88. Watson and Bird, "We Couldn't Run, So We Hoped We Could Hide," 46.

89. Asher Byrnes and Garrett Underhill, "Civil Defense Muddle," *New Republic,* 15 Jan. 1962, 3.

90. Promotional Flyer, "Fallout Survival Show," *Dallas Morning News,* 17 Nov. 1961.

91. R. E. Holt to Lyndon B. Johnson, 10 Nov. 1961, Vice Presidential Papers—1961 Subject File, Box 74, Defense—National Civilian Folder, LBJL.

92. "Radio Stations to Get Federal Aid for Shelters," 7.

93. Gallup, *Gallup Poll,* 1732.

94. Rose, *One Nation Underground,* 192.

95. Berrien, Schulman, and Amarel, "Fallout-Shelter Owners," 207.

96. "Confusion on Olympus," *New Republic,* 15 Jan. 1962, 13.

97. "Survival: Are Shelters the Answer?" *Newsweek,* 6 Nov. 1961, 19.

98. Kaplan, *Wizards of Armageddon,* 311.

99. *"Sauve Qui Peut," New Republic,* 15 Jan. 1962, 29. For more on ties between religious imagery and nuclear war, see Boyer, *When Time Shall Be No More,* and Lifton, *Broken Connection.*

100. Rose, *One Nation Underground,* 94.

101. "Toward the Garrison State," *Progressive,* Feb. 1962, 40.

102. Serling, "Shelter," *The Twilight Zone,* MT&R.

103. "That Long-Awaited Booklet," *New Republic,* 15 Jan. 1962, 13.

104. Flemming oral history interview, 26, DDELOHP. See also "The Narrow Limits of Nuclear Knowledge," *Progressive,* Feb. 1962, 30.

105. Robert L. McManus, "1962 Governor's Conference—For Release in the Afternoon Papers," 2 July 1962, Office Records, 1959–73, Nelson Rockefeller Papers, Civil Defense Folder, Microfilm Reel 156, RA.

106. "Postattack Situation," 19–20.

107. Julius Duscha, "McNamara Explains His Shelter Program," *Washington Post,* 2 Aug. 1961, A7.

108. Detzer, *Brink,* 194.

109. United Press International, "A-Shelter Project Hit as Saving Men Only," *Washington Post,* 3 Aug. 1961, 2.

110. "Report by the PSAC Panel on Civil Defense," National Security Files, Box 295, Report by the PSAC Panel on Civil Defense Folder-II-34, JFKL.

111. Mack and Baker, *Occasion Instant,* 10.

112. "Personal and Otherwise," *Harper's Bazaar*, Nov. 1957, 24.

113. Mack and Baker, *Occasion Instant*, 18.

114. Ibid., 31–32.

115. Ford, *Button*, 28.

116. Gallard, "October's Dark Abyss," *Chicago Sun-Times*, 28 Oct. 1995, 20.

117. "U.S. Nuclear Weapons Accidents (1950–1980) Acknowledged by the Pentagon," Operations—Atomic Weapons Accident Subject File, 6E–6F, USMCHC.

118. *On the Beach*.

119. Papers of the President of the United States (Ann Whitman File), Cabinet Series, Box 15, 12/11/59 Folder, DDEL.

120. For the Eisenhower administration's position on the possibility of a doomsday machine, see "Infoguide: *On the Beach*," United States Information Agency, 4 Dec. 1959, 1–3, White House Office, Cabinet Secretariat: Records, 1953–60, Box 22, CP 64, DDEL. In 1961, analyst Herman Kahn told a House panel that creation of a doomsday machine capable of killing mankind probably would occur by 1971. See "Civil Defense—1961," Hearing of the House of Representatives, Subcommittee on Military Operations, Committee on Government Operations, 7 Aug. 1961, *Congressional Record*, 167.

121. "Minutes of Cabinet Meeting," 11 Dec. 1959, 2, Cabinet Series, Box 15, Cabinet Meeting of December 11, 1959, Folder, DDEL.

122. Burdick and Wheeler, *Fail-Safe*, 98.

123. United Press International Dispatch, 7 Apr. 1958, White House Office, Office of the Staff Secretary, Subject Series, Department of Defense, Box 1, Vol. II (6) Folder, DDEL.

124. Kennedy liked this novel and joked that some military men might wish to seize power. He felt a coup was possible if an inexperienced leader made many errors. See Sorensen, *Kennedy*, 606–7, and Reeves, *President Kennedy*, 305. Within weeks of the crisis, JFK had read both *Fail-Safe* and *Seven Days in May*. See Sulzberger, *Last of the Giants*, 935.

125. Serling, "Time Enough at Last," *The Twilight Zone*, MT&R.

126. Aronson, *Press and the Cold War*, 37.

127. Kraus, Mehling, and El-Assal, "Mass Media and the Fallout Controversy," 198.

128. Harris, Proshansky, and Raskin, "Some Attitudes of College Students."

129. Erskine, "Polls," 156.

130. Caroline Bird, "Nine Places to Hide," *Esquire*, Jan. 1962, 55–57, 128–30.

131. "If Bombs Do Fall—Who'll Run Things," 46–49.

132. "If Bombs Do Fall: What Happens to Your Savings, Property, Investments?" *U.S. News & World Report*, 13 Nov. 1961, 81–83.

133. "Toward the Garrison State," *Progressive*, Feb. 1962, 43.

134. *Exercise Spadefork*, 2–4, 12, 15–16, 18, 33, 35, 41, 46.

CHAPTER TWO

1. Edward A. McDermott to Steuart L. Pittman, 29 Oct. 1962, Office of Emergency Preparedness Records, Central Correspondence Files 1962–64, Box 2, Civil Defense Office Folder, NAII.

2. In a 30 October 1962 memo, Office of Emergency Planning director Edward A. McDermott wrote to Office of Civil Defense chief Steuart Pittman using the language of

bureaucratic warfare to repeat each agency's role. See McDermott to Pittman, Washington, 30 Oct. 1962, Office of Emergency Planning Records, Correspondence Files 1962–64, Box 2, Civil Defense Office (DOD) Folder, NA.

3. Leonard L. Reese Jr. to Edward A. McDermott, Washington, 29 Oct. 1962, 2, Office of Emergency Planning Records, Microfilm Roll 1, JFKL.

4. Leonard L. Reese Jr. to E. J. Quindlen, Washington, 23 Oct. 1962, Office of Emergency Planning Records, Microfilm Roll 1, JFKL.

5. Ralph E. Spear, "OEP Bulletin 9300," 23 Oct. 1962, Office of Emergency Planning Records, Microfilm Roll 1, JFKL.

6. Pittman later faulted the administration for providing too little public leadership on civil defense during the crisis. See Pittman, "Government and Civil Defense," 70.

7. Blair, Pike, and Schwartz, "Targeting and Controlling the Bomb," 213.

8. Hugh Sidey, "I'm Staying Right Here," *Time*, 13 Feb. 1989, 40.

9. Since no enemy south of the United States had nuclear weapons before the crisis, no radar scanned southern skies for incoming weapons until Wednesday, 24 October 1962. See Department of Defense, "Department of Defense Operations during the Cuban Crisis," 11, National Security Files, Box 55, Cuba Subjects—Cuban Testimony, Defense and Military Resources Folder, JFKL.

10. To assure that one person in the presidential line of succession always was safe, the administration considered a rotating schedule keeping one cabinet member in a bunker at all times, but the plan was never implemented. See Emergency Planning Committee, "Report to the President on a Re-examination of Federal Policy with Respect to Emergency Plans and Continuity of Government in the Event of Nuclear Attack on the United States," 11 June 1962, 6, Presidential Office Files, Box 94, Emergency Planning Committee on Assumptions for Non-Military Planners Folder, JFKL. For details on fears of losing everyone in the line of succession, see ibid.

11. To prove to doubters that the government could be run from underground, Dwight Eisenhower, in an elaborate publicity stunt, actually had performed his duties in bomb-proofed headquarters under Raven Rock Mountain at Fort Ritchie, Md., during "Operation Alert 1955." See Pike, Blair, and Schwartz, "Defending against the Bomb," 313–14.

12. Blair, Pike, and Schwartz, "Targeting and Controlling the Bomb," 212.

13. Ted Gup, "The Doomsday Blueprints," *Time*, 10 Aug. 1992, 35.

14. Blair, Pike, and Schwartz, "Targeting and Controlling the Bomb," 212.

15. Until 1992, this facility was manned by government employees who pretended to be running a TV repair shop. In reality, the staff kept the facility ready for a congressional relocation through steps such as constantly keeping up with the prescription drug needs of all members of Congress and keeping supplies of all needed drugs on hand at all times. See ibid., 214.

16. Ed Vallandingham, tour guide, public tour of Greenbrier resort bunker, 11 Mar. 1998.

17. Gup, "Doomsday Blueprints," 34–37.

18. The line of succession is as follows: the vice president, the Speaker of the House, the Senate president pro tem, and then cabinet members in the order in which their departments were created, which would place the secretary of state first.

19. "Report of the Task Group on the Survivable Communications Requirements," 20

Aug. 1962, 10, National Security Files—Meetings and Memoranda File, Box 333, NSAM 127 Folder, Emergency Plan for Continuity of Government 9/62–10/62, JFKL.

20. Edward A. McDermott to Paul Mefford, 23 Nov. 1963, Office of Emergency Preparedness Records, Central Correspondence Files 1962–64, Box 1, General Book Folder, NAII.

21. "Unanswerable Questions about Whom to Shelter," *New York Times*, 13 Aug. 1980, A22.

22. E. L. Kennan, Daily Report to Edward A. McDermott, 26 Oct. 1962, Office of Emergency Preparedness Records, Executive Correspondence and Memos 1961–63, Box 3, OEP Director Sept.–Oct. 1962 Folder, NAII.

23. Leonard L. Reese Jr. to Edward A. McDermott, Washington, 29 Oct. 1962, 1, Office of Emergency Planning Records, Microfilm Roll 1, JFKL.

24. Robert Y. Phillips to Edward A. McDermott, Washington, 23 Oct. 1962, Office of Emergency Planning Records, Microfilm Roll 1, JFKL.

25. Leonard L. Reese Jr. to E. J. Quindlen, Washington, 23 Oct. 1962, Office of Emergency Planning Records, Microfilm Roll 1, JFKL.

26. Associated Press, "Homefront Mobilization Plans Ready to Cope with Nuclear Attack on U.S.," *Philadelphia Evening Bulletin*, 25 Oct. 1962, 11.

27. Edward A. McDermott to Heads of Departments and Agencies Having Nonmilitary Defense Responsibilities, Washington, 25 Oct. 1962, Vice Presidential Papers, National Security Files, Box 283A, 10/25/62–10/10/63 Folder, LBJL.

28. Robert Y. Phillips to Edward A. McDermott, Washington, 26 Oct. 1962, Office of Emergency Planning Records, Microfilm Roll 1, JFKL.

29. Salinger, *With Kennedy*, 256.

30. Edward A. McDermott to All Office of Emergency Preparedness Regional Directors, 31 Oct. 1962, Office of Emergency Preparedness Records, Central Correspondence Files 1962–64, Box 1, Regional Book Folder, NAII.

31. Eugene J. Quindlen, Memorandum to the Staff, 30 Oct. 1962, Office of Emergency Preparedness Records, Executive Correspondence and Memos 1961–63, Box 3, OEP Book Oct.–Dec. 1962 Folder, NAII.

32. William B. Rice, Bulletin to Executive Staff, Staff and Regional Office Directors, 24 Oct. 1962, Office of Emergency Preparedness Records, Executive Correspondence and Memos 1961–63, Box 3, OEP Book Oct.–Dec. 1962 Folder, NAII.

33. Leonard L. Reese Jr. to Col. Justice M. Chambers, 31 Oct. 1962, Office of Emergency Preparedness Records, Executive Correspondence and Memos 1961–63, Box 3, Deputy Director—July–Dec. Folder, NAII.

34. Civilian agencies' duties at various DEFCON levels depended on their wartime responsibilities. Disagreement about whether DEFCON alerts affected the Office of Civil Defense went up the ladder to Pittman. See Ralph E. Spear to Edward A. McDermott, 24 Oct. 1962, Office of Emergency Planning Records, Executive Correspondence and Memos, Box 3, OEP Director—Sept.–Oct. 1962 Folder, NAII.

35. "Senior Duty Watch," 22 Oct. 1962, Office of Emergency Planning Records, Microfilm Roll 1, JFKL.

36. At the Greenbrier, there are rumors that many members of Congress checked into the resort during the crisis, but there is no evidence to back that assertion. It is doubtful

that any lawmakers who chose to get closer to the bunker would register using their own names.

37. J. L. Bourassa to William B. Rice, Washington, 13 Mar. 1964, Office of Emergency Planning Records, Microfilm Roll 1, JFKL.

38. "Senior Duty Watch," 22 Oct. 1962.

39. The Emergency News Service's goal was to "refine plans leading to the establishment of a stand-by emergency domestic information system." As a result of the crisis, it generated plans for a large exercise to identify communication problems. See Jack Rosenthall, "Exercise for W. H. Information Group," 1 Nov. 1962, and J. M. Chambers to Robert McNamara, 25 Oct. 1962, both in Office of Emergency Planning Records, Microfilm Roll 1, JFKL.

40. J. L. Bourassa to William B. Rice, Washington, 13 Mar. 1964, Office of Emergency Planning Records, Microfilm Roll 1, JFKL.

41. John J. O'Neill, "Report on Colonel Chambers' Request for Information," 24 Oct. 1962, Office of Emergency Planning Records, Microfilm Roll 1, JFKL.

42. Robert Y. Phillips to Edward A. McDermott, Washington, 30 Oct. 1962, Office of Emergency Planning Records, Microfilm Roll 1, JFKL.

43. Paul Revelle, "Report on Transportation Agencies' Situation at 4:30 P.M. Last Evening," 24 Oct. 1962, Office of Emergency Planning, Microfilm Roll 1, JFKL.

44. John E. Cosgrove to Eugene L. Quindlen, Washington, 6 Nov. 1962, Office of Emergency Planning Records, Microfilm Roll 1, JFKL.

45. Associated Press, "Homefront Mobilization Plans Ready to Cope," 11.

46. John K. Cosgrove to Edward A. McDermott, Washington, 25 Oct. 1962, Office of Emergency Planning Records, Microfilm Roll 1, JFKL.

47. "Meeting RCDMS Held Boston 9/23," Office of Emergency Planning Records, Microfilm Roll 1, JFKL.

48. Acting Regional Director to Deputy Director, Everett, Washington, 25 Oct. 1962, Office of Emergency Planning Records, Microfilm Roll 1, JFKL.

49. Regional planners struggled to find relocation sites while receiving mixed signals from federal agencies. See ibid.

50. Bill Rice to Joe ?, Washington, 24 Oct. 1962, Office of Emergency Planning Records, Microfilm Roll 1, JFKL.

51. Edward A. McDermott to Steuart Pittman, 30 Oct. 1962, Office of Emergency Preparedness Records, Central Correspondence Files 1962–64, Box 2, Civil Defense Office Folder, NAII.

52. "Outline of Remarks by Edward A. McDermott," Washington, 27 Oct. 1962, Office of Emergency Planning Records, Microfilm Roll 1, JFKL.

53. To gauge officials' ability to gather quickly, Eisenhower unexpectedly called a National Security Council meeting at Mount Weather in 1960. One member never arrived; another made it only because his wife, wearing only a nightgown, drove him; and one member refused to take the call announcing relocation of the meeting. See "Thursday May 5, 1960," Papers of the President of the United States (Ann Whitman File), Box 11, May 1960 Folder, DDEL.

54. Robert Y. Phillips to Edward A. McDermott, Washington, 25 Oct. 1962, Office of Emergency Planning Records, Microfilm Roll 1, JFKL.

55. "Helicopter Pickup Points in the Event of an Emergency Evacuation of the Vice President," 1 Nov. 1962, Vice President Security Files, Box 5, Emergency Evacuation Instructions Folder, LBJL.

56. Edward A. McDermott to Heads of Departments and Agencies Having Nonmilitary Defense Responsibilities, Washington, 25 Oct. 1962, Vice Presidential Papers, National Security Files, Box 283A, 10/25/62–10/10/63 Folder, LBJL.

57. Salinger, *With Kennedy*, 256.

58. Sidey, "I'm Staying Right Here," 40.

59. Salinger, *With Kennedy*, 256. Also see *Nightline*, ABC News, 30 Jan. 1989, which revealed that Soviet officials apparently confronted this same issue during the crisis. Salinger has reported that two close aides to Khrushchev urged their wives to leave Moscow because of a possible attack on 27 October 1962. *Nightline* tape available at MT&R.

60. Rusk, *As I Saw It*, 244.

61. Tazewell Shepard, "Memorandum for Mrs. Evelyn Lincoln," 26 Oct. 1962, Presidential Office Files, Box 114, Cuba General 10/24/62–12/31/62 Folder, JFKL.

62. Edward A. McDermott to Earl Warren, Washington, 30 Oct. 1962, Office of Emergency Planning Records, Microfilm Roll 1, JFKL.

63. See *Nightline*, 30 Jan. 1989, MT&R.

64. Allyn, Blight, and Welch, eds., *Back to the Brink*, 77.

65. Leonard L. Reese Jr. to Edward A. McDermott, Washington, 29 Oct. 1962, 1, Office of Emergency Planning Records, Microfilm Roll 1, JFKL.

66. Ted Gup, "The Doomsday Plan," *Time*, 10 Aug. 1992, 32.

67. Nash, *Other Missiles of October*, 126.

68. Ibid., 87.

69. Blight, *Shattered Crystal Ball*, 20.

70. Kramer, "'Lessons' of the Cuban Missile Crisis," 59.

71. Gribkov, "View from Moscow and Havana," 45–46.

72. Ross, *American Government in Crisis*, 115.

73. "Cuba Fact Sheet," 1, National Security Files—Countries, Box 36, Cuba General 10/26/62–10/27/62 Folder, JFKL.

74. "Actions of Military Services in Cuban Crisis Outlined," Department of Defense, 29 Nov. 1962, 9, Document CC02628, NSA.

75. *Studies in the Employment of Air Power*, 372.

76. Ross, *American Government in Crisis*, 195.

77. "Background Briefing on Cuban Situation," The Pentagon, 22 Oct. 1962, 2, Document K160-951-5, AFHRC.

78. "Actions of Military Services in Cuban Crisis Outlined," 4.

79. Burchinal oral history interview, 117, AFHRC.

80. "Actions of Military Services in Cuban Crisis Outlined," 4.

81. May and Zelikow, eds., *Kennedy Tapes*, 178.

82. Johnson, LeMay, Burchinal, and Catton oral history interview, AFHRC.

83. In all, 183 U.S. vessels were at sea in the Caribbean. They carried 85,000 people. See "Actions of Military Services in Cuban Crisis Outlined," 6.

84. Some Soviet submarines were operating with minimal oxygen supplies, and frayed nerves reportedly almost led the Soviets to use nuclear torpedoes. See Alexander Mov-

govoi, "The Cuban Samba of the Quartet of Fox Trots," *Military Parade, Moscow, 2002,* NSA.

85. Ford, *Button,* 51.

86. "Actions of Military Services in Cuban Crisis Outlined," 6.

87. May and Zelikow, eds., *Kennedy Tapes,* 261–62.

88. Powell oral history interview, 12, AWC.

89. White, ed., *Kennedys and Cuba,* 200.

90. Young, *When the Russians Blinked,* 117.

91. Hersh, *Dark Side of Camelot,* 341.

92. Powell oral history interview, 24, AWC.

93. Maggio interview by author.

94. Sagan, *Limits of Safety,*136.

95. "Documentary History, Ninth Air Defense Division," Oct. 1961–Dec. 1962, Attachment 1 and Attachment 2, Document K-Div-9-Hi, AFHRC.

96. Sagan, *Limits of Safety,* 128.

97. Ibid., 130.

98. Ibid., 131–32.

99. Ibid., 99.

100. The spacecraft's presence on an intercontinental ballistic missile pad during the crisis created a stir in the Soviet military. Some wanted to remove the Mars craft to replace it with a missile; however, spacecraft experts won Khrushchev's approval to proceed with the planned 24 October launch. See Harford, *Korolev,* 151–52.

101. "Changed Plans," *Army Navy Air Force Journal and Register,* 27 Oct. 1962, 39.

102. "Broad Spectrum of Armed Forces Responses in the Cuban Missile Crisis," *Army Navy Air Force Journal and Register,* 3 Nov. 1962, 2–3.

103. "Actions of Military Services in Cuban Crisis Outlined," 19.

104. Ibid., 2.

105. John M. McGuire, "The Day the Cold War Almost Ignited: Soldier Recalls Mystery of '62 Missile Crisis," *St. Louis Post-Dispatch,* 27 Oct. 1997, 3E.

106. "Railway Scene in Area Recalls Wartime Era," *Commercial Appeal,* 28 Oct. 1962, 15.

107. Powell oral history interview, 30, AWC.

108. Blanchard, "American Civil Defense 1945–75," 282.

109. Schlesinger Jr., *Thousand Days,* 391.

110. Blanchard, "American Civil Defense 1945–1984," 8.

111. There were about 4,700 requests for civil defense information in January 1961, and queries on 1 August totaled 5,382. See Asher Byrnes and Garrett Underhill, "Civil Defense Muddle," *New Republic,* 15 Jan. 1962, 8.

112. Newman, "Civil Defense and the Congress," 35.

113. "Hazards of Selling Survival Products," *Business Week,* 24 Feb. 1962, 62.

114. Schlesinger Jr., *Thousand Days,* 749.

115. Pittman, "Government and Civil Defense," 55.

116. Civil defense programs did not stop with the missile crisis, but there never again was such an outpouring of public interest. Congress remained reluctant to spend on these programs, but by the end of the Johnson administration, 270,000 buildings had been identified as possible shelters; owners of 105,000 buildings had committed to let parts

of their property serve as shelters; two weeks worth of supplies had been produced for 60 million people at a cost of $2.50 per person; and 2,600 state and local emergency operating centers had been set up. See ibid., 58–59.

117. Blanchard, "American Civil Defense 1945–1984," 9.

118. Gouré, *Civil Defense in the Soviet Union*, 80.

119. Ibid., 85.

120. Ibid., 87.

121. Ibid., 101.

122. Ibid., 139.

123. In the U.S. government, the size and efficacy of the Soviet civil defense program was a topic of speculation and debate throughout the Cold War. The Soviet Union was believed to have a program suitable for protecting 10 to 15 million citizens in the late 1950s. See "Discussion at the 359th Meeting of the National Security Council, Thursday, March 20, 1958," Papers of the President of the United States (Ann Whitman File), NSC Series, Box 9, 359th Meeting of the National Security Council Folder, DDEL. There was also disagreement in the U.S. intelligence community about the existence of mass evacuation plans. See "Economic Intelligence Report: Civil Defense in the USSR," Papers of the President of the United States (Ann Whitman File), NSC Series, Box 4, Civil Defense (2) Folder, DDEL. Like U.S. leaders, Soviet military planners apparently based much of their Cold War strategy on memories of World War II. The model for Soviet responses was Germany's decision to break its alliance with the Soviet Union and begin a two-front war by attacking the Soviets. Fear of surprise attack drove up the Soviet missile stockpiles during the early 1960s. See Kaplan, "Soviet Civil Defense Myth," 42. In the 1980s, a Federal Emergency Management Agency report estimated that the Soviets spent about seven times as much as the United States per capita on civil defense. See *Comparison of Soviet and U.S. Civil Defense Programs*.

124. Central Intelligence Agency, "Soviet Civil Defense and Air-Raid Shelter Construction," 14 Mar. 1958, 1, National Security Council, Policy Papers, Box 24, NSC5807/1 Shelter Program (6) Folder, DDEL.

125. Curtis E. Harvey, "Civil Defense Abroad in Review," in Wigner, ed., *Survival and the Bomb*, 159–61.

126. Ibid., 161–62.

127. U.S. Congress, House, Committee on Appropriations, *Hearings, Independent Offices Appropriations for FY 1962*, 614.

128. A poll taken in the crisis's wake showed 25 percent considering action, but 72 percent still had not even begun to plan for such an emergency. See Peter B. Greenough, "Huge Dual-Purpose Civil Defense Program Proposed," *Boston Globe*, 25 Nov. 1962, 72.

129. Charles Grutzner, "Crisis Spotlights Civil Defense Lag," *New York Times*, 24 Oct. 1962, 26.

130. May and Zelikow, eds., *Kennedy Tapes*, 338.

131. Pittman told the council that thirty-five cities, including New York and Washington, had adequate shelters, a statement typical of government efforts to reassure the public. Those cities may well have had enough buildings with basements to house the population, but that did not mean those shelter areas had been identified, marked, or stocked with supplies. See "City Said to Have Enough Shelters," *New York Times*, 20 Oct. 1962, 25.

132. May and Zelikow, eds., *Kennedy Tapes*, 338.

133. Ros Gilpatric and John F. Kennedy telephone conversation, Washington, 23 Oct. 1962, Presidential Office Files, Box 14A, Cuba General 10/23/62 Folder, JFKL.

134. "Report on Implications for U.S. Foreign and Defense Policy of Recent Intelligence Estimates," 23 Aug. 1962, Paul H. Nitze Papers, Box 152, Folder 4, LOC.

135. Clarfield and Wiecek, *Nuclear America*, 256–57.

136. McGeorge Bundy, "Executive Committee Record of Action," Oct. 23, 1962, 6 P.M. Meeting No. 2, Document CC00965, NSA.

137. *Nightline*, American Broadcasting Co., Hosted by Ted Koppel, 24 Oct. 1996, MT&R.

138. *War Room Journal*, 25 Oct. 1962, Document CC01320, NSA.

139. Pittman oral history interview, 17, JFKLOHP.

140. May and Zelikow, eds., *Kennedy Tapes*, 339.

141. Associated Press, "Governors Get CD Briefing at White House," *Washington Star*, 27 Oct. 1962, A23.

142. John E. Cosgrove, Memorandum to Regional Book, 14 Nov. 1962, Office of Emergency Preparedness Records, Central Correspondence Files 1962–64, Box 11, Regional Book Folder, NAII.

143. Robert L. McManus, Press Release, "Governors' Conference Committee of Civil Defense and Post-Attack Recovery," 27 Oct. 1962, Nelson Rockefeller Papers, Record Group III 1525, Gubernatorial Press Office, Public Relations Files, Box 13, Folder 236, RA.

144. H. R. Gallagher, "Emergency Actions Taken," 26 Oct. 1962, Office of Emergency Planning Records, Microfilm Roll 1, JFKL.

145. Steuart Pittman to Robert McNamara, Washington, 29 Oct. 1962, Office of Emergency Planning Records, Microfilm Roll 1, JFKL.

146. "Six-Point Accelerated CD Program Described to State and Local Officials," *Information Bulletin*, Department of Defense, 29 Oct. 1962, 2–3, Office of the Defense Civil Preparedness Agency, Office of Civil Defense, Records of Assistant Secretary of Defense for Civil Defense Steuart L. Pittman 1961–64, Box 1, CHRON November 1962 Folder, NAII.

147. Office of Civil Defense, *Annual Report of the Office of Civil Defense, July 1, 1962 to June 30, 1963*, Document CC03201, NSA.

148. David Olinger, "The Cold War Was a Fearful Time for Children," *St. Petersburg Times*, 10 Dec. 1989, 1D.

149. Edward F. Phelps Jr. to Edward McDermott, Washington, 26 Oct 1962, Office of Emergency Planning Records, Microfilm Roll 1, JFKL.

150. Gordon Chase to McGeorge Bundy, Washington, 26 Oct. 1962, 1, the Declassified Documents Reference System.

151. Steuart Pittman, "Civil Defense Measures Related to Cuba," 24 Oct. 1962, Attachment 1, Office of Emergency Planning Records, Microfilm Roll 1, JFKL.

152. Ibid., Attachment 2.

153. McGeorge Bundy, "National Security Action Memorandum No. 200," 28 Oct. 1962, National Security Files, Box 274, General 9/62–12/62 Folder, JFKL.

154. William P. Durkee to State and Local Civil Defense Directors, Washington, 5 Nov. 1962, State Records, Office of Civil Defense, Box 1, Administration OCDM National Folder, SHSOW.

155. McGeorge Bundy, "National Security Action Memorandum No. 200," 28 Oct. 1962, National Security Files, Box 274, General 9/62–12/62 Folder, JFKL.

156. "Department of Defense Operations during the Cuban Crisis," Document CC02925, NSA.

157. Associated Press, "U.S. Lowers Shelter Standards, Seeks Protection for 120 Million," *Philadelphia Evening Bulletin*, 28 Oct. 1962, 2. The minimum protection level stood at 1,000 as recently as 1958. See Rose, *One Nation Underground*, 32.

158. "A Report on National Civil Defense Readiness by Steuart L. Pittman, Assistant Secretary of Defense to the Committee on Civil Defense and Post-Attack Recovery of the National Governors' Conference, October 27, 1962," Presidential Office Files, Box 96, Civil Defense Folder, JFKL.

159. Leonard L. Reese Jr. to Edward A. McDermott, Washington, 29 Oct. 1962, 2, Office of Emergency Planning Records, Microfilm Roll 1, JFKL.

CHAPTER THREE

1. Bardyl Tirana, director of the U.S. Defense Civil Preparedness Agency, 1979 testimony. See U.S. Congress, Senate, Committee on Banking, Housing, and Urban Affairs, *Transcript of Proceedings: Hearing on Civil Defense.*

2. The estimate of 10 million evacuees can be found in Roger Sullivan, "Memorandum to Distribution," 10 Jan. 78, Paul H. Nitze Papers, Box 65, Folder 5, LOC. See also Blanchard, "American Civil Defense 1945–75."

3. Eugene L. Meyer, "When the Bomb Falls, Head for Paw Paw," *Washington Post*, 8 Mar. 1980, A1.

4. United Press International, Wire Dispatch, 6 May 1981.

5. Hackworth, *About Face*, 429.

6. Associated Press, "Ma Forgets Her Kids," *Philadelphia Inquirer*, 29 Oct. 1962, 7.

7. John Compton in *Children Write about John F. Kennedy*, edited by William G. Walsh (Brownsville: Springman-King Publishing Co., 1964), 119.

8. "Please Don't Call *Times* for Cuba Information," *New York Times*, 25 Oct. 1962, 20.

9. Howard James, "Calls Deluge Civil Defense Offices Here," *Chicago Tribune*, 24 Oct. 1962, pt. 1, p. 10.

10. "Civil Defense Interest Jumps," *New Orleans Times-Picayune*, 27 Oct. 1962, sec. 1, p. 9.

11. Rose, *One Nation Underground*, 199.

12. "Civil Defense Units Push Preparedness Plan," *Commercial Appeal*, 27 Oct. 1962, 16.

13. "The Editor's Column," *Texas Defense Digest*, Nov.–Dec. 1962, 2.

14. George M. Mawhinney, "Radio Drama Causes Panic," *Philadelphia Inquirer*, 31 Oct. 1938, 1.

15. "Civil Defense Annual Report—1962," 21, Office of the Mayor, Civil Defense Council, Annual Reports—1962 Folder, CA.

16. Art Peters, "Officials Admit Phila. Unprepared for Nuclear Attack," *Philadelphia Tribune*, 27 Oct. 1962, 1.

17. "Drop Jim Crow Setup in New Orleans Civil Defense," *Jet*, 8 Nov. 1962, 10.

18. Davis Merritt, "'In Case of Attack, Stay Put,'" *Charlotte Observer*, 26 Oct. 1962, 1C.

19. "Civil Defense Speakers Available," *Los Angeles Times*, 28 Oct. 1962, sec. B, p. 3.

20. Dwight Jensen, "Civil Defense Guide Ready for City Use," *Des Moines Register*, 25 Oct. 1962, 1.

21. "Booklet Tells How to Prepare for A-Attack," *Washington Star*, 25 Oct. 1962, A1.

22. "Civil Defense Instructions to Be Rerun on Television," *Houston Post*, 28 Oct. 1962, 12.

23. Associated Press, "Cuba Crisis Taught Civil Defense Lesson in Chaos, Panic and Apathy," *Philadelphia Evening Bulletin*, 30 Jan. 1963, 47.

24. "Bomb Shelter Data Held up in 14 Towns," *Philadelphia Evening Bulletin*, Delaware County Edition, 25 Oct. 1962, 30.

25. "Predicts Russia Will Yield to Blockade," *Chicago Tribune*, 23 Oct. 1962, 5.

26. Reichert-Facilides interview by author.

27. Robert Condon, Press Release of the City of New York Office of Civil Defense, 26 Dec. 1962, Records of the Office of the Mayor (Wagner, Robert F., Jr.), Subject Files 1954–65, Box 34, Civil Defense Fallout Shelter Folder, MA.

28. James, "Calls Deluge Civil Defense Offices Here."

29. "26 City Weekly Report No. 5," 20 Sept. 1962, Records of the Defense Civil Preparedness Agency, Regional Coordination Division, Studies and Reports Relating to Fallout Shelters 1962–63, Box 1, 26 City Reports McConnell Folder, NAII.

30. "307 Buildings in L.A. Licensed as Shelters," *Los Angeles Times*, 25 Oct. 1962, 18.

31. Don Bolles, "CD Mobilized," *Arizona Republic*, 24 Oct. 1962, 1.

32. Associated Press, "Cuba Crisis Taught Civil Defense Lesson in Chaos, Panic and Apathy," *Philadelphia Evening Bulletin*, 30 Jan. 1963, 47.

33. "Transcript of Proceedings of Meeting of New York Civil Defense Commission," 23 Oct. 1962, 31, Nelson Rockefeller Papers, Record Group III 1525, Gubernatorial Press Office, Public Relations Files, Box 13, Folder 232, RA.

34. Wisconsin Office of Civil Defense to Gil Czarnecki, Madison, 4 Dec. 1962, State Records, Office of Civil Defense, Northwest Area Command Control Folder, SHSOW.

35. William K. Chipman to Station Manager, Madison, 27 Oct. 1962, State Records, Gaylord Nelson, Box 18, Folder 8, SHSOW.

36. John A. McCone, "Memorandum for the File," 23 Oct. 1962, in McAuliffe, ed., *CIA Documents on the Cuban Missile Crisis*, 291–92.

37. "Duluth Not Prime Target Area, Says CD Director," *Duluth News Tribune*, 24 Oct. 1962, 6.

38. United Press International, "Jacksonville Ready to Evacuate If—," *Charlotte Observer*, 25 Oct. 1962, 3A.

39. Brugioni, *Eyeball to Eyeball*, 323–24.

40. Communications Division, the City of New York Office of Civil Defense, "Annual Report 13," Records of the Office of the Mayor (Wagner, Robert F., Jr.), Subject Files 1954–65, Box 37, Civil Defense–Telephone Information Folder, MA.

41. Robert Condon, Press Release of the City of New York Office of Civil Defense, 26 Dec. 1962, Records of the Office of the Mayor (Wagner, Robert F., Jr.), Subject Files 1954–65, Box 34, Civil Defense Fallout Shelter Folder, MA.

42. "Six-Point Accelerated CD Program Described to State and Local Officials," *Information Bulletin*, Department of Defense, 29 Oct. 1962, 3, Office of the Defense Civil Pre-

paredness Agency, Office of Civil Defense, Records of Assistant Secretary of Defense for Civil Defense Steuart L. Pittman 1961–64, Box 1, CHRON November 1962 Folder, NAII.

43. The nation also had 31,400 monitoring stations to register levels of radiation so that survivors would know when it was safe to leave shelters, but they amounted to only about 30 percent of the network needed to provide thorough information. See "Six-Point Accelerated Civil Defense Program," 5.

44. Rutledge Carter, "Shorted Siren Wails, Switchboards Jammed," *Patriot*, 27 Oct. 1962, 1.

45. "Defense Alert Scares Suburb," *Chicago Tribune*, 27 Oct. 1962, 1.

46. Joshua L. Weinstein, "1962 Missile Crisis Had Residents Stocking Up," *St. Petersburg Times*, 25 Oct. 1987, 1.

47. Associated Press, "Blast of Siren Triggers Scare," *Lubbock Avalanche Journal*, 24 Oct. 1962, 2A.

48. L. D. Kerr, "Sirens OK—If Working," *Arkansas Democrat*, 24 Oct. 1962, 1.

49. Associated Press, "Bomb Sirens Blow the Job," *Detroit Free Press*, 25 Oct. 1962, 1A.

50. Arthur E. Norgaard to William K. Chipman, Green Bay, 23 Nov. 1962, State Records, Bureau of Civil Defense, Box 12, Brown 1962–65 Folder, SHSOW.

51. "City, County Shape Civil Defense Plans," *Midland Reporter-Telegram*, 24 Oct. 1962, 1.

52. Justin Roberts, "Crowds Gather in Plaza; Protest Protesters," *Daily Californian*, 23 Oct. 1962, 1.

53. Joe Campbell, "Birmingham Lacks Adequate Shelters," *Birmingham News*, 27 Oct. 1962, 1.

54. Joseph P. Barnett and Mont Morton, "Merchants Report Rise in CD Provision Sales," *State*, 25 Oct. 1962, 1D, 6D.

55. Universal-International News, *1962*.

56. "CD Chief: Towns Must Rely on Own Preparedness," *State*, 26 Oct. 1962, 1.

57. "Could House Only 73,000 in Shelters," *Des Moines Register*, 25 Oct. 1962, 4.

58. James Wise to William H. Avery, 13 Nov. 1962, Records of the Defense Civil Preparedness Agency, Office of Civil Defense, Records of the Assistant Secretary of Defense for Civil Defense Steuart L. Pittman 1961–64, Box 1, CHRON November 1962 Folder, NAII.

59. U.S. Congress, House, Committee on Government Operations, *Hearings*, 87th Cong., 138.

60. "Transcript of Proceedings of Meeting of the New York Civil Defense Commission," 22.

61. Del W. Harding, "As a Fallout Shelter, This One's No Hotel!" *Rocky Mountain News*, 26 Oct. 1962, 6.

62. Marion Gaines, "Speed up Civil Defense or Drop It, State Urged," *Atlanta Constitution*, 26 Oct. 1962, 1.

63. "More Shelters Are Offered," *Washington Star*, 26 Oct. 1962, A1.

64. The quest for shelter space was complicated by 1960s building designs, which tended toward brick schools with many windows and offered inadequate fallout protection. See "Transcript of Proceedings of Meeting of the New York Civil Defense Commission," 18.

65. Marion Ellis, "Gaston Civil Defense Efforts Accelerated," *Charlotte Observer*, 27 Oct. 1962, 1B.

66. "2:05 P.M. Report," WNBC Radio, 24 Oct. 1962, National Broadcasting Company Records, Box 266, WNBC—24 Oct. 1962 Folder, SHSOW.

67. Press Release, State of New York, 23 Oct. 1962, Records of the Office of the Mayor (Wagner, Robert F., Jr.) Subject Files 1954–65, Box 32, Civil Defense 1960 Folder, MA.

68. "Transcript of Proceedings of Meeting of the New York Civil Defense Commission," 2.

69. United Press International, "U.S. Keeps Close Eye on Suspected Cubans," *Philadelphia Evening Bulletin*, 24 Oct. 1962, 26.

70. "The City's Standby Alert," *Philadelphia Evening Bulletin*, 24 Oct. 1962, 34.

71. "Increased Security Here Urged by Port Council," *Philadelphia Evening Bulletin*, 24 Oct. 1962, 30.

72. "Crisis Stirs CD Interest," *Anchorage Daily News*, 28 Oct. 1962, 1.

73. United Press International, "Jacksonville Ready to Evacuate If—."

74. "CD Groups in Area Ready to Deal with Emergencies," *New Orleans Times-Picayune*, 25 Oct. 1962, 1.

75. J. C. Wolfe, "County Police Units Plan for Emergency," *St. Paul Pioneer Press*, 28 Oct. 1962, sec. 2, p. 11.

76. "Virginians Show Anxiety but No Panic," *Richmond Times-Dispatch*, 28 Oct. 1962, 4B.

77. Saul Pett, "'Good-by' and 'If' Become Words of Special Meaning," *Washington Star*, 28 Oct. 1962, A1.

78. "City, County Shape Civil Defense Plans," 1.

79. Associated Press, "Civilian Defense Planned in Texas," *San Antonio Express*, 24 Oct. 1962, 1C. See also "Fallout Shelter Work Isn't Picking up Much," *Charlotte Observer*, 26 Oct. 1962, 1C.

80. "N.O. Designates 42 CD Shelters," *New Orleans Times-Picayune*, 26 Oct. 1962, 1.

81. In New Jersey, home-shelter backers had formed a "Moles' Club" to convert skeptics. See William K. Chipman to F. Corning Knote, 1 Dec. 1962, Madison, Wisc., State Records, Office of Civil Defense, Box 9, Out-of-State—62 Folder, SHSOW.

82. "Don't Panic, But Here's What to Do If 'Emergency' Erupts," *Miami Herald*, 28 Oct. 1962, 4C.

83. "Raid Advice: Take Cover—Then Pray," *Chicago Tribune*, 24 Oct. 1962, 2.

84. Joe Treaster, "Fallout Shelter—Ready Made," *Miami Herald*, 29 Oct. 1962, 1C.

85. Detzer, *Brink*, 193.

86. Lydel Sims, "Crisis-Created Curiosity Offers Puzzle to Police," *Commercial Appeal*, 26 Oct. 1962, 1.

87. "Builder of $16,000 Shelter Is in Demand as Consultant," *Philadelphia Evening Bulletin*, 26 Oct. 1962, 11.

88. Associated Press, "Bomb Shelter Monument to 1960's Missile Fear," 2 Aug. 1982.

89. Peter B. Greenough, "Huge Dual-Purpose Civil Defense Program Proposed," *Boston Globe*, 25 Nov. 1962, 72.

90. "Civil Defense Leaders Speed Area Programs," *Washington Post*, 26 Oct. 1962, 1.

91. Associated Press, "Hughes Orders State CD Action to Meet Perils," *Philadelphia Evening Bulletin*, 30 Oct. 1962, New Jersey Edition, 78.

92. Susan Ager, "Making (Uneasy) Peace with the Bomb," *Detroit Magazine*, 4 Aug. 1985, 10.

93. Juan Ponce, "Bread, Not Bombs, Worry Puerto Ricans," *Miami Herald*, 25 Oct. 1962, 18A.

94. *The Huntley-Brinkley Report*, 25 Oct. 1962, National Broadcasting Company Records, Box 534, H.B. (N.Y. Only) 1962, Oct. 15–30 Folder, SHSOW.

95. Jack Smith, "City Feels Panic, Calm in Crisis," *Los Angeles Times*, 28 Oct. 1962, 2.

96. "Wave of Buying Hits Some Markets in LA," *Los Angeles Times*, 25 Oct. 1962, 18.

97. "McNayr Criticized for Attack Alert," *Miami Herald*, 26 Oct. 1962, 2A.

98. Americans were not alone in panic buying; rushes were reported in Poland, then a Communist nation. See Arthur J. Olsen, "Poles Start Run on Food Stores," *New York Times*, 26 Oct. 1962, 18.

99. "McNayr Criticized for Attack Alert," 2A.

100. Janet Koltun, "Stocked Basements Urged," *Washington Star*, 25 Oct. 1962, B1.

101. "Just Call It Calorie Crisis," *Dallas Morning News*, 27 Oct. 1962, sec. 1, p. 6.

102. Arnold E. Chase to Fay M. Bean, 26 Oct. 1962, Washington, U.S. Department of Labor, Bureau of Labor Statistics Records, Reel No. 53, JFKL.

103. Blanchard, "American Civil Defense 1945–75," 328–29.

104. "Big Sale of Guns at Bakersfield," *San Francisco Chronicle*, 28 Oct. 1962, 12.

105. "Crisis Builds Gun Demand," *Dallas Morning News*, 28 Oct. 1962, sec. 1, p. 5.

106. Weinstein, "1962 Missile Crisis Had Residents Stocking Up," 1.

107. "Virginians Show Anxiety but No Panic," 4B.

108. "N.O. Designates 42 CD Shelters," 1.

109. Kent Biffle, "Run on Emergency Supplies Reported by Dallas Stores," *Dallas Morning News*, 25 Oct. 1962, 9.

110. Ellen Middlebrook, "Cuba Crisis Touches Off Run on Water and Foods," *Houston Post*, 25 Oct. 1962, sec. 1, p. 1.

111. Barnett and Morton, "Merchants Report Rise in CD Provision Sales," 1D, 6D.

112. Edward F. Phelps Jr. to Edward A. McDermott, Washington, 24 Oct. 1962, Office of Emergency Planning Records, Microfilm Roll 1, JFKL.

113. Willard Lawson, "Cuban Crisis Creates Run on Survival Items Here," *Anchorage Daily News*, 25 Oct. 1962, 1–2.

114. "Interest in Civil Defense Rises, but Most People Avoid Scare Buying," *Wall Street Journal*, 26 Oct. 1962, 1.

115. Associated Press, "Nation's Food Stocks Ample, Freeman Says," *Los Angeles Times*, 28 Oct. 1962, 3.

116. Dan Thomasson, "Official Assures Denverites," *Rocky Mountain News*, 26 Oct. 1962, 5.

117. *Estimated Number of Days' Supply of Food and Beverages in Retail Stores*, 2.

118. "General Principles and Guidelines for the Conservation of Food under a Freeze Order in a Cut-Off Situation—For Use by State Defense Food Boards," 16 Nov. 1962, 7, U.S. Agricultural Marketing Service Records, Special Services Division Records Relating

to Emergency Preparedness 1963–65, Box 1, Cuban Crisis Orders and Authorities Recommendations Folder, NAII.

119. Ibid., 6.

120. "Summary of Food Situation," 23 Oct. 1962, U.S. Agricultural Marketing Service Records, Special Services Division Records Relating to Emergency Preparedness 1963–65, Box 1, Cuban Crisis FM Project Control Folder, NAII.

121. "Notes for Meeting K with Secretary 10/23/62," U.S. Agricultural Marketing Service Records, Special Services Division, Records Relating to Emergency Preparedness 1963–65, Box 1, Cuban Crisis FM Project Control Folder, NAII.

122. "Six-Point Accelerated CD Program Described to State, Local Officials," 4.

123. Edward A. McDermott to John F. Kennedy, Washington, 14 June 1962, President's Office Files, Box 85, Office of Emergency Planning Records, 1/62–6/62 Folder, JFKL.

124. The crisis prompted accelerated production of shelter supplies over the following months, with the goal of having 10,000 boxcars of supplies within six months. See "Six-Point Accelerated CD Program Described to State, Local Officials," 2.

125. Edward F. Phelps Jr. to Edward A. McDermott, Washington, 26 Oct. 1962, Office of Emergency Planning Records, Microfilm Roll 1, JFKL.

126. "Suggested Broadcast Script on 'Cut-Off,' Situation 'Freeze' Order," 16 Nov. 1962, 1, U.S. Agricultural Marketing Service Records, Special Services Division Records Relating to Emergency Preparedness 1963–65, Box 1, Cuban Crisis Orders and Authorities Recommendations Folder, NAII.

127. "Operating Instructions for Postattack Consumer Rationing-Draft," Feb. 1963, 10, U.S. Agricultural Marketing Service Records, Special Services Division Records Relating to Emergency Preparedness 1963–65, Box 1, Cuban Crisis Rationing Folder, NAII.

128. Ibid., 11.

129. Ibid., General Freeze Order, 1.

130. Edward F. Phelps to Edward A. McDermott, Washington, 26 Oct. 1962, Office of Emergency Planning Records, Microfilm Roll 1, JFKL.

131. Charles H. Kendall to Edward A. McDermott, Washington, 23 Oct. 1962, Office of Emergency Planning Records, Microfilm Roll 1, JFKL.

132. Edward A. McDermott, "Civilian Readiness Measures Memorandum No. 1," 23 Oct. 1962, Office of Emergency Planning Records, Microfilm Roll 1, JFKL.

133. Edward F. Phelps Jr. to Edward A. McDermott, Washington, 22 Oct. 1962, Office of Emergency Planning Records, Microfilm Roll 1, JFKL.

134. Edward A. McDermott, "Memorandum for the President," 14 June 1962, Presidential Office Files, Box 85, Office of Emergency Planning Records, 1/62–6/62 Folder, JFKL.

135. "Post Office Department: Executive Order #11002," undated, Office of Emergency Planning Records, Microfilm Roll 1, JFKL.

136. "Department of the Interior: Executive Order #10997," undated, Office of Emergency Planning Records, Microfilm Roll 1, JFKL.

137. "Department of Health, Education, and Welfare: Executive Orders #10958 and #11001," undated, Office of Emergency Planning Records, Microfilm Roll 1, JFKL.

138. Leonard L. Reese Jr. to Edward A. McDermott, Washington, 29 Oct. 1962, Office of Emergency Planning Records, Microfilm Roll 1, JFKL.

139. "Doctors Map A-War Plans," *Las Vegas Sun*, 26 Oct. 1962, 13.

140. "List of Doctors Given to Civil Defense, Police," *Los Angeles Times*, 28 Oct. 1962, sec. 1, p. 3.

141. "Hospitals, Stocks Held in Reserve," *Dallas Morning News*, 27 Oct. 1962, sec. 1, p. 6.

142. J. K. Shafer, Memorandum to Edward A. McDermott, 26 Oct. 1962, Office of Emergency Preparedness Records, Executive Correspondence and Memos 1961–63, Box 3, OEP Director Sept.–Oct. 1962 Folder, NAII.

143. Ralph L. Garrett, "Summary of Studies of Public Attitudes toward and Information about Civil Defense" (Washington: Office of Civil Defense, 1963), 6, Records of the Defense Civil Preparedness Agency, Office of Civil Defense, Federal/Federally Funded Publications Re: To Civil Defense, 1959–64, Box 2, Summary of Studies of Public Attitudes toward and Information about Civil Defense Folder, NAII.

144. Ibid., 9.

145. Ibid., 14.

146. Ibid., 15.

147. Oakes, *Imaginary War*, 69.

148. Robert H. Mast, *Impact of the Cuban Missile Crisis: Patterns of Public Response*, (Washington: National Emergency Training Center, 1966), 12.

149. Ibid., 13.

150. Ibid., 9.

151. Brelis, *Run, Dig or Stay?*, 178–79.

152. Oschmann interview by author, 11 Mar. 1995.

153. Williams interview by author.

154. John Bloomquist, telegram to John F. Kennedy, 27 Oct. 1962, Central Files, Box 597, 9/1/62–1/31/63 Folder, JFKL.

155. Tom Stotler, telegram to John F. Kennedy, 27 Oct. 1962, Central Files, Box 597, 9/1/62–1/31/63 Folder, JFKL.

156. J. Earl Manning, telegram to John F. Kennedy, 27 Oct. 1962, Central Files, Box 597, 9/1/62–1/31/63 Folder, JFKL.

157. Paul B. Hartenstein, Memorandum to Mayor Joseph S. Clark Jr., 15 Mar. 1955, Mayor's Files—1955, Box A-475, Civil Defense 1955 Folder, CA.

158. Women Strike for Peace, "Protection in a Nuclear Age," Records of Women Strike for Peace, A2, Box 1, Literature circa 1962 Folder, PC.

159. In the first thirty days after the crisis, when anxiety about war remained high, there was a 600 percent increase in the posting of shelter areas. Within three months, 40,000 buildings with the capacity to shelter 25 million people had been marked and supplies were in place for 3 million—still less than 4 percent of the population. Public interest in civil defense would never again reach such high levels. See Jerome S. Cahill, "Public Reaction to Cuba Crisis May Boost CD," *Philadelphia Inquirer*, 31 Mar. 1963, 8.

CHAPTER FOUR

1. "CBS News Special Report," 6 June 1961, MT&R.

2. Reston, "Reminiscences of James Barrett Reston," Lecture, 26 Apr. 1962, CUOHP, 16.

3. Ibid., 18.

4. McGrory, Lisagor, and Herman oral history interview, 74, JFKLOHP.

5. Kraft oral history interview, 27, JFKLOHP.

6. Edwin Bayley, "The Kennedy Administration and the Press," undated speech, Edwin Bayley Papers, Box 14, Speeches 1962–66 Folder, SHSOW.

7. Bayley oral history interview, 14, JFKLOHP.

8. Edward R. Murrow to McGeorge Bundy, Washington, 24 June 1961, National Security Files—Countries, Box 35A, Cuba General 6/61–12/61 Folder, JFKL.

9. For a more sinister interpretation of Kennedy's power over the press, see Hersh, *Dark Side of Camelot*, 107.

10. "How Our Free Press Uses Its Freedom in the Cuban Crisis," *I. F. Stone's Weekly*, 12 Nov. 1962, 1.

11. David Lawrence, "Managed News vs. Deception," *Washington Star*, 20 Mar. 1963, A23.

12. Edwin Newman, "Noon News Report," National Broadcasting Company, 21 Oct. 1962, National Broadcasting Company Records, Box 458, 1962 Oct. 21–27 Folder, SHSOW.

13. Robert F. Kennedy, *Thirteen Days*, 111.

14. May and Zelikow, eds., *Kennedy Tapes*, 239.

15. Salinger, *With Kennedy*, 252–53.

16. Bundy, *Danger and Survival*, 196.

17. Schlesinger, *Thousand Days*, 809.

18. Clifton Daniel, "A Footnote to History: The Press and National Security," an address to the World Press Institute, Macalester College, St. Paul, Minn., 1 June 1966, Cuba: Bay of Pigs 1960–72 Folder, p. 12, *NYTA*.

19. Clifton Daniel, managing editor of the *New York Times*, revealed in 1966 that JFK had told *Times* publisher Orvil Dryfoos that he regretted the newspaper's decision not to publish details of the invasion, which he called "a colossal mistake." *Times* reporter Tad Szulc had prepared an article calling an invasion "imminent," but editors toned it down, fearing that it might alert Castro and enable him to defeat the invaders. See Associated Press, "Editor's Decision on Cuba Related," *New York Times*, 2 June 1966, 14, and "When Is News News?" *Nation*, 10 June 1966, 730. Among Cuban refugees in Miami, knowledge of invasion preparations was so widespread that the *Times*'s James Reston feared newspapers would lose credibility by ignoring it. See Reston, Testimony to Committee, 19 Mar. 1963, U.S. Congress, House, Committee on Government Operations, *Hearings*, 88th Cong., 57.

20. Abel, *Missile Crisis*, 109.

21. Unsigned memo, undated, George Ball Papers, Box 147, George Ball Notebook, SGML.

22. Associated Press, "50 Million Set as TV Viewers," *Los Angeles Times*, 24 Oct. 1962, pt. 1, p. 9.

23. "Must and Will Unite," editorial, *New York Herald Tribune*, reprinted in "Excerpts from Newspaper Editorials on Decision," *New York Times*, 24 Oct. 1962, 26.

24. Associated Press, "Newspapers Give Solid Backing to President," *Sacramento Bee*, 24 Oct. 1962, A12.

25. David Lawrence, "Retreat," *U.S. News & World Report*, 24 Sept. 1962, 136.

26. For more on Senator Keating's activities, see Mark Jonathan White, *Cuban Missile Crisis*, 89–114.

27. "Showdown-Backdown," *Newsweek*, 5 Nov. 1962, 34.

28. "TV-Radio: Week to Remember: Medium Alerted to Cuban Crisis," *Variety*, 31 Oct. 1962, 29.

29. "For the Record," *TV Guide*, 3–9 Nov. 1962, A1.

30. Hartford N. Gunn Jr., "The Future of Educational Television," Report submitted to the Ford Foundation, 20 Dec. 1962, 9, Newton Minow Papers, Box 45, WGBH-Cambridge, MA 1961, Oct.-1963, Apr. Folder, SHSOW.

31. "TV-Radio: Week to Remember," 29.

32. Paar, *Jack Paar Program*.

33. Allyn, Blight, and Welch, eds., *Back to the Brink*, 88.

34. Salinger, *With Kennedy*, 270.

35. "T.R.B. from Washington," *New Republic*, 3 Nov. 1962, 2.

36. Tim Weiner, "C.I.A. Had Ability to Plant Bay of Pigs News, Documents Show," *New York Times*, 24 Mar. 2001, 7A.

37. John Troan, Scripps-Howard News Service, "Missiles Could Reach Denver in 13 Minutes," *Rocky Mountain News*, 24 Oct. 1962, 7.

38. Neal Shine, "How A-Blast Would Sear Detroit Area," *Detroit Free Press*, 29 Oct. 1962, 1A.

39. "Hot War Seen Delaying Race to Reach Moon," *Washington Star*, 26 Oct. 1962, A5.

40. William L. Ryan, Associated Press, "One Week May Alter All Future," *Tulsa World*, 29 Oct. 1962, 1.

41. "No Time for Contrived Drama," *Variety*, 31 Oct. 1962, 29.

42. "CBS News Special Report," 23 Oct. 1962, MT&R.

43. Ibid., 25 Oct. 1962.

44. *The Huntley-Brinkley Report*, 22 Oct. 1962, National Broadcasting Company Records, Box 534, H.B. (N.Y. Only) 1962, Oct. 15–30 Folder, SHSOW.

45. In 1962, the *Times* came under fire because of Herbert Matthews, an ex-*Times* reporter in Cuba who had written glowing articles about Castro when he took power in 1959. Radio call-in shows featured tirades against Matthews, and the *St. Louis Globe-Democrat* published a poetic editorial skewering him. See the Orvil Dryfoos Papers, Microfilm Roll 2, *NYTA*, and "Silent 'Prophet,'" *St. Louis Globe-Democrat*, 24 Oct. 1962, 12A. For details on the *Times*'s decision that it could no longer maintain a reporter in Cuba, see Emmanuel R. Freedman to Turner Catledge, 10 Sept. 1962, Cuba 1962 Folder, *NYTA*.

46. "CBS News Special Report," 1 Nov. 1962, MT&R.

47. "Bottled Water, Canned Goods in Demand Here," *Laredo Times*, 25 Oct. 1962,1.

48. David Wise, "For Press—Caution," *New York Herald Tribune*, 25 Oct. 1962, 1.

49. Sorensen, *Kennedy*, 319.

50. Rowe, Statement to Committee, 19 Mar. 1963, U.S. Congress, House, Committee on Government Operations, *Hearings*, 88th Cong., 22.

51. Salinger, *With Kennedy*, 301.

52. This was not the administration's only attempt to tighten restrictions on the press. In 1961, Kennedy complained that newspapers were giving the enemy military information that once could have been acquired only "through theft, bribery or espionage," and he urged the media to examine whether each article was "in the interest of national security." He encouraged development of some organization, such as a watchdog group, that could provide advice on whether publishing certain information represented a national

security risk. Kennedy thought this group, chosen by media executives, could get national security clearance to verify information and ascertain its impact on U.S. foreign affairs. See Peter Kihss, "President Finds Some Resisting Call to Sacrifice," *New York Times*, 16 June 1961, 1. When JFK sought advice from journalist Arthur Krock, the *New York Times* columnist told Kennedy that he first needed the agreement that the nation faced a "clear and present danger" of a shooting war. Ultimately, media executives rejected the idea, saying such a panel was unnecessary. See Arthur Krock, "Private Memorandum," 5 May 1961, Arthur Krock Papers, Box 27, Re: Cuba Folder, SGML.

53. Gene Miller, "U.S. Navy Guns' Pointed Message: Don't Try to Fly South of Key West," *Miami Herald*, 25 Oct. 1962, 1A.

54. John H. Colburn, "Government Censorship and Manipulation of News," Prepared for the American Society of Newspaper Editors and the American Newspaper Publishers Association, U.S. Congress, House, Committee on Government Operations, *Hearings*, 88th Cong., 12.

55. "How Much Censorship? How Much Distortion?" *Newsweek*, 12 Nov. 1962, 29. This was not a case of clear-cut distortion because the missile ranges intelligence officers supplied to Kennedy were much closer to the new, higher figures. See McAuliffe, ed., *CIA Documents on the Cuban Missile Crisis*, 271.

56. Many journalists remained stung by the embarrassment they suffered when reporting on the Bay of Pigs invasion. At that time, press releases misled the media, prompting journalists to report wrongly that mass uprisings against Castro were under way. That information's main source was Lem Jones, who Arthur Schlesinger Jr. said was "putting out in the name of the [Cuban Revolutionary] Council press releases dictated over the phone by the CIA." See Schlesinger, *Thousand Days*, 275.

57. Walt W. Rostow to Dean Rusk, Washington, 24 Oct. 1962, George Ball Papers, Box 147, George Ball Notebook, SGML.

58. Salinger, *With Kennedy*, 292.

59. Ibid., 294.

60. "NSC Executive Committee Record of Action, November 2, 1962, 11 A.M. Meeting, No. 17," 2 Nov. 1962, Lyndon B. Johnson Papers, Vice Presidential Security File, Box 8, Policy Papers and Background Studies (IV) Folder, LBJL.

61. "Last Articles of Sub Series Withheld," *Los Angeles Times*, 28 Oct. 1962, 1.

62. Associated Press, "NBC Postponing 'Tunnel' Program," *Washington Star*, 23 Oct. 1962, A5.

63. Ralph McGill, telegram to John F. Kennedy, 27 Oct. 1962, Central Files, Box 50, CO55-10/26/62–10/28/62 Folder, JFKL.

64. Ralph McGill to McGeorge Bundy, Atlanta, 12 Nov. 1962, Ralph McGill Papers, Box 11, Item No. 14, RWWL.

65. McGrory, Lisagor, and Herman oral history interview, 73, JFKLOHP.

66. United Press International, "Pentagon Denies Rightists Caused Action on Cuba," *Philadelphia Evening Bulletin*, 1 Nov. 1962, 2.

67. Luce oral history interview, 32, JFKLOHP.

68. Kern, Levering, and Levering, *Kennedy Crises*, 130.

69. Assorted Letters, Walter Lippmann Papers, Box 190, Folder 282, YUL.

70. Anatoly Dobrynin to Soviet Foreign Ministry, Washington, 1 Nov. 1962, Archive of

Foreign Policy, Russian Federation, Moscow, provided to Cold War International History Project, translation by Vladimir Zaemsky.

71. *John Scali*; Arthur M. Schlesinger Jr. Papers, Box W-5, ABC News Reports Folder, JFKL.

72. Scali oral history interview, JFKLOHP.

73. *John Scali*.

74. Allyn, Blight, and Welch, eds., *Back to the Brink*, 112–13.

75. For more details on Scali's role in the process, see the JFK Assassination Records, Roger Hilsman Papers, Record Number 1761003010242I, NAII.

76. Anatoly Dobrynin to Soviet Foreign Ministry, Washington, 25 Oct. 1962, Archive of Foreign Policy, Russian Federation, Moscow; copy obtained by NHK (Japanese Television), provided to Cold War International History Project, translation by Vladimir Zaemsky.

77. Fursenko and Naftali, *"One Hell of a Gamble,"* 261.

78. Ibid., 249.

79. Ibid., 263.

80. Elie Abel, "3 P.M. report," National Broadcasting Company, 28 Oct. 1962, Elie Abel Papers, Box 3, Elie Abel Scripts, Sept.–Dec. 1962 Folder, Boston University's Twentieth Century Archives, ML.

81. *Today News*, 25 Oct. 1962, National Broadcasting Company Records, Box 551, Today News, Oct. 22–26 Folder, SHSOW.

82. "Foreign Policy of JFK," American Broadcasting Company, 28 Oct. 1962, Howard K. Smith Papers, Box 51, 1962, Oct. 28, "Foreign Policy of JFK" Folder, SHSOW.

83. Hallin, *Uncensored War*, 25.

84. Donald Wilson, "Memorandum for the President," 2 Nov. 1962, reprinted in Elliston, *Psywar on Cuba*, 146.

85. "Castro Airs Plea to Negro," *Pittsburgh Courier*, 27 Oct. 1962, 1.

86. "The U.S. Puts It on the Line," *Life*, 2 Nov. 1962, 35–36.

87. "The Backdown," *Time*, 2 Nov. 1962, 27.

88. "The Lessons Learned," *Newsweek*, 12 Nov. 1962, 21.

89. Ibid., 35.

90. "Cuba and Berlin," *New Republic*, 3 Nov. 1962, 1.

91. "After Quarantine," *Nation*, 3 Nov. 1963, 277.

92. William Randolph Hearst Jr., "Tough Line with Soviet Pays Off," *San Francisco Examiner*, 28 Oct. 1962, 1.

93. Robert Y. Phillips to Edward McDermott, Washington, 26 Oct. 1962, Office of Emergency Planning Records, Microfilm Roll 1, JFKL.

94. John F. Kennedy to James Hagerty, Washington, 24 Oct. 1962, Office of Emergency Planning Records, Microfilm Roll 1, JFKL.

95. Colburn, "Government Censorship and Manipulation of News," 9.

96. Salinger, *With Kennedy*, 257.

97. "How Much Censorship? How Much Distortion?" *Newsweek*, 12 Nov. 1962, 29.

98. Lee Hills, telegram to John F. Kennedy, 31 Oct. 1962, Central Files, Box 50, CO55-10/30/62–11/1/62 Folder, JFKL.

99. Salinger, *With Kennedy*, 296–97.

100. Chester V. Clifton, Note, 22 Oct. 1962, Presidential Office Files, Box 115, Cuba Notes and Doodles Folder, JFKL.

101. "Role of Press in National Security Discussed by Representatives of ANPA, ASNE and NEA," *American Newspaper Publishers Association General Management Bulletin*, 17 Dec. 1962, 239.

102. United Press International, "'Managed News' Hearings Due to Start on March 18," *New York Times*, 16 Feb. 1963, 5.

103. Carroll J. Bateman, "Techniques of Managing the News," *Public Relations Journal*, Aug. 1963, 6.

104. "Lectures and Discussions in the Graduate School of Journalism, Columbia University," 22 Apr. 1963, 8, CUOHP.

105. Pierpoint oral history interview, 12, JFKLOHP.

106. Charles Bartlett, "News Managing? Eternal Question," *Chicago Sun-Times*, 28 Feb. 1963, 38.

107. Charles S. Rowe, "Interim Report of the Associated Press Managing Editors Freedom of Information Committee," 17 Apr. 1963, Records of the Associated Press Managing Editors, Box 41, APME Study Reports—FOI Folder, SHSOW.

108. John S. Knight, "The Press Must Get the Facts," *Charlotte Observer*, 28 Oct. 1962, 3B.

109. Drew Pearson, 26 Oct. 1962, reprinted in Aronson, *Press and the Cold War*, 171.

110. Salinger, *With Kennedy*, 298–99.

111. "Memorandum for Executive Committee Meeting, November 29, 1962," Lyndon B. Johnson Papers, Vice Presidential Security File, Box 8, Policy Papers and Background Studies (1) Folder, LBJL.

112. Salinger, *With Kennedy*, 298–99.

113. Colonel Burris to Lyndon B. Johnson, Washington, 5 Nov. 1962, Lyndon B. Johnson Papers, Vice Presidential Security File, Box 6, Memos to the VP from Col. Burris, 7/62–4/63 Folder, Document 112, LBJL.

114. John Chamberlain, "LBJ's Tough Stand during Cuban Crisis," *Journal American*, 13 Jan. 1964, 14.

115. Stewart Alsop and Charles Bartlett, "The White House in the Cuban Crisis," *Saturday Evening Post*, 8 Dec. 1962, 15–20.

116. "Transcript of an interview with Ambassador Adlai E. Stevenson," *Today*, National Broadcasting Company, 5 Dec. 1962, Adlai Stevenson Papers, Box 346, Folder 4, SGML.

117. Drew Pearson, "Kennedy's PR Techniques Revealed in Stevenson Flap," Syndicated Column, 17 Dec. 1962, 1, Drew Pearson Papers, Box G121, 1 of 3, Kennedy, John F., Miscellaneous 1 Folder, LBJL.

118. Martin, *Adlai Stevenson and the World*, 747–48.

119. "The Big Flap—Doves, Hawks, 'Dawks,' 'Hoves,'" *Newsweek*, 17 Dec. 1962, 18.

120. Charles Bartlett to John F. Kennedy, Washington, 29 Oct. 1962, Presidential Office Files, Box 28, Bartlett, Charles L., 9/62–10/62 Folder, JFKL.

121. Associated Press, "Stevenson," 10 Dec. 1962, Vice Presidential Papers, 1962 Subject File, Box 135, Foreign Relations Cuba, Folder 1 of 8, LBJL.

122. John F. Kennedy to Adlai Stevenson, Washington, 5 Dec. 1962, Adlai Stevenson Papers, Box 47, Folder 5, SGML.

123. United Press International, "Stevenson," 12 Dec. 1962, Adlai Stevenson Papers, Box 340, Folder 4, SGML.

124. "The Stranger on the Squad," *Time*, 14 Dec. 1962, 15.

125. Drew Pearson, "Stevenson Opposed 'Pearl Harbor' Strike at Cuba," Syndicated Column, 17 Dec. 1962, 2, Drew Pearson Papers, Box G121, 1 of 3, Kennedy, John F., Miscellaneous 1 Folder, LBJL.

126. Beschloss, *Crisis Years*, 502.

127. Gilbert Harrison, "Why Stevenson?" *New Republic*, 15 Nov. 1962, 10.

128. Arthur Krock, Editorial for Broadcast, National Broadcasting Company, 9 Dec. 1962, Arthur Krock Papers, Box 14, *New York Times* Folder, SGML.

129. May and Zelikow, eds., *Kennedy Tapes*, 198.

130. It is impossible to know whether JFK thought his secret deal on the Turkish missiles would enhance or damage historians' evaluation of his role in the crisis. Clearly, making such a deal public would have hurt his political standing in 1962, but historians generally have seen the deal as a sign that Kennedy was willing to be more careful and pragmatic than his Cold War rhetoric suggested. See "Excerpts from President Kennedy's Press Conference of December 12, 1962," Adlai Stevenson Papers, Box 47, Folder 5, SGML.

131. Pierpoint oral history interview, JFKLOHP.

132. Paper, *Promise and the Performance*, 40.

133. Hersh, *Dark Side of Camelot*, 370.

134. "Query Editor," *Newsweek* Atlanta Bureau, 25 Oct. 1962, *Newsweek* Atlanta Bureau Records, Box 5, Item 2, RWWL.

135. Reprinted in Hammond, *Public Affairs*, 131.

136. Stevenson was not alone in experiencing conflicts with the president. Robert Kennedy more than once attacked Undersecretary of State Chester Bowles after his disagreement with the Kennedys over the Bay of Pigs. RFK's efforts to intimidate Bowles occurred in front of witnesses but were not played out in the media. In spite of that, President Kennedy passed on the details of one confrontation to Ben Bradlee, a journalist and friend. See Hilty, *Robert Kennedy*, 415.

137. Arthur M. Schlesinger Jr. popularized this label, often used to characterize the Nixon administration, in his 1973 book, *The Imperial Presidency*.

CHAPTER FIVE

1. Paper, *Promise and the Performance*, 275.

2. "J. F. K. on the Stump," *Time*, 19 Oct. 1962, 17.

3. Schlesinger, *Thousand Days*, 757.

4. *Face the Nation*, MT&R.

5. George B. McManus, Memo, 5 Nov. 1962, JFK Assassination Records, Record Number 1781000310006, NAII.

6. This poll measured reactions only of respondents familiar with the president's plans. See George Gallup, "Americans Back Kennedy on Cuba Blockade Decision," *Philadelphia Evening Bulletin*, 24 Oct. 1962, 30.

7. "Gallup Poll Being Released Sunday, October 14," National Security File—Countries, Box 36, Cuba General 10/15/62–10/23/62 Folder, JFKL.

8. Fletcher Knebel, "Washington Crisis: 154 Hours on the Brink of War," *Look*, 13 Dec. 1962, 50.

9. "Cuba and the Monroe Doctrine," *Christianity and Crisis*, 15 Oct. 1962, 173.

10. Stanley Lubell, "Majority Favor Forced Dismantling of Cuba Bases If UN Effort Fails," *Philadelphia Evening Bulletin*, 28 Oct. 1962, 10.

11. To provide the illusion of a totally united America, some leaders sought to silence the other emerging crisis in America: African Americans' push for equal rights. The mayors of Miami, Chicago, Dallas, and New York issued special pleas to African Americans to unite with white Americans in this time of crisis; however, Roy Wilkins, executive secretary of the National Association for the Advancement of Colored People, responded, "We don't see any reason why in this emergency we should not go full steam ahead." See Larry Still, "The Spotlight Is Diverted but Rights Fight Goes On," *Jet*, 8 Nov. 1962, 15–16.

12. "Union League Applauds Vote Supporting Kennedy," *Philadelphia Evening Bulletin*, 24 Oct. 1962, 63.

13. Press release, Texas Association of Broadcasters, 22 Oct. 1962, Lyndon B. Johnson Papers, Vice Presidential Papers, 1961–63, 1962 Subject File, Box 136, Foreign Relations Cuba 5 of 8 Folder, LBJL.

14. Assorted telegrams to Lyndon Johnson, 12 Nov. 1962, Vice Presidential Papers, 1962 Subject File, Box 135, Foreign Relations Cuba 4 of 8 Folder, LBJL.

15. George Gallup, "President Kennedy's Popularity," 5 Dec. 1962, *Gallup Poll*, 1793.

16. For most presidents who succeeded Kennedy, such ratings would be considered quite good. However, in this moment of triumph, Kennedy's approval rating was lower than it had been after the disastrous Bay of Pigs invasion in 1961, when 83 percent approved of his performance and only 5 percent disapproved. See ibid., 5 May 1961, 1786.

17. While the tapes show no eagerness to pursue quiet negotiations, the rationalization for this course of action can be seen in various administration memoirs. See Robert F. Kennedy, *Thirteen Days*; Schlesinger Jr., *Thousand Days*; and Sorensen, *Kennedy*.

18. Sorensen oral history interview, 51, CUOHP.

19. Revisionists and even some members of the Kennedy administration later saw the Cuban Missile Crisis's confrontational strategy as a bad foreign policy model that contributed to the arms race and to the Kennedy and Johnson administrations' tendency to see the Vietnam War as a conflict essentially between the United States and the Soviet Union. For concise revisionist critiques, see Stone, "Brink," 12–16; Nathan, "Missile Crisis," 265–81; and Barton J. Bernstein, "Week We Almost Went to War," 13–21.

20. Richard Russell, "Statement of Senator Richard B. Russell Re President's Address on the Cuban Situation," 23 Oct. 1962, Vice Presidential Papers, 1962 Subject File, Box 135, Foreign Relations Cuba 1 of 8 Folder, LBJL.

21. See Hartsock, "Masculinity, Heroism, and the Making of War," 147–48. See also Mart, "Tough Guys and American Cold War Policy," 357, and Rosenberg, "'Foreign Affairs' after World War II," 66. For more on perceived Cold War ties between Communism and homosexuality, see D'Emilio, *Sexual Politics, Sexual Communities*. For a discussion of ties between Cold War politics and the maintenance of heterosexual social order, see Elaine Tyler May, *Homeward Bound*.

22. Dean, *Imperial Brotherhood*, 169.

23. Ibid., 182–83.

24. Ibid., 170.

25. Hamilton, *JFK*, 258–59.

26. Hellmann, *Kennedy Obsession*, 15.

27. John F. Kennedy, "The Soft American," *Sports Illustrated*, 26 Dec. 1960, 17. See also John F. Kennedy, "The Vigor We Need," ibid., 16 July 1962, 12–14.

28. Carol McMurtrey, "The People Back JFK," *Austin American*, 23 Oct. 1962, 1A.

29. Research Division, Republican National Committee, "Some Notes on U.S. Policy toward Cuba," Oct. 1962, 9, Kenneth B. Keating Papers, II:1027:7, UOR.

30. The Cold War's perceived need for secrecy shielded the public from a full understanding of the administration's secret war with Cuba. During the crisis, the clandestine Operation Mongoose sent three two- to five-man teams into Cuba in small craft and ten more teams awaited assignments aboard a submarine. The nation's leaders oversaw plans to sabotage or sink Cuban ships in ports and at sea. Intelligence officials running Operation Mongoose even sought to provide popular resistance backing by producing a theme song. See "Operation Mongoose: Main Points to Consider," 26 Oct. 1962, JFK Assassination Records, Record Number 1781000310010, NAII.

31. The Manion Forum, Newsletter, 14 Sept. 1962, Kenneth B. Keating Papers, II:948:2, UOR.

32. The Manion Forum, Newsletter, 28 Sept. 1962, Right-Wing Pamphlets, Box 3, Folder 38, YUL.

33. The Kennedy administration was never sure who Keating's sources were. He told reporters that 95 percent of his sources were in the federal government and less than 5 percent were refugees. See "Inside Story on Cuba. . . . Why the U.S. Almost Got Caught," *U.S. News & World Report*, 19 Nov. 1962, 86. Keating died in 1975 without ever revealing his sources, and almost forty years later, that information remains secret. Many of his documents from this period were removed from his papers before they were donated to the University of Rochester in the 1980s. Mark Jonathan White has speculated that his informants included Cuban emigrants and Pentagon and CIA officials, possibly even CIA director John McCone. See Mark Jonathan White, *Cuban Missile Crisis*, 94–100.

34. From Press Dispatches, "More Red Arms Going to Cuba," *New York Herald Tribune*, 24 Aug. 1962, 2.

35. Kenneth B. Keating, "Soviet Troops in Cuba, Keating Reveals," Address to U.S. Senate, 31 Aug. 1962, Kenneth B. Keating Papers, IX:26:51, UOR.

36. Mark Jonathan White, *Cuban Missile Crisis*, 98. The White House speculated on this possibility during the crisis; see "Soviet MRBM's in Cuba," 31 Oct. 1962, JFK Assassination Records, Record Number 1781000210496, NAII.

37. Kennedy, "The President's News Conference of September 13, 1962," *Public Papers of the Presidents: John F. Kennedy, 1962*, 378.

38. McGeorge Bundy read from Keating's speech at an Ex Comm meeting. See May and Zelikow, eds., *Kennedy Tapes*, 64.

39. Despite errors and unproven allegations in his barrage of statements, Keating had been ahead of the administration on details of the missile installation, a 1963 confidential

memo by McGeorge Bundy conceded. See McGeorge Bundy to the Secretary of State, Secretary of Defense, and Director of the Central Intelligence Agency, Washington, 19 Feb. 1963, Document CC02949, NSA.

40. Robert S. Allen and Paul Scott, "Four IRBM Missile Bases Ready in Cuba, Threatening," *Miami News*, 16 Mar. 1962, 1A.

41. L. Mendel Rivers to John A. McCone, Washington, 8 June 1962, L. Mendel Rivers Papers, Box 16, State Department—Foreign Affairs—Cuba—1962 Folder, LOC.

42. "Briefing Paper for *Issues and Answers* Appearance—9 Sept. 1962," Paul H. Nitze Papers, Box 147, Folder 4, LOC.

43. Research Division, Republican National Committee, "The Buildup of Communist Offensive Strength in Cuba—The Accusations and the Denials," Oct. 1962, 1, Kenneth B. Keating Papers, II:1027:7, UOR.

44. McGeorge Bundy, "Memorandum on Cuba for the Press Conference," 13 Sept. 1962, National Security Files, Box 26, Cuba General 9/62 Folder, JFKL.

45. "'Cuba' Issue Most Cited by Congressmen, Editors," *Congressional Quarterly Weekly Reports* (Week ending 19 Oct. 1962), 1933.

46. William Randolph Hearst Jr., "Tough Line with Soviets Pays Off," *San Francisco Examiner*, 28 Oct. 1962, 1.

47. Lyle C. Wilson, United Press International, "Kennedy's New Image," *Atlanta Journal*, 23 Oct. 1962, 9.

48. United States Congress, "Joint Resolution," S.J. Res. 230, 3 Oct. 1962, Office of Emergency Planning Records, Microfilm Roll 1, JFKL.

49. Charles H. Percy, "Kennedy Talk 'Is Unrelated to Action,'" *U.S. News & World Report*, 29 Oct. 1962, 113.

50. Kennedy, "Remarks at the Indianapolis Airport," *Public Papers of the Presidents: John F. Kennedy, 1962*, 456.

51. Kennedy clearly did not want to discuss Cuba as he campaigned because he knew it was an area of vulnerability. However, what the editors of *Time* did not know during his final campaign swing was that he probably avoided the subject because he knew that there were Soviet missiles in Cuba and he did not want to tip his hand. See "Still Waiting to Hear," *Time*, 26 Oct. 1962, 24.

52. Sorensen, *Kennedy*, 252.

53. John and probably Robert Kennedy knew the sessions were being recorded and may have held back blatantly political comments, but the other participants were unaware that a secret taping system was recording their words for posterity. For Dillon's comments, see C. Douglas Dillon to Theodore Sorensen, Washington, 18 Oct. 1962, Theodore Sorensen Papers, Box 48, Cuba—General—10/17/62–10/27/62 Folder, JFKL.

54. Pierre Salinger, news conference, 22 Oct. 1962, Pierre Salinger Papers, Box 50, Press Briefings/JFK 10/17/62–10/23/62 Folder, JFKL.

55. Harry S. Truman, "Statement by Former President Harry S. Truman," 25 Oct. 1962, Post-Presidential Papers, Speeches—General Folder, HSTL.

56. Joe Doster, "Briefing on Cuba to Stall Politicking," *Charlotte Observer*, 25 Oct. 1962, 1B.

57. Nelson need not have worried; he won anyway. For more on his concerns, see Gay-

lord A. Nelson to Hubert H. Humphrey, Madison, 23 Oct. 1962, State Records, Gaylord Nelson Papers, Box 134, Folder 2, SHSOW.

58. Clymer, *Edward M. Kennedy*, 142.

59. There are no records of how many Democrats actually used these drafts. See Paterson and Brophy, "October Missiles and November Elections," 108.

60. In early 1963, when officials took steps to remove the missiles from Turkey, there was concern that the public would learn about the deal. See Jeffrey C. Kitchen to George Ball, Washington, 4 Jan. 1963, George Ball Papers, Box 148, Miscellaneous Papers Book, SGML; and Steering Group on Implementing the Nassau Decisions, "Jupiter Missiles," 4 Jan. 1964, George Ball Papers, Box 154, Nassau Conference Notebook, SGML. For more on the missiles in Turkey, see Nash, *Other Missiles of October*.

61. "National Security Action Memorandum No. 181," 23 Aug. 1962, National Security Files, Box 338, NSAM 181 Cuba (A) 8/23/62 Folder, JFKL.

62. Max Lerner, "GOP Dream," *New York Post*, 16 Oct. 1962, 45.

63. "2:05 P.M. Report," WNBC Radio, 24 Oct. 1962, National Broadcasting Company Records, Box 266, WNBC Radio—Oct. 24, 1962 Folder, SHSOW.

64. Ralph McGill, "A President with Steel," *Atlanta Constitution*, 29 Oct. 1962, 1.

65. Paterson and Brophy, "October Missiles and November Elections," 87.

66. "1962 Elections—Mixed Pattern of Results," 2128.

67. "U.S. Switch on Cuba Finds G.O.P. Skeptics," *Washington Star*, 27 Oct. 1962, A2.

68. Associated Press, "Republicans Score Timing of Blockade," *New York Times*, 27 Oct. 1962, 1.

69. Hal Gulliver, "Collegians Protest over Cuba," *Atlanta Constitution*, 25 Oct. 1962, 1.

70. Research Division, Republican National Committee, "The Buildup of Communist Offensive Strength in Cuba—The Accusations and the Denials," Oct. 1962, 4, Kenneth B. Keating Papers, II:1027:7, UOR.

71. During the 1960 race, Nixon was incensed during one televised debate because Kennedy had criticized Eisenhower for failing to act on Cuba, and Nixon believed that Kennedy had been briefed on administration plans for a covert operation to back a refugee invasion of the island. Then-director of the CIA, Allen Dulles, later said he had given JFK a general briefing but had not informed him of Bay of Pigs planning. See Post-Presidential Papers, Special Name Series, Box 14, Nixon, Richard M., 1962 Folder, DDEL.

72. Transcript of interview with Dwight D. Eisenhower by Malcolm Moos, 8 Nov. 1966, Post-Presidential Papers, Augusta Walter Reed Series, JFK, 1962–67 (2) Folder, DDEL.

73. Clifton F. White, *Suite 3505*, 80.

74. Dwight D. Eisenhower, Memorandum of Conversation with Director of Central Intelligence Agency, 22 Oct. 1962, Post-Presidential Papers, Augusta Walter Reed Series, Box 2, Memoranda on Conferences, 1961–63 Folder, DDEL.

75. Associated Press, "Eisenhower Backs Kennedy," *Philadelphia Evening Bulletin*, 24 Oct. 1962, 15.

76. Dwight D. Eisenhower, "Memorandum on Telephone Conversation," 29 Oct. 1962, Post-Presidential Papers, Augusta Walter Reed Series, Cuba (1) Folder, DDEL.

77. Dwight D. Eisenhower, Memorandum, 5 Nov. 1962, Post-Presidential Papers, Augusta Walter Reed Series, Cuba (1) Folder, DDEL.

78. Dwight D. Eisenhower, Memorandum, 2 Nov. 1962, Post-Presidential Papers, Augusta Walter Reed Series, Box 2, Memoranda on Conferences, 1961–63 Folder, DDEL.

79. Associated Press, "Russians Use Broken Promises as Basic Tactic, Eisenhower Warns," *Philadelphia Evening Bulletin*, 30 Oct. 1962, 13.

80. Dwight D. Eisenhower to Joyce Hall, 30 Oct. 1962, Post-Presidential Papers, Secretary's Series, H Folder, DDEL.

81. United Press International, "Nixon Backs Stand Made by President," *Wichita Eagle*, 23 Oct. 1962, 2A.

82. United Press International, "Gov. Rockefeller Backs President's Vigorous Stand," *Wichita Eagle*, 23 Oct. 1962, 2A.

83. Nelson Rockefeller, "Statement by Governor Nelson Rockefeller," 22 Oct. 1962, Nelson Rockefeller Papers, Record Group III 1525, Gubernatorial Press Releases, Box 13, Folder 238, RA.

84. Steuart L. Pittman to Robert S. McNamara, Washington, 29 Oct. 1962, Office of Emergency Planning Records, Microfilm Roll 1, JFKL.

85. Richard Nixon, "Statement by Richard Nixon Regarding President Kennedy's Cuban Statement—October 22, 1962," RNL.

86. Richard Nixon, "Statement by Richard Nixon," 24 Oct. 1962, RNL.

87. Richard Nixon, "Statement of Richard Nixon: Win with Nixon Rally—Hollister," 29 Oct. 1962, Committee to Re-Elect Gov. Brown Records, Box 4, Press Releases—Nixon for Governor #2 Folder, BL.

88. "Civil Defense and California: Brown at D.C. Briefing, Plans Broadcast Report," *San Francisco Examiner*, 28 Oct. 1962, 1.

89. Richard Nixon, "Statement Issued by Richard Nixon—San Diego," 28 Oct. 1962, Committee to Re-Elect Gov. Brown Records, Box 4, Press Releases—Nixon for Governor #1 Folder, BL.

90. Democrats for Nixon, Press Release, 29 Oct. 1962, Committee to Re-Elect Gov. Brown Records, Box 2, Nixon Campaign Folder, BL.

91. Richard Nixon, "Statement by Richard Nixon: Win With Nixon Rally—East Los Angeles," 31 Oct. 1962, Committee to Re-Elect Gov. Brown Records, Box 4, Press Releases—Nixon for Governor #2 Folder, BL.

92. Richard Nixon, "Statement by Richard Nixon: Cerritos College," 1 Nov. 1962, Committee to Re-Elect Gov. Brown Records, Box 4, Press Releases—Nixon for Governor #2 Folder, BL.

93. Richard Nixon, "Statement by Richard Nixon," 3 Nov. 1962, RNL.

94. Sorensen, *Kennedy*, 669–70.

95. Kenneth B. Keating to Luther Hodges, Washington, 23 Oct. 1962, Kenneth B. Keating Papers, II:828:2, UOR.

96. James Daniel, "Kenneth Keating Critic of Our Cuban Policy," *Reader's Digest*, May 1963, 197.

97. Kenneth B. Keating to the editor of the *Jamestown Post-Journal*, 26 Feb. 1963, Reel 159, Name File, Gubernatorial Office Records, Nelson Rockefeller Papers, RA.

98. United Press International, "CD Is Not a Campaign Issue Says Director," *Anchorage Daily News*, 26 Oct. 1962, 2.

99. John G. McCullough, "Dilworth Calls Scranton Unfit in Cuban Crisis," *Philadelphia Evening Bulletin*, 25 Oct. 1962, 1.

100. "Candidate's Stand on Cuba Criticized by TV Viewers," *New York Times*, 24 Oct. 1962, 22.

101. Fletcher Knebel, "Potomac Fever," *Washington Post*, 30 Oct. 1962, A11.

102. Clifton F. White, *Suite 3505*, 82.

103. Reeves, *President Kennedy*, 429.

104. "Congressional Quarterly Fact Sheet on Kennedy Gains/Losses," *Congressional Quarterly Weekly Reports* (Week ending 9 Nov. 1962): 2133.

105. Cato, "From Washington Straight," *National Review*, 6 Nov. 1962, 347.

106. M. Stanton Evans, "Election Forecast," *National Review*, 6 Nov. 1962, 349.

107. Adams oral history interview, 22, Earl Warren Oral History Office, Regional Oral History Office, BL.

108. McGirr, *Suburban Warriors*, 119.

109. Ambrose, *Nixon*, 650–54.

110. *California Poll*.

111. Brown oral history interview, tape no. 2, LBJL.

112. This trend would continue in 1964, with Goldwater claiming victories in Alabama, Georgia, Louisiana, Mississippi, and South Carolina. The 1966 off-year elections gave the GOP another boost in the South, consolidating Republican strength in the region. After 1964, the only Democrats elected president have been moderate southerners who could make inroads among southern voters who might otherwise vote Republican.

113. "GOP's Goldwater: Busting out All Over," *Newsweek*, 20 May 1963, 29.

114. Paterson and Brophy, "October Missiles and November Elections," 92.

115. Angus Campbell, "Prospects for November: Why We Can Expect More of the Same," *New Republic*, 8 Oct. 1962, 13.

116. Patterson and Brophy, "October Missiles and November Elections," 87–119.

117. "What the Election Means," Transcript, Columbia Broadcasting System, 7 Nov. 1962, 16, Charles Collingwood Papers, Box 4, "CBS Reports" 4/61–11/62 Folder, SHSOW.

118. "American National Election Study, 1962."

119. "Statement of the Committee for the Monroe Doctrine," Right-Wing Pamphlets, Box 13, Folder 215, YUL.

120. Curtis B. Dall, Liberty Lobby newsletter, 5 Nov. 1962, Right-Wing Pamphlets, Box 7, Folder 115, YUL.

121. "Information and Public Affairs Matters Growing out of the Cuban Situation," Unsigned, 29 Nov. 1962, Vice Presidential Security File, Box 8, Policy Papers and Background Studies (I) Folder, Document 18, LBJL.

122. General Anatoly Gribkov, quoted in Blight, Allyn, and Welch, *Cuba on the Brink*, 61.

123. Freedman, *Kennedy's Wars*, 166.

CHAPTER SIX

1. Escalona, "Growing up with the Threat of Nuclear War," 606.

2. Until the Cold War's end, all-out nuclear war remained a somewhat diminished pos-

sibility, but because civil defense largely had been rejected by the time baby boomers' children reached school, the idea of nuclear war played a smaller role in their daily lives.

3. "Adjustment," *New Yorker*, 18 Aug. 1945, 17.

4. Relin, "Era of Fear," 11.

5. Hart, "Career Aspirations in Cataclysmic Times," 46.

6. *One Minute to Midnight: The Real Story of the Cuban Missile Crisis*, National Broadcasting Company, 23 Oct. 1992, MT&R.

7. *Biography*.

8. Sigel, "Image of a President," 220.

9. *Kids' Letters to President Kennedy*, 158.

10. Ibid., 18.

11. Ibid., 154.

12. Hugh Wilson, "Keeping Tabs on Space Traffic," *Boys' Life*, May 1962, 15.

13. Lane, "What Are We Doing to Our Children?" 8.

14. *Two Faces*, 5.

15. Kopich, *Red Iceberg*, 8.

16. Ibid., 5.

17. *Treasure Chest*'s publisher targeted a scholastic audience, but it never won a big role in the classroom. See Reitberger and Fuchs, *Comics*, 141.

18. "Godless Communism," *Treasure Chest of Fun and Fact*, 28 Sept. 1961, 3–8.

19. Ibid., 23 Nov. 1961, 12.

20. Winkler, *Life under a Cloud*, 98–99.

21. *Operation Survival!*

22. "Mad's Picture of the Issue," *Mad*, June 1962, 49.

23. Joe Orlando, "Nuclear Jitters," *Mad*, Apr. 1962, 48.

24. Phil Hahn and Joe Orlando, "A Mad Guide to Russia," *Mad*, December 1961, 19–20.

25. Haber, *Our Friend the Atom*, 145–46. Also see Walt Disney Productions, *Our Friend the Atom*.

26. Haber, *Our Friend the Atom*, 13.

27. *Weekly Reader*, 138.

28. "Cuban Problem Grows Worse," *My Weekly Reader*, R-6, 8 Oct. 1962, 1.

29. "The Monroe Doctrine: The Communist Arms Build-up in Cuba Has Hurled a New Challenge," *Senior Scholastic*, 31 Oct. 1962, 7.

30. David Olinger, "The Cold War Was a Fearful Time for Children," *St. Petersburg Times*, 10 Dec. 1989, 1D.

31. Juchem, *Organizing Colorado Schools for Civil Defense*, 16, Virgil L. Couch Papers, Box 17, Publications by State and Local Agencies 1951–58 (10) Folder, DDEL.

32. Boy Scouts of America, *Annual Report*, 56–57.

33. "More Mental Than Material," *Safety Education*, Apr. 1962, 49.

34. Brown, "'A is for Atom,'" 79.

35. Freud and Burlingham, *Infants without Parents*, 72. For more on children's responses to war, see Tuttle, *"Daddy's Gone to War."*

36. "Let Our Children Go!" *Nation*, 7 Oct. 1961, 219.

37. Reifel, "Children Living with the Nuclear Threat," 76.

38. Adams, "Adolescent Opinion on National Problems," 397–400.

39. Elder, "Summary of Research," 122.

40. Allerhand, "Children's Reactions," 127–29.

41. Harris and Associates, *Pilot Study of American Knowledge*, 7, 19.

42. Bruce Watson, "Caves of the Cold War," *Sacramento Bee*, 10 Apr. 1994, F01.

43. Adon Taft, "How Children Look at Cuban Crisis," *Miami Herald*, 27 Oct. 1962, 18A.

44. Jean A. Thompson, "Impact on the Child's Emotional Life," 31.

45. Gross, *My Generation*, 31.

46. Brown, "'A is for Atom,'" 80–81.

47. Olinger, "Cold War was a Fearful Time for Children," 1D.

48. Harry G. Toland, "What About School Children in an Attack? CD Has Pinpointed Peril but Done Little," *Philadelphia Evening Bulletin*, 7 Nov. 1961, 40.

49. "Manual for the Organization and Operation of Mass Care Centers," Philadelphia Civil Defense Council Education and Welfare Service Records, Sept. 1959, 2, Urban Archives, Philadelphia, Pa.

50. "Since There's a Chance of Nuclear War," 84.

51. "If Warned of Nuclear Attack," 71.

52. "Civil Defense in Schools," 1-T.

53. "The Truth about Civil Defense," Civil Defense Protest Committee, undated, Social Action Vertical File, Box 10, Civil Defense Protest Committee Folder, SHSOW.

54. Mr. And Mrs. J. A. Smith to John J. Theobald and James McQuillen, New York, 27 Jan. 1962, Social Action Vertical File, Box 10, Civil Defense Protest Committee Folder, SHSOW. For more on the almost-spontaneous involvement of mothers in civil defense protests, see Garrison, "Our Skirts Gave Them Courage," 201–26.

55. Sheryl James, "Fallout Lingers through the Decades," *St. Petersburg Times*, 3 Sept. 1990, 1D.

56. Escalona, "Growing up with the Threat of Nuclear War," 601–2. A study done between 1977 and 1980 by two doctors, William Beardslee and John Mack, showed that of 1,100 fifth through twelfth graders interviewed in Boston, Baltimore, and Los Angeles, 40 percent said they were aware of the existence of nuclear arms by age twelve. Also, about half of 389 high school students said that nuclear weaponry affected their thoughts about the future. No comparable study is available for youths in the early 1960s, but if anything, awareness of nuclear arms probably was higher because students engaged in civil defense drills then. See Beardslee and Mack, *Impact on Children*. Other studies done in the 1980s showed that 10 to 15 percent of adolescents thought about nuclear war daily and concluded that thinking about the subject might be too painful for some teens. These surveys showed that fear of nuclear war decreased with age. See Hanna, *Psychosocial Impact of the Nuclear Threat*, and Goldberg et al., "Thinking about the Threat of Nuclear War," 503–12.

57. Allerhand, "Children's Reactions," 127–29.

58. Carey, "Psychological Fallout," 22.

59. Children had less chance of surviving nuclear war because their bones and organs would absorb more radioactive elements. See "Fallout and School Shelters," *Safety Education*, Apr. 1962, 44.

60. Harris, Proshansky, and Raskin, "Some Attitudes of College Students," 29–30.

61. Henkel and DiSanto, *Student Attitudes toward Civilian Defense*, 14–15.

62. Oschmann interview by author, 11 Mar. 1995.

63. Beschloss, *Crisis Years*, 487.

64. Jean Dietz, "What Can Parents Tell Their Children in Crisis?" *Boston Globe*, 25 Oct. 1962, 1 and 10.

65. "Schools and Crises," 55–56.

66. Barnett interview by author.

67. Dingfelder interview by author.

68. Scicchitano interview by author.

69. "Query Editor," Newsweek Atlanta Bureau, undated, *Newsweek* Atlanta Bureau Records, Box 5 (Cuba), 4 Folder, RWWL.

70. Beschloss, *Crisis Years*, 487.

71. "Advice to Boy, 14, Guide in Crisis," *Boston Globe*, 25 Oct. 1962, 10.

72. Olinger, "Cold War Was a Fearful Time for Children," 1D.

73. Boyer, *By the Bomb's Early Light*, xix.

74. Roberta Applegate, "Youngsters Turn to Parody, Not Panic," *Miami Herald*, 25 Oct. 1962, 1.

75. Charles Lane, "The Master of the Game: Strobe's World," *New Republic*, 7 Mar. 1994, 19.

76. Gross, *My Generation*, 37.

77. Jeff Klinkenberg, "Doomsday Loomed in Miami," *St. Petersburg Times*, 11 Oct. 1992, 1F.

78. Sharp interview by author.

79. Obst, *Too Good to Be Forgotten*, 32–40.

80. Weber interview by author.

81. There was little improvement in civil defense in the schools during or after the crisis. Two years later, the United States had only 9 million shelter spaces in schools—many of them unstocked and unlicensed—to house 49.25 million children in public and private schools. See the National Commission on Safety Education, *Current Status of Civil Defense in Schools*.

82. David Breated, "School Shelter Funds Short, Parents Face Bill up to $9," *Washington Star*, 31 Oct. 1962, A1.

83. "Shelter Choice Reasons Given," *New Orleans Times-Picayune*, 28 Oct. 1962.

84. Edward Luckenbaugh, "Cumberland Plans School Civil Defense Warning System," *Patriot*, 26 Oct. 1962, 27.

85. "CD Radio in Schools Proposed," *Dallas Morning News*, 25 Oct. 1962, sec. 1, p. 13.

86. "Fire Chief Will Head County CD," *Richmond Times-Dispatch*, 26 Oct. 1962, 14.

87. Daniel Greene, "Fallout-Shelter Schools Are Urged for County," *Washington Star*, 24 Oct. 1962, A16. Just months before the crisis, the nation got its first underground school. The Abo School in Artesia, New Mexico, had classroom space to accommodate 540 students in first through sixth grades. In the event of nuclear attack, the facility could house 2,000 people for two weeks. See Bernard Ross, Statement, U.S. Congress, Senate, Committee on Armed Services, *Hearings before Subcommittee No. 3*, 4273.

88. Ellen Bartlett, "The Wailing Siren," *Boston Globe*, 22 Oct. 1988, 75.

89. "Schools to Recess in Case of Attack," *Wichita Eagle*, 25 Oct. 1962, 5A.

90. "Prejean Maps Disaster Plan," *New Orleans Times-Picayune*, 24 Oct. 1962, sec. 1, p. 21.

91. United Press International, "Jacksonville Ready to Evacuate If—," *Charlotte Observer*, 25 Oct. 1962, 3A.

92. "Parents Deluge Schools with Crisis Queries," *Los Angeles Times*, 25 Oct. 1962, 1.

93. "Homes OKd as Pupils' CD Haven," *Patriot*, 30 Oct. 1962, 13.

94. National Commission on Safety Education of the NEA, *Current Status of Civil Defense in Schools*, 5.

95. Lois Dickert, "They Thought the War Was On!" *McCall's*, Apr. 1963, 96–203.

96. Milton Schwebel, "What Do They Think?" in Child Study Association of America, ed., *Children and the Threat of Nuclear War*, 26–29.

97. Schwebel, "Effects of the Nuclear War Threat," 610.

98. Schwebel, "What Do They Think?" 30–32.

99. Nehnevajsa and Berkowitz, *Cuban Crisis*, 8–9.

100. Ibid., 11.

101. Ibid., 60.

102. Ibid., 16–17.

103. Joan Jenks, "Tell Your Children the Facts—Calmly," *Miami Herald*, 25 Oct. 1962, 14A.

104. Willard Lawson, "Cuban Crisis Creates Run on Survival Items Here," *Anchorage Daily News*, 25 Oct. 1962, 1.

105. Carey, "Psychological Fallout," 22.

106. Brown, "'A is for Atom,'" 81.

107. Florida State University could make a rare claim: it had twenty-two shelters to house all 10,000 people who worked and attended classes there at a cost of just $1 per person. See William H. Watson, "Civil Defense at Florida State University," *Safety Education*, Apr. 1962, 52–54.

108. Mary McGowan, "Nation's Students Scared by New Cuban Crisis," *Daily Californian*, 24 Oct. 1962, 1.

109. Arthur Grossman, "Joint Air Raid Drill SC Topic Tonight," *Temple University News*, 25 Oct. 1962, 1.

110. Gitlin, *Sixties*, 98.

111. "Kennedy and Cuba in College Press," *Daily Pennsylvanian*, 29 Oct. 1962, 3.

112. Manuel Carballo, "A Dialogue in Havana," *Daily Princetonian*, 25 Oct. 1962, 2.

113. Chesler and Schmuck, "Student Reactions to the Cuban Crisis," 473.

114. Ibid., 475.

115. Chatfield, *American Peace Movement*, 111.

116. Wessel, *Peace Movement*, 2679.

117. Schwebel, ed., *Behavioral Science and Human Survival*, 185.

118. Swerdlow, *Women Strike for Peace*, 15.

119. Ibid., 21.

120. Ibid., 90.

121. Dagmar Wilson to Gerard Piel, 24 Oct. 1962, New York, Women Strike for Peace Records, A3, Box 7, Correspondence—10/62 Folder, PC.

122. Swerdlow, *Women Strike for Peace*, 262.

123. Katz, *Ban the Bomb*, 77.

124. Patricia P. Nelson to National Committee for a Sane Nuclear Policy, DG58, SANE Records, Series J, Box 8, SANE Washington Office—Correspondence—Cuban Crisis Folder, PC.

125. "SANE Action during the Cuban Crisis: A Daily Diary," SANE Records, DG58, Series B, Box 36, Cuba 1962 Folder, PC.

126. Katz, *Ban the Bomb*, 80.

127. Boyer, "From Activism to Apathy," 840.

128. "National Secretary's Report," Student Peace Union, 30 Nov. 1962, Student Peace Union Records, Box 1, SPU-1962–63 Development Folder, NYUA.

129. "Constitution," Student Peace Union, undated, Student Peace Union Records, Box 1, SPU-1960–61 N.C. and Convention Folder, NYUA.

130. "Even the Fruits of Victory Would Be in Our Mouth—Kennedy," Student Peace Union, Social Protest Collection, Box 24, Folder 36, BL.

131. United Press International, "Campuses Stirred up by Crisis," *Dallas Morning News*, 25 Oct. 1962, 10.

132. Associated Press, "Eggs Hit 2 on Faculty," *New York Times*, 25 Oct. 1962, 25.

133. "Cuba Protest Parade Set by Students," *Chicago Tribune*, 25 Oct. 1962, 1.

134. "Cuba Blockade: SPU Protests Coast to Coast," *Student Peace Union Bulletin*, Nov. 1962, 1, Student Peace Union Records, Box 1, SPU-1962–63 Development Folder, NYUA.

135. "SPU Cuba Pickets Called 'Impressive,'" *Temple University News*, 1 Nov. 1962, 2.

136. Boyer, "From Activism to Apathy," 838.

137. Gitlin, *Sixties*, 99.

138. Associated Press, "Fist Fights over Cuba at Indiana U," *Des Moines Register*, 25 Oct. 1962, 9.

139. Associated Press, "Two Seized in Indiana," *New York Times*, 25 Oct. 1962, 25.

140. Hal Gulliver, "Collegians Protest over Cuba," *Atlanta Constitution*, 25 Oct. 1962, 1.

141. "Query Editor," Newsweek Atlanta Bureau, undated, *Newsweek* Atlanta Bureau Records, Box 5 (Cuba), 4 Folder, RWWL.

142. "First 'Crisis Nerves' Calm as Reactions Start Sounding," *Patriot*, 26 Oct. 1962, 4.

143. United Press International, "Peace Marchers Jeered," *New York Times*, 27 Oct. 1962, 7.

144. "Students March Today in Capital in Protest over Cuban Blockade," *New York Times*, 27 Oct. 1962, 7.

145. Weart, *Nuclear Fear*, 259.

146. United Press International, "500 Picket White House; 3 Arrested, One Removed," *Richmond Times-Dispatch*, 28 Oct. 62, 14A.

147. "S.F. Rallies on Cuba Blockade—For and Against," *San Francisco Chronicle*, 28 Oct. 1962, 1.

148. Emanuel Perlmutter, "Rally Held Here by 8,000 Pacifists," *New York Times*, 29 Oct. 1962, 20.

149. "Not Everyone Heeds the Call," *Temple University News*, 26 Oct. 1962, 2.

150. Mary McGowan, "The Children's Hour," *Daily Californian*, 25 Oct. 1962, 2.

151. Eliot Fremont-Smith, "War/Peace Books: I," *Village Voice*, 1 Nov. 1962, 11.

152. "University Students Demonstrate," *Atlanta Constitution*, 25 Oct. 1962, 14.

153. Schneider, *Cadres of Conservatism*, 64.

154. Tom Hayden and Dick Flacks, "Cuba and USA," *Common Sense* 4, no. 2 (December 1962), 11–12.

155. Martin Luther King Jr., *Why We Can't Wait*, 7.

156. McGruder interview by author.

157. Kleidman, *Organizing for Peace*, 221.

158. "Political Action: Was the Time Right?" *Student Peace Union Bulletin*, Nov. 1962, 4.

159. Sanford Gottlieb, "The Peace Candidates and the 1962 Elections," National Committee for a Sane Nuclear Policy, 13 Nov. 1962, SANE Records, DG58, Series A, Box 11, Releases 1962 Folder, PC.

CONCLUSION

1. "The Talk of the Town," *New Yorker*, 3 Nov. 1962, 43.

2. Elmo Roper to Lyndon Johnson, undated, Washington, Lyndon B. Johnson Papers, Vice Presidential Papers, 1962 Subject File, Box 136, Foreign Relations—Cuba Folder, LBJL.

3. "CBS News Special Report," 1 Nov. 1962, MT&R.

4. Allyn, Blight, and Welch, eds., *Back to the Brink*, 137.

5. Art Buchwald, "The Doves and the Hawks," Herald Tribune Syndicate, Nov. 1962, Art Buchwald Papers, Box 4, Folder 1, SHSOW.

6. Allison and Zelikow, *Essence of Decision*, 339.

7. Nathan, "Missile Crisis," 259.

8. Robert F. Kennedy, *Thirteen Days*, 44.

9. Count done by author.

10. Count done by author, with some figures drawn from Weart, *Nuclear Fear*, 260.

11. "Civil Defense and Cold War Attitudes," University of Pittsburgh, June 1964, 90, in Nehnevajsa, *Civil Defense and Society*, 88.

12. Rose, *One Nation Underground*, 201.

13. Americans did not know that at the time, nuclear tactical weapons remained in Cuba until 20 November. See "News Release, 12 Oct. 2002, 1 P.M. EST," NSA. Removal of Soviet weapons did not eliminate all nuclear weapons from the island. The Pentagon revealed in 1999 that the United States had nuclear weapons components in Cuba at the time of the crisis in the form of depth-charge weapons to be used against submarines. See Robert Burns, "Pentagon Reveals Weapons Locations," Associated Press, 19 Oct. 1999.

14. Garthoff, *Reflections on the Cuban Missile Crisis*, 73.

15. See Robert F. Kennedy, *Thirteen Days*; Sorensen, *Kennedy*; and Schlesinger Jr., *Thousand Days*.

bibliography

PRIMARY SOURCES

MANUSCRIPT COLLECTIONS

Abilene, Kans.
  Dwight D. Eisenhower Library
    Virgil L. Couch Papers
    John Foster Dulles Papers
    Dwight D. Eisenhower, Papers of the President of the United States
    ———, Post-Presidential Papers
    Oral History Project
      Dr. Arthur Flemming oral history interview by Thomas Soapes,
        24 November 1978
Atlanta, Ga.
  Georgia Department of Archives and History
    Georgia Department of Defense Records
  Martin Luther King Jr. Center
    Martin Luther King Jr. Papers
  Robert W. Woodruff Library
    Ralph McGill Papers
    Newsweek Atlanta Bureau Records
Austin, Tex.
  Lyndon Johnson Library
    Lyndon Johnson, Papers of the President of the United States
    ———, Vice Presidential Papers
    Office of Emergency Planning Records
    Oral History Project
      George Ball oral history interview
      Edmund G. Brown oral history interview by Joe B. Frantz, 19 August 1970
      C. Farris Bryant oral history interview by Joe B. Frantz, 5 March 1971
      Douglas Dillon oral history interview by Paige Mulhollan, 13 September 1974
    Drew Pearson Papers
Berkeley, Calif.
  Bancroft Library
    Earl Adams oral history interview by Amelia R. Fry, 1975
    Committee to Re-Elect Gov. (Edmund) Brown Records
    Social Protest Collection
Boston, Mass.
  John F. Kennedy Library

John F. Kennedy, Papers of the President of the United States
Office of Emergency Planning Records
Oral History Project
    Dean Acheson oral history interview by Lucius D. Battle, 27 April 1964
    Anthony Akers oral history interview by William E. Moss, 1971
    Edwin Bayley oral history interview by Larry J. Hackman, 10 October 1968
    Liz Kovacs oral history interview by Sheldon Stern, 7 June 1978
    Joseph Kraft oral history interview by John F. Stewart, 9 January 1967
    Peter Lisagor oral history interview by Ronald J. Grele, 12 May 1966
    Henry Luce oral history interview by John L. Steele, 11 November 1965
    John J. McCloy oral history interview by Paige Mulhollan, 8 July 1969
    Mary McGrory, Peter Lisagor, and George Herman oral history interview
        by Fred Holborn, 4 August 1964
    George Meany oral history interview by Arthur Goldberg, 16 July 1964
        and 18 August 1964
    Paul Nitze oral history interview by Dorothy Fosdick, 11 July 1964
    Robert Pierpoint oral history interview by Sheldon Stern, 18 November 1982
    Steuart L. Pittman oral history interview by William W. Moss, 18 September
        1970
    John Scali oral history interview by Sheldon Stern, 17 November 1982
    Theodore Sorensen oral history interview by Herbert Parmet, 17 May 1977
    Donald Wilson oral history interview by James Greenfield, 2 September 1964
Presidential Office Files
David Reardon Papers
Pierre Salinger Papers
Arthur M. Schlesinger Jr. Papers
Theodore Sorensen Papers
U.S. Department of Labor, Bureau of Labor Statistics Records
U.S. Secret Service Records
Adam Yarmolinsky Papers
Mugar Library, Boston University
Elie Abel Papers
Carlisle, Pa.
Army War College
    General Herbert Powell oral history interview by Lieutenant Colonel Hubert
        Bartron and Lieutenant Colonel Robert McCue, 27 May 1975
College Park, Md.
National Archives II
Defense Civil Preparedness Agency Records
John F. Kennedy Assassination Records
Office of Emergency Planning Records (Records of the Office of Emergency
    Preparedness)
Rockefeller Commission Records
U.S. Agricultural Marketing Service Records
U.S. Department of Defense Records

Independence, Mo.
    Harry S. Truman Library
        Harry S. Truman Post-Presidential Papers
Madison, Wisc.
    State Historical Society of Wisconsin
        Associated Press Managing Editors Records
        Edwin Bayley Papers
        Art Buchwald Papers
        Charles Collingwood Papers
        National Broadcasting Company Records
        Newton Minow Papers
        Gaylord Nelson Papers
        Howard K. Smith Papers
        Social Action Vertical File
        State Records, Office of Civil Defense
        Wisconsin Division of Emergency Resource Management Planning Project
           Records
Montgomery, Ala.
    Air Force Historical Research Center
        General David A. Burchinal oral history interview by Colonel John B. Schmidt
           and Lieutenant Colonel Jack Strasser, 11 April 1975
        General Bennie L. Davis oral history interview
        "Documentary History, Ninth Air Defense Division," October 1961–December
           1962
        Generals Leon Johnson, Curtis LeMay, David A Burchinal, Jack J. Catton oral
           history interview by Richard H. Kohn and Joseph P. Harahan, 15 June 1984
        Pentagon Documents
        General Horace M. Wade oral history interview by Hugh N. Ahmann,
           10–12 October 1978
New Haven, Conn.
    Yale University Library
        Walter Lippmann Papers
        Right-Wing Pamphlets Collection
New York, N.Y.
    Columbia University Oral History Project
        Dwight D. Eisenhower oral history interview by Dr. Philip A. Crowl, 28 July 1965
        "Lectures and Discussions in the Graduate School of Journalism"
        James Reston, "Reminiscences of James Barrett Reston," Lecture, 26 April 1962
        Theodore Sorensen oral history interview by Herbert Parmet, 1977
        James Jeremiah Wadsworth oral history interview by John T. Mason Jr., 1976
    Municipal Archives
        Robert F. Wagner Papers
    Museum of Television & Radio
        "CBS News Extra: U.S. Quarantines Cuba," 22 October 1962
        "CBS News Special Report," 12 April 1961

"CBS News Special Report," 23 October 1962

"CBS News Special Report," 25 October 1962

"CBS News Special Report," 1 November 1962

"CBS News Special Report: Return of President Kennedy after Summit Talks in Europe," 6 June 1961

CBS Washington Report, 28 October 1962

Face the Nation: John F. Kennedy, 30 October 1960

"Madman, Parts 1 and 2," *The Defenders*

Nightline, 30 January 1989

————, 24 October 1996

One Minute to Midnight: The Real Story of the Cuban Missile Crisis, 23 October 1992

Rod Serling, "The Shelter," *The Twilight Zone*

————. "Time Enough at Last," *The Twilight Zone*

New York Times Archives

   Cuba Files

   Orvil Dryfoos Papers

New York University Archives

   Student Peace Union Records

Palo Alto, Calif.

   Hoover Institution

      Ray S. Cline Papers

      Edward O'Donnell Papers

Philadelphia, Pa.

   City Archives

      Joseph S. Clark Jr. Papers

   Urban Archives

      Philadelphia Civil Defense Council Education and Welfare Service Records

Pocantico Hills, N.Y.

   Rockefeller Archives

      John C. Bugher Papers

      Nelson Rockefeller Papers

      Rockefeller Brothers Fund Records

Princeton, N.J.

   Seeley G. Mudd Library

      George Ball Papers

      Allen Dulles Papers

      Arthur Krock Papers

      Adlai Stevenson Papers

Rochester, N.Y.

   University of Rochester Rare Books Department

      Kenneth B. Keating Papers

Swarthmore, Pa.

   Peace Collection

      SANE Records

Women Strike for Peace Records

Washington, D.C.

   Library of Congress

      W. Averell Harriman Papers

      Paul H. Nitze Papers

      L. Mendel Rivers Papers

      Eric Sevareid Papers

   National Archives

   National Security Archive

      Cuban Missile Crisis Documents

   U.S. Marine Corps Historical Center

      Operations—Atomic Weapons Accident Subject File

   U.S. Naval Institute

      Admiral William Davis Irvin oral history interview by John T. Mason Jr.,
         12 October 1978

      Vice Admiral William P. Mack oral history interview [no interviewer named],
         23 March 1979

      Admiral Gerald E. Miller oral history interview by John T. Mason Jr., 22 March
         1976

Yorba Linda, Calif.

   Richard Nixon Library and Birthplace Collections

      Richard Nixon Papers

GOVERNMENT DOCUMENTS

U.S. Congress. House. *House Joint Resolution 447*. Washington: U.S. House of
   Representatives, 12 June 1961.

————. Committee on Appropriations. *Hearings, Independent Offices Appropriations for
   FY 1962*. 87th Cong., 1st sess. Washington: Government Printing Office, 1961.

————. Committee on Government Operations. *Hearings before a Subcommittee of the
   Committee on Government Operations*. 87th Cong., 2nd sess., Washington:
   Government Printing Office, 1962.

————. *Hearings before a Subcommittee of the Committee on Government Operations*.
   88th Cong., 1st sess., Washington: Government Printing Office, 1963.

U.S. Congress. Senate. Committee on Armed Services. *Hearings before Subcommittee
   No. 3 on H.R. 3516*. 88th Cong., 1st sess., Washington: Government Printing Office,
   1963.

————. Committee on Banking, Housing, and Urban Affairs. *Transcript of Proceedings:
   Hearing on Civil Defense*. 96th Cong., 1st sess. Washington: Government Printing
   Office, 1979.

U.S. Department of State. *Foreign Relations of the United States*. Vol. 8, 1961–63.
   Washington: Government Printing Office, 1996.

INTERVIEWS

Barnett, Barbara. Interview by author. 16 March 1995.

Dingfelder, Bill. Interview by author. 10 September 2001.

Maggio, Vincent. Interview by author. 6 September 2001.

McGruder, Bob. Interview by author. 23 March 1995.

Oschmann, Louis Henry. Interview by author. 11 March 1995.

———. Interview by author. 20 April 2000.

Reichert-Facilides, Otto. Interview by author. 14 March 1995.

Scicchitano, Bill. Interview by author. 4 September 2001.

Sharp, Marion. Interview by author. 5 September 2001.

Weber, Mariel. Interview by author. 12 June 2000.

Williams, Clois. Interview by author. 20 March 1995.

CURRENT PERIODICALS

Abilene (Texas) Reporter News

American Heritage

Anchorage Daily News

Arizona Republic

Arkansas Democrat

Army Navy Air Force Journal and Register

Associated Press

Atlanta Constitution

Atlanta Daily World

Atlanta Journal

Austin Statesman

Birmingham (Ala.) News

Boston Globe

Boston Traveler

Boys' Life

Bradenton (Fla.) Herald

Business Week

Charlotte Observer

Chicago Sun-Times

Chicago Tribune

Cincinnati Enquirer

Common Sense

Consumer Reports

Daily Californian, University of California at Berkeley

Daily Pennsylvanian, University of Pennsylvania

Daily Princetonian

Dallas Morning News

Desert Wings, Edwards AFB, Lancaster, Calif.

Des Moines Register

Detroit Free Press

Detroit Magazine

Duluth News Tribune

Esquire

Florida Times-Union

Forward Times

Geneva (N.Y.) Times

Harper's Bazaar

Harper's Magazine

Hartford Courant

Houston Post

Idaho Statesman

I. F. Stone's Weekly

Inter Press Service

Jet

Jet Journal, Miramar NAS, Oceanside, Calif.

(New York) Journal American

Kansas City Times

Laredo (Texas) Times

Las Vegas Sun

Life

Look

Los Angeles Times

Louisville Courier-Journal

Lubbock (Texas) Avalanche Journal

Mad

McCall's

Memphis Commercial Appeal

Miami Herald

Miami News

Midland (Texas) Reporter-Telegram

Milwaukee Journal

My Weekly Reader

The Nation

National Review

New Orleans Times-Picayune
The New Republic
Newsweek
New Yorker
New York Herald Tribune
New York Mirror
New York Post
New York Times
Omaha World-Herald
Paris (Texas) News
Parris Island, Parris Island Marine
  Base, S.C.
The (Harrisburg, Pa.) Patriot
Peace News
Philadelphia Daily News
Philadelphia Evening Bulletin
Philadelphia Tribune
Pittsburgh Courier
Popular Science
The Progressive
Quantico Sentry, Quantico Marine
  Base, Va.
Reader's Digest
Richmond Times-Dispatch
Rocky Mountain News
Rolling Stone
The Roundup, Reese AFB, Lubbock, Tex.
Sacramento Bee

St. Louis Globe-Democrat
St. Louis Post-Dispatch
St. Paul Pioneer Press
St. Petersburg Times
San Antonio Express
San Francisco Examiner
San Francisco Chronicle
Saturday Evening Post
Saturday Review
Scranton (Pa.) Tribune
Senior Scholastic
Smithsonian
The (Columbia, S.C.) State
Strata Courier, Mountain Home AFB,
  Idaho
Temple University News
Time
Tulsa World
TV Guide
United Press International
U.S. News & World Report
Valley Bomber, Castle AFB, Merced, Calif.
Variety
Village Voice
Wall Street Journal
Washington Post
Washington Star
Wichita Eagle

SECONDARY SOURCES

Abel, Elie. *The Missile Crisis*. Philadelphia: J. P. Lippincott Co., 1966.

Adams, James F. "Adolescent Opinion on National Problems." *Personnel and Guidance Journal* 43 (December 1963): 397–400.

Alfred P. Sloan Foundation Seminar. Videotape by Alfred P. Sloan Foundation, 22 November 1983; moderator, Richard Neustadt; participants, Dean Rusk, McGeorge Bundy, Edwin M. Martin, Donald M. Wilson.

Allerhand, Melvin E. "Children's Reactions to Societal Crises: Cold War Crisis." *American Journal of Orthopsychiatry* 35 (January 1965): 127–29.

Allison, Graham, and Philip Zelikow. *Essense of Decision: Explaining the Cuban Missile Crisis*. 2nd ed. New York: Longman, 1999.

Allyn, Bruce J., James G. Blight, and David A. Welch, eds. *Back to the Brink: Proceedings of the Moscow Conference on the Cuban Missile Crisis, January 27–28, 1989*. Lanham, Md.: University Press of America, 1992.

Ambrose, Stephen. *Nixon: The Education of a Politician 1913–1962*. Vol. 1. New York: Simon & Schuster, 1987.

"American National Election Study, 1962." Survey Research Center of the Institute of Social Research, University of Michigan, 1962.

Andrew, Christopher. *For the President's Eyes Only: Secret Intelligence and the American Presidency from Washington to Bush*. New York: HarperCollins, 1995.

"Archive of Nuclear Data." *Natural Resources Defense Council.* <http://nrdc.org/nuclear/nudb/datainx.asp>. 25 May 2002.

Aronow, Saul, Frank R. Ervin, and Victor W. Sidel, eds. *The Fallen Sky: Medical Consequences of Thermonuclear War*. New York: Hill and Wang, 1963.

Aronson, James. *The Press and the Cold War*. Indianapolis: Bobbs-Merrill, 1970.

Bateman, Carroll J. "Techniques of Managing the News." *Public Relations Journal* 18 (August 1963): 6.

Beardslee, W. R., and J. E. Mack. *The Impact on Children and Adolescents of Nuclear Developments*. Washington: American Psychiatric Association, 1982.

Benson, Robert Louis, and Michael Warner, eds. *Venona: Soviet Espionage and the American Response 1939–1957*. Washington: National Security Agency/Central Intelligence Agency, 1996.

Bernstein, Barton J. "The Week We Almost Went to War." *Bulletin of the Atomic Scientists* 32 (February 1976): 13–21.

Bernstein, Irving. *Promises Kept*. New York: Oxford University Press, 1991.

Berrien, F. K., Carol Schulman, and Marianne Amarel. "The Fallout-Shelter Owners: A Study of Attitude Formation." *Public Opinion Quarterly* 26 (Winter 1962): 206–16.

Beschloss, Michael R. *The Crisis Years: Kennedy and Khrushchev, 1960–1963*. New York: HarperCollins, 1991.

Biography: John F. Kennedy Jr. A&E and CBS News Productions. 22 December 1999, narrator, Harry Smith; executive producers, Josh Howard and Tom Seligson.

Blair, Bruce G., John E. Pike, and Stephen I. Schwartz. "Targeting and Controlling the Bomb." In *Atomic Audit: The Costs and Consequences of U.S. Nuclear Weapons Since 1940*, edited by Stephen I. Schwartz, 197–268. Washington: Brookings Institution Press, 1998.

Blanchard, B. Wayne. "American Civil Defense 1945–75: The Evolution of Programs and Policies." Ph.D. diss., University of Virginia, 1980.

Blight, James G. *The Shattered Crystal Ball: Fear and Learning in the Cuban Missile Crisis*. Savage, Md.: Rowman & Littlefield Publishers Inc., 1990.

Blight, James G., Bruce J. Allyn, and David A. Welch. *Cuba on the Brink*. New York: Pantheon Books, 1993.

Blight, James G., and David A. Welch. *On the Brink*. New York: Hill and Wang, 1989.

Bottome, Edgar M. *The Missile Gap: A Study of the Formulation of Military and Political Policy*. Rutherford, N.J.: Fairleigh Dickinson University Press, 1971.

Boyer, Paul. *By the Bomb's Early Light: American Thought and Culture at the Dawn of the Atomic Age*. Chapel Hill: University of North Carolina Press, 1994.

———. *Fallout*. Columbus: Ohio State University, 1998.

———. "From Activism to Apathy: The American People and Nuclear Weapons, 1963–1980." *Journal of American History* 70 (March 1984): 821–44.

———. *When Time Shall Be No More*. Cambridge, Mass.: Harvard University Press, 1994.

Boy Scouts of America. *Annual Report of the Boy Scouts of America—1962*. Washington: Government Printing Office, 1963.

Branch, Taylor. *Parting the Waters: America in the King Years, 1954–1963*. New York: Simon & Schuster, 1988.

Brelis, Dean. *Run, Dig or Stay? A Search for an Answer to the Shelter Question*. Boston: Beacon Press, 1962.

Brians, Paul. *Nuclear Holocausts: Atomic War in Fiction*. Kent, Ohio: Kent State University Press, 1987.

Brown, JoAnne. "'A Is for Atom, B Is for Bomb': Civil Defense in American Public Education, 1948–63." *Journal of American History* 75 (June 1988): 68–90.

Brugioni, Dino A. *Eyeball to Eyeball*. Edited by Robert F. McCort. New York: Random House, 1990.

Bundy, McGeorge. *Danger and Survival*. New York: Random House, 1988.

Burdick, Eugene, and Harvey Wheeler. *Fail-Safe*. New York: McGraw-Hill Book Co., 1962.

Bush, Robert H. *Industry-Government Co-Operation in Emergencies: Governor's Conference Industrial Survival*. Iowa City, Iowa: The Bureau of Labor and Management, 1963.

Butler, G. Paul, ed. *Best Sermons*. Vol. 7, 1959–60. New York: Thomas Y. Cromwell Co., 1959.

By, for, and about Women in Civil Defense: Grandma's Pantry Belongs in Your Kitchen. Washington: Government Printing Office, 1958.

The California Poll. University of California State Data Program in cooperation with Field Research Corp., 30 October 1962–1 November 1962.

Campbell, David. *Writing Security*. Minneapolis: University of Minnesota Press, 1992.

Carey, Michael J. "Psychological Fallout." *The Bulletin of the Atomic Scientists* 38 (January 1982): 20–24

Central Intelligence Agency. *The Secret Cuban Missile Crisis Documents*. Washington: Brassey's, 1994.

Chang, Laurence, and Peter Kornbluh, eds. *The Cuban Missile Crisis, 1962: A National Security Archive Documents Reader*. New York: New Press, 1998.

Chatfield, Charles. *The American Peace Movement: Ideals and Activism*. New York: Twayne Publishers, 1992.

Chesler, Mark, and Richard Schmuck. "Student Reactions to the Cuban Crisis and Public Dissent." *Public Opinion Quarterly* 28 (1964): 467.

Child Study Association of America, ed. *Children and the Threat of Nuclear War*. New York: Duell, Sloan and Pearce, 1964.

Civil Defense Education Project. *Education for National Survival*. Washington: U.S. Department of Health, Education and Welfare, 1956.

"Civil Defense in Schools." *Scholastic Teacher* 7 March 1962: 1-T.

Clarfield, Gerard H., and William M. Wiecek. *Nuclear America: Military and Civilian Nuclear Power in the United States, 1940–1980*. New York: Harper & Row, 1984.

Clymer, Adam. *Edward M. Kennedy*. New York: William Morrow, 1999.

Colburn, John H. "Government Censorship and Manipulation of News." Prepared for the American Society of Newspaper Editors and the American Newspaper

Publishers Association. Reprinted in *Hearings before a Subcommittee of the Committee on Government Operations, House of Representatives*. Washington: Government Printing Office, 1963.

Cold War International History Project, comp. "Russian Documents on the Cuban Missile Crisis." Bulletin 8–9, *Cold War in the Third World and the Collapse of Detente*.

Cold War International History Project, Woodrow Wilson International Center for Scholars, <http://wwics.si.edu/index.cfm?fusaction=topics.home&topic_id =1409>.

A Comparison of Soviet and U.S. Civil Defense Programs. Washington: Federal Emergency Management Agency, 1988.

"'Congressional Quarterly Fact Sheet on Kennedy Gains/Losses.'" *Congressional Quarterly Weekly Reports* 18 (Week ending 9 November 1962): 2133.

A Conversation with President Kennedy. American Broadcasting Company, Columbia Broadcasting System, and National Broadcasting Company, 17 December 1962.

Craig, Campbell. *Destroying the Village: Eisenhower and Thermonuclear War*. New York: Columbia University Press, 1998.

"Cuba and the Monroe Doctrine." *Christianity and Crisis* 22 (15 October 1962): 173.

"'Cuba' Issue Most Cited by Congressmen, Editors." *Congressional Quarterly Weekly Reports* 18 (Week ending 19 October 1962): 1933.

Daniel, Clifton. "A Footnote to History: The Press and National Security." An address to the World Press Institute, Macalester College, St. Paul, Minn., 1 June 1966. *New York Times* Archives.

Daniel, James, and John G. Hubbell. *Strike in the West*. New York: Holt, Rinehart and Winston, 1963.

Dean, Robert D. *Imperial Brotherhood: Gender and the Making of Cold War Foreign Policy*. Amherst: University of Massachusetts Press, 2001.

——— "Masculinity as Ideology: John F. Kennedy and the Domestic Politics of Foreign Policy." *Diplomatic History* 22 (Winter 1998): 29–62.

The Declassified Documents Reference System. Washington: Carrollton Press Inc., 1976.

D'Emilio, John. *Sexual Politics, Sexual Communities: The Making of a Homosexual Minority in the United States, 1940–1970*. Chicago: University of Chicago Press, 1983.

Detzer, David. *The Brink: Cuban Missile Crisis, 1962*. New York: Thomas Y. Crowell, 1979.

Dinerstein, Herbert S. *The Making of a Missile Crisis: October 1962*. Baltimore: Johns Hopkins University Press, 1976.

Divine, Robert A., ed. *The Cuban Missile Crisis*. Chicago: Quadrangle Books, 1971.

Dobrynin, Anatoly. *In Confidence*. New York: Random House, 1995.

"The Editor's Column." *Texas Defense Digest* 10 (November–December 1962): 2.

Elder, J. H. "A Summary of Research on Reactions of Children to Nuclear War." *American Journal of Orthopsychiatry* 35 (January 1965): 120–23.

Elliston, Jon, ed. *Psywar on Cuba: The Declassified History of U.S. Anti-Castro Propaganda*. Melbourne, Australia: Ocean Press, 1999.

Engelhardt, Tom. *The End of Victory Culture*. New York: BasicBooks, 1995.

Erskine, Hazel Gaudet. "The Polls: Atomic Weapons and Nuclear Energy." *Public Opinion Quarterly* 27 (Winter 1963): 155–89.

Escalona, Sibylle K. "Growing up with the Threat of Nuclear War." *American Journal of Orthopsychiatry* 52 (October 1982): 600–607.

Estimated Number of Days' Supply of Food and Beverages in Retail Stores, 1962. Washington: U.S. Department of Agriculture, 1963.

Exercise Spadefork. Washington: Office of Emergency Management, 1962. Office of Emergency Planning Records, Box 6, OEP: NREC Reports (2) Folder, LBJL.

"Fallout and School Shelters." *Safety Education* 41 (April 1962): 40–47.

The Family Fallout Shelter. Washington: Office of Civil and Defense Mobilization, 1959.

Farber, David. *The Age of Great Dreams: America in the 1960s.* New York: Hill and Wang, 1994.

Ford, Daniel. *The Button.* New York: Simon & Schuster, 1985.

Frank, Pat. *Alas, Babylon.* New York: Perennial Classics, 1999.

Freedman, Lawrence. *Kennedy's Wars.* New York: Oxford University Press, 2000.

Freud, Anna, and Dorothy T. Burlingham. *Infants without Parents.* New York: International University Press, 1944.

———. *War and Children.* Edited by P. R. Lehrman. New York: International University Press, 1944.

Fursenko, Aleksandr, and Timothy Naftali. *"One Hell of a Gamble": Khrushchev, Castro, and Kennedy, 1958–1964.* New York: W. W. Norton & Co., 1997.

Gaddis, John Lewis. *We Now Know: Rethinking Cold War History.* Oxford: Clarendon Press, 1997.

Gaddis, John Lewis, Philip H. Gordon, Ernest R. May, and Jonathan Rosenberg, eds. *Cold War Statesmen Confront the Bomb.* Oxford: Oxford University Press, 1999.

Gallup, George. *The Gallup Poll: Public Opinion, 1935–1971.* Vol. 3. New York: Random House, 1972.

Garrison, Dee. "Our Skirts Gave Them Courage." In *Not June Cleaver*, edited by Joanne Meyerowitz, 201–26. Philadelphia: Temple University Press, 1994.

Garthoff, Raymond L. *Reflections on the Cuban Missile Crisis.* Washington: Brookings Institution, 1987.

Giglio, James N. *The Presidency of John F. Kennedy.* Lawrence: University Press of Kansas, 1991.

Gitlin, Todd. *The Sixties: Years of Hope, Days of Rage.* New York: Bantam Books, 1987.

"Godless Communism." *Treasure Chest of Fun and Fact.* 28 September 1961, 3–8.

"Godless Communism." *Treasure Chest of Fun and Fact.* 23 November 1961, 12.

"Godless Communism." *Treasure Chest of Fun and Fact.* 12 April 1962, 33.

Goldberg, S., S. LaCombe, D. Levinson, K. R. Parker, C. Ross, and F. Sommers. "Thinking about the Threat of Nuclear War: Relevance to Mental Health." *American Journal of Orthopsychiatry* 55 (1985): 503–12.

Gouré, Leon. *Civil Defense in the Soviet Union.* Berkeley: University of California Press, 1962.

Gribkov, General Anatoli I. "The View from Moscow and Havana." In *Operation ANADYR: U.S. and Soviet Generals Recount the Cuban Missile Crisis*, edited by Alfred Friendly Jr., 3–78. Chicago: Edition Q Inc., 1994.

Gross, Michael. *My Generation.* New York: Clay Street Books, 2000.

Guthman, Edwin O., and Jeffrey Shulman, eds. *Robert Kennedy in His Own Words*. Toronto: Bantam Books, 1988.

Haber, Heinz. *Our Friend the Atom*. New York: Simon & Schuster, 1956.

Hachiya, Michihiko. *Hiroshima Diary*. Edited by W. Wells. Chapel Hill: University of North Carolina Press, 1955.

Hackworth, David. *About Face*. New York: Simon & Schuster, 1989.

Hallin, Daniel C. *The Uncensored War: The Media and Vietnam*. Berkeley: University of California Press, 1989.

Hamilton, Nigel. *JFK: Reckless Youth*. New York: Random House, 1992.

Hammond, William M. *Public Affairs: The Military and the Media, 1962-1968: United States Army in Vietnam*. Washington: Center of Military History, 1968.

Hanna, S. D. *The Psychosocial Impact of the Nuclear Threat on Children*. Akron: Akron City Hospital, 1983.

Harford, James. *Korolev: How One Man Masterminded the Soviet Drive to Beat America to the Moon*. New York: John Wiley & Sons, 1997.

Harris, Louis, and Associates. *A Pilot Study of American Knowledge and Attitudes toward Communism in Russia and in the United States*. Prepared for the National Broadcasting Co., January 1962.

Harris, Robert A., Harold M. Proshansky, and Evelyn Raskin. "Some Attitudes of College Students Concerning the Hydrogen Bomb." *The Journal of Psychology* 22 (1956): 29–33.

Hart, Susan L. "Career Aspirations in Cataclysmic Times." *The Career Development Quarterly* 39 (September 1990): 44–59.

Hartsock, Nancy C. M. "Masculinity, Heroism, and the Making of War." In *Rocking the Ship of State: Toward a Feminist Peace Politics*, edited by Adrienne Harris and Ynestra King, 147–48. Boulder, Colo.: Westview Press, 1989.

Haynes, John Earl, and Harvey Klehr. *Venona: Decoding Soviet Espionage in America*. New Haven: Yale University Press, 1999.

Hellmann, John. *The Kennedy Obsession: The American Myth of JFK*. New York: Columbia University Press, 1997.

Henkel, Ramon E., and Joseph E. DiSanto. *Student Attitudes toward Civilian Defense*. Madison: University of Wisconsin, 1962.

Henriksen, Margot A. *Dr. Strangelove's America: Society and Culture in the Atomic Age*. Berkeley: University of California Press, 1997.

Hersh, Seymour M. *The Dark Side of Camelot*. Boston: Back Bay Publishers, 1997.

Hershberg, James. "More New Evidence on the Cuban Missile Crisis: More Documents from the Russian Archives." Compiled by the Cold War International History Project, Bulletin 8–9, *Cold War in the Third World and the Collapse of Detente*.

Highlights of the U.S. Civil Defense Program. Washington: Office of Civil Defense, 1963.

Hilty, James W. *Robert Kennedy: Brother Protector*. Philadelphia: Temple University Press, 1997.

Hopkins, Donn Emery. "Urban Dispersal in the United States for Military Purposes." M.A. thesis, University of California, 1956.

Horelick, Arnold L. *The Cuban Missile Crisis: An Analysis of Soviet Calculations and Behavior*. Santa Monica: Rand Corporation, 1963.

"If Warned of Nuclear Attack, Schools Should Send Children Home to Parents." *The Nation's Schools* 35 (February 1962): 71.

Immerman, Richard H., and Robert R. Bowie. *Waging Peace, 1956-61*. Garden City, N.Y.: Doubleday & Co., 1965.

Jacobsen, Carl G., ed. *Strategic Power: USA/USSR*. New York: St. Martin's Press, 1990.

Javits, Jacob. "Construction of Civil Defense Shelters." *Congressional Record—Senate, 1959*: 5889.

John Scali. American Broadcasting Company News, 13 August 1964, Howard K. Smith, narrator.

Johnson, Lyndon B. *Public Papers of the Presidents, 1963-64*. 2 vols. Washington: Government Printing Office, 1965.

Johnson, Robert H. *Improbable Dangers: U.S. Conceptions of Threat in the Cold War and After*. New York: St. Martin's Press, 1994.

Juchem, Marguerite R. *Organizing Colorado Schools for Civil Defense*. Denver: Colorado State Department of Education, 1953.

Kahn, Herbert. *On Thermonuclear War*. Princeton: Princeton University Press, 1960.

Kaplan, Fred. "The Soviet Civil Defense Myth: Part 2." *Bulletin of the Atomic Scientists* 34 (April 1978): 41-51.

———. *The Wizards of Armageddon*. New York: Simon & Schuster, 1983.

Katz, Milton S. *Ban the Bomb*. New York: Greenwood Press, 1986.

Kennan, George F. *The Nuclear Delusion: Soviet-American Relations in the Atomic Age*. New York: Pantheon Books, 1976.

Kennedy, John F. *Prelude to Leadership: The European Diary of John F. Kennedy*. Washington: Regnery Publishing Inc., 1995.

———. *Public Papers of President John F. Kennedy*. 3 vols. Washington: Government Printing Office, 1964.

———. "The Soft American." *Sports Illustrated* 7 (26 December 1960): 15-18.

Kennedy, Robert F. *Thirteen Days*. New York: W. W. Norton & Co., 1969.

Kern, Montague, Patricia W. Levering, and Ralph B. Levering. *The Kennedy Crises: The Press, the Presidency, and Foreign Policy*. Chapel Hill: University of North Carolina Press, 1983.

Khrushchev, Nikita. *Khrushchev Remembers*. Edited by Strobe Talbott. Boston: Little, Brown and Co., 1970.

———. *Khrushchev Remembers: The Glasnost Tapes*. Edited by J. L. Schecter and V. V. Luchkov. Boston: Little, Brown and Co., 1990.

———. *Khrushchev Speaks*. Edited by Thomas P. Whitney. Ann Arbor: University of Michigan Press, 1963.

Khrushchev, Sergei. *Nikita Khrushchev and the Creation of a Superpower*. University Park, Pa.: Pennsylvania State University Press, 2000.

Kids' Letters to President Kennedy. New York: William Morrow, 1961.

King, Larry. *Larry King Live*. Cable News Network, 23 January 1992, Transcript 481.

King, Martin Luther, Jr. *Why We Can't Wait*. New York: New American Library, 2000.

Kleidman, Robert. *Organizing for Peace*. Syracuse, N.Y.: Syracuse University Press, 1993.

Knebel, Fletcher, and Charles W. Bailey II. *Seven Days in May*. New York: Harper & Row, 1962.

Kopich, John. *The Red Iceberg*. St. Paul: Impact Press, 1960.

Kramer, Mark. "The 'Lessons' of the Cuban Missile Crisis for Warsaw Pact Nuclear Operations." *Cold War International History Project Bulletin*, Spring 1995: 59.

Kraus, Sidney, Reuben Mehling, and Elaine El-Assal. "Mass Media and the Fallout Controversy." *Public Opinion Quarterly* 27 (Winter 1963): 191–205.

Lane, Howard A. "What Are We Doing to Our Children?" *The National Elementary Principal* 30 (June 1951): 4–7.

Larson, David L. *The Cuban Missile Crisis of 1962: Selected Documents, Chronology and Bibliography*. Lanham, Md.: University Press of America, 1963.

Leininger, Harold V., Edwin P. Laug, Raymond D. Chapman, Homer J. McConnell, Alan T. Spiher, and Stephen E. Koelz. *Operation Plumbbob: Effect of Fallout Contamination on Processed Foods, Containers, and Packaging*. Washington: Food and Drug Administration, 1958.

————. *Operation Plumbbob: Effect of Fallout Contamination on Raw Agricultural Products*. Washington: Food and Drug Administration, 1958.

Lifton, Robert Jay. *The Broken Connection: On Death and the Continuity of Life*. New York: Simon & Schuster, 1979.

————. *Death in Life: Survivors of Hiroshima*. New York: Random House, 1967.

Mack, Raymond W., and George W. Baker. *The Occasion Instant*. Washington: National Academy of Sciences—National Research Council Publication 945, 1961.

Mannix, Patrick. *The Rhetoric of Antinuclear Fiction*. Lewisburg, Pa.: Bucknell University Press, 1992.

Mart, Michelle. "Tough Guys and American Cold War Policy: Images of Israel, 1948–1960." *Diplomatic History* 20 (Summer 1996): 357–80.

Martin, John Bartlow. *Adlai Stevenson and the World*. Garden City: Anchor Books, 1978.

Mast, Robert H. *Impact of the Cuban Missile Crisis: Patterns of Public Response*. Washington: Office of Civil Defense, 1966.

May, Elaine Tyler. *Homeward Bound: American Families in the Cold War Era*. New York: BasicBooks, 1988.

May, Ernest R. *"Lessons" of the Past: The Use and Misuse of History in American Foreign Policy*. London: Oxford University Press, 1973.

May, Ernest R., and Philip D. Zelikow, eds. *The Kennedy Tapes: Inside the White House during the Cuban Missile Crisis*. Cambridge, Mass.: Belknap Press of Harvard University Press, 1997.

McAuliffe, Mary S., ed. *CIA Documents on the Cuban Missile Crisis, 1962*. Washington: Central Intelligence Agency, 1992.

McConnell, E. Rolland, George O. Sampson, and John M. Sharf. *Operation Teapot: The Effect of Nuclear Explosions on Commercially Packaged Beverages*. Washington: Food and Drug Administration, 1956.

McCoy, Donald R., and Richard T. Ruetten. *Quest and Response: Minority Rights and the Truman Administration*. Lawrence: University Press of Kansas, 1973.

McEnaney, Laura. *Civil Defense Begins at Home: Militarization Meets Everyday Life in the Fifties*. Princeton: Princeton University Press, 2000.

McGirr, Lisa. *Suburban Warriors: The Origins of the New American Right*. Princeton: Princeton University Press, 2001.

McNamara, Robert S., and B. VanDeMark. *In Retrospect: The Tragedy and Lessons of Vietnam.* New York: Random House, 1995.

Mead, Margaret. *And Keep Your Powder Dry.* New York: William Morrow, 1942.

Medland, William J. *The Cuban Missile Crisis of 1962.* New York: Praeger, 1988.

Miller, Walter M., Jr. *A Canticle for Leibowitz.* Philadelphia: Lippincott, 1959.

"Morality at the Shelter Door." *Christianity and Crisis* 21 (13 November 1961): 197.

"More Mental Than Material." *Safety Education* 41 (April 1962): 48–50.

Nash, Philip. *The Other Missiles of October: Eisenhower, Kennedy, and the Jupiters, 1957-1963.* Chapel Hill: University of North Carolina Press, 1997.

Nathan, James A., ed. *The Cuban Missile Crisis Revisited.* New York: St. Martin's Press, 1992.

——. "The Missile Crisis: His Finest Hour Now." *World Politics* 27 (January 1975): 265–81.

National Commission of Safety Education. *Current Status of Civil Defense in Schools.* Washington: National Education Association, 1966.

Nehnevajsa, Jiri. *Civil Defense and Society.* Pittsburgh: University of Pittsburgh, 1964.

Nehnevajsa, Jiri, and Morris I. Berkowitz. *The Cuban Crisis: Meaning and Impact.* Pittsburgh: University of Pittsburgh, 1962.

Newman, Stanley L. "Civil Defense and the Congress: Quiet Reversal." *Bulletin of the Atomic Scientists* 18 (November 1962): 33–37.

Niebuhr, Reinhold. *The Children of Light and the Children of Darkness: A Vindication of Democracy and a Critique of Its Traditional Defense.* New York: Scribner's Sons, 1960.

"1962 Elections—Mixed Pattern of Results." *Congressional Quarterly Weekly Reports* 18 (Week Ending 9 November 1962): 2128.

Nitze, Paul. *From Hiroshima to Glasnost.* New York: Grove Weidenfeld, 1989.

Oakes, Guy. *The Imaginary War: Civil Defense and American Cold War Culture.* New York: Oxford University Press, 1994.

Obst, David. *Too Good to Be Forgotten: Changing America in the '60s and '70s.* New York: John Wiley & Sons, 1998.

On the Beach. Film, Stanley Kramer, director, with Gregory Peck, Ava Gardner, Fred Astaire, and Anthony Perkins. United Artists, 1959.

Operation Doorstep. Film produced by Byron Inc., 1953.

Operation Survival! New York: Graphic Information Service Inc., 1957.

Our Friend the Atom. Walt Disney Productions, 1957.

Paar, Jack. *The Jack Paar Program.* National Broadcasting Company, 2 November 1962, Museum of Television and Radio, New York.

Paper, Lewis J. *The Promise and the Performance.* New York: Crown Publishers Inc., 1975.

Parmet, Herbert S. *JFK: The Presidency of John F. Kennedy.* New York: Dial Press, 1983.

Paterson, Thomas G., and William J. Brophy. "October Missiles and November Elections: The Cuban Missile Crisis and American Politics, 1962." *The Journal of American History* 72 (June 1986): 87–119.

Pellegrino, Charles. "Reality Check." *Star Trek: The Next Generation: Dyson Sphere.* New York: Pocket Books, 1999, 204–5.

Philbeck, Robert H., and Delbert M. Doty. *Operation Teapot: The Effect of Nuclear*

Explosions on Meat and Meat Products. Washington: Food and Drug Administration, 1956.

Pike, John E., Bruce G. Blair, and Stephen I. Schwartz. "Defending against the Bomb." In *Atomic Audit: The Costs and Consequences of U.S. Nuclear Weapons Since 1940*, edited by Stephen I. Schwartz, 269–326. Washington: Brookings Institution Press, 1998.

Pittman, Steuart. "Government and Civil Defense." In *Who Speaks for Civil Defense?* edited by Eugene P. Wigner, 47–74. New York: Scribner's Sons, 1968.

"Political Action: Was the Time Right?" *Student Peace Union Bulletin*. November 1962, 4.

"The Postwar Era: Between an Unfree World and None: Increasing Our Chances." *Foreign Affairs* 64 (1985): 962.

Presbyterian Church of the United States. *Minutes of the General Assembly and Report of Assembly Agencies*. New York: Presbyterian Church of the United States, 1954.

Public Papers of the Presidents of the United States: John F. Kennedy, 1961–1963. Washington: Government Printing Office, 1962–64.

"Radio Stations to Get Federal Aid for Shelters." *The Keystone Defender* 11 (September–October 1962): 7.

Reeves, Richard. *President Kennedy: Profile in Power*. New York: Simon & Schuster, 1993.

Reifel, Stuart. "Children Living with the Nuclear Threat." *Young Children* 39 (July 1984): 74–80.

Reitberger, Reinhold, and Wolfgang Fuchs. *Comics: Anatomy of a Mass Medium*. Boston: Little, Brown and Co., 1972.

Relin, David Oliver. "The Era of Fear." *Scholastic Update* 123 (7 September 1990): 11.

Rogers, Rita R., William Beardslee, Doyle I. Carson, Jerome Frank, John Mack, and Michael Mufson. *Psychosocial Aspects of Nuclear Developments*. Washington: American Psychiatric Association, 1981.

"Role of Press in National Security Discussed By Representatives of ANPA, ASNE and NEA." *American Newspaper Publishers Association General Management Bulletin*, 17 December 1962, 239.

Rose, Kenneth D. *One Nation Underground: The Fallout Shelter in American Culture*. New York: New York University Press, 2001.

Rosenberg, Emily. "'Foreign Affairs' after World War II: Connecting Sexual and International Politics." *Diplomatic History* 18 (Winter 1994): 59–70.

Roshwald, Mordecai. *Level 7*. New York: McGraw-Hill Book Co., 1959.

Ross, Bernard H. *American Government in Crisis: An Analysis of the Executive Branch of Government during the Cuban Missile Crisis*. Ann Arbor: University Microfilms, 1972.

Rusk, Dean, and Richard Rusk. *As I Saw It*. Edited by Daniel S. Papp. New York: W. W. Norton & Co., 1990.

Sagan, Scott D. *The Limits of Safety*. Princeton: Princeton University Press, 1993.

Salinger, Pierre. *With Kennedy*. Garden City, N.Y.: Doubleday & Co., 1966.

Schlesinger, Arthur M. *Paths to the Present*. New York: MacMillan, 1949.

Schlesinger, Arthur M., Jr. *A Thousand Days: John F. Kennedy in the White House*. Boston: Houghton-Mifflin Co., 1965.

Schmitt, H. P. *Operation Teapot: Effects of Nuclear Explosions on Frozen Foods*. Washington: Food and Drug Administration, 1956.

Schneider, Gregory L. *Cadres of Conservatism*. New York: New York University Press, 1999.

Schools and Civil Defense. Washington: National Commission on Safety Education, 1964.

"Schools and Crises." *High Points* 45 (March 1963): 55–56.

Schwebel, Milton. "Effects of the Nuclear War Threat on Children and Teenagers: Implications for Professionals." *American Journal of Orthopsychiatry* 52 (October 1982): 608–18.

———, ed. *Behavioral Science and Human Survival*. Palo Alto, Calif.: Science and Behavior Books, 1965.

Shesol, Jeff. *Mutual Contempt*. New York: W. W. Norton & Co., 1997.

Shute, Nevil. *On the Beach*. London: Heinemann, 1957.

Sidey, Hugh. Introduction to *Prelude to Leadership: The European Diary of John F. Kennedy*. Washington: Regnery Publishing Inc., 1995.

Sigel, Roberta S. "Image of a President: Some Insights into the Political Views of School Children." *American Political Science Review* 62 (March 1968): 216–26.

"Since There's a Chance of Nuclear War, Schools Should Prepare Students for It," *The Nation's Schools* 35 (January 1962): 84.

Slotkin, Richard. *Gunfighter Nation: The Myth of the Frontier in Twentieth-Century America*. New York: Harper Perennial, 1993.

Smith, General William Y. "The View from Washington." In *Operation ANADYR: U.S. and Soviet Generals Recount the Cuban Missile Crisis*, edited by Alfred Friendly Jr., 79–162. Chicago: Edition Q Inc., 1994.

Solomon, Zahava. *Combat Stress Reaction: The Enduring Toll of War*. New York: Plenum Press, 1993.

Sorensen, Theodore C. *Kennedy*. New York: Harper & Row, 1965.

Stone, I. F. "The Brink." *New York Review of Books* 6 (April 1966): 12–16.

Studies in the Employment of Air Power. Vol. 6. Montgomery: Air University, 1988.

Sulzberger, C. L. *The Last of the Giants*. New York: MacMillan, 1970.

Swerdlow, Amy. *Women Strike for Peace*. Chicago: University of Chicago Press, 1993.

Thompson, Jean A. "The Impact on the Child's Emotional Life." *The National Elementary Principal* 30 (June 1951): 30–33.

Thompson, Robert Smith. *The Missiles of October*. New York: Simon & Schuster, 1992.

Trachtenberg, Marc. *A Constructed Peace*. Princeton: Princeton University Press, 1999.

The Truth about Cuba Committee Inc., *Bulletin on Cuba*, 5 November 1962.

Tuttle, William M. *"Daddy's Gone to War."* New York: Oxford University Press, 1993.

Two Faces. Houston: Christian Anti-Communist League, 1961.

Universal-International News. *1962*. Vol. 35, no. 87 of *Universal-International News Newsreel*, 25 October 1962; reporter, Ed Herlihy.

Utley, Robert M. *Cavalier in Buckskin*. Norman: University of Oklahoma Press, 1988.

Utz, Curtis A. *Cordon of Steel: The U.S. Navy and the Cuban Missile Crisis*. Washington: Navy Historical Center, 1993.

Wagner, Ruth H. *Put Democracy to Work*. London: Abelard Schumen, 1961.

Weart, Spencer R. *Nuclear Fear: A History*. Cambridge. Mass.: Harvard University Press, 1988.

Weekly Reader: 60 Years of News for Kids, 1928–1988. New York: World Almanac, 1988.

Weinstein, Allen, and Alexander Vassilev. *The Haunted Wood: Soviet Espionage in American—the Stalin Era*. New York: Random House, 1999.

Wessel, A. E. *The Peace Movement*. Rand Corporation booklet. December 1962.

What You Should Know about Radioactive Fallout. Washington: Office of Civil and Defense Mobilization, May 1958.

White, Clifton F. *Suite 3505: The Story of the Draft Goldwater Movement*. New Rochelle: Arlington House, 1967.

White, Mark Jonathan. "Approaching the Abyss: The Cuban Missile Crisis and the Men Who Made and Resolved It." Ph.D. diss., State University of New Jersey, Graduate School–New Brunswick, 1992.

——. *The Cuban Missile Crisis*. London: MacMillan Press Ltd., 1996.

——, ed. *The Kennedys and Cuba: The Declassified Documentary History*. Chicago: Ivan R. Dee, 1999.

Wigner, Eugene P., ed. *Survival and the Bomb: Methods of Civil Defense*. Bloomington: Indiana University Press, 1969.

——. *Who Speaks for Civil Defense?* New York: Scribner's Sons, 1968.

Winkler, Allan M. *Life under a Cloud*. Urbana: University of Illinois Press, 1993.

Winn, Marie. *Children without Childhood*. New York: Pantheon Books, 1981.

Wofford, Harris. *Of Kennedys and Kings*. New York: Farrar, Straus & Giroux, 1980.

Young, Major John M. *When the Russians Blinked: The U.S. Maritime Response to the Cuban Missile Crisis*. Washington: History and Museums Division, U.S. Marine Corps, 1990.

Zaloga, Steven J. *Target America: The Soviet Union and the Strategic Arms Race, 1945–1964*. Novato, Calif.: Presidio, 1973.

Zubok, Vladislav, and Constantine Pleshakov. *Inside the Kremlin's Cold War: From Stalin to Khrushchev*. Cambridge, Mass.: Harvard University Press, 1996.

index

68; and Eisenhower administration, 19, 26–38, 53, 59, 86, 182 (n. 11), 184 (n. 153); and Kennedy administration, 26, 28, 59, 86; evacuation of civilians, 26, 30, 62–63, 64, 65, 68–69, 75; and private shelters, 31, 32, 33, 59, 60, 77; and public shelters, 34, 35, 43, 60–67, 70–78; Office of Civil Defense, 42–43, 48, 51, 64–66, 183 (n. 34); during Cuban Missile Crisis, 42–53, 62–86, 117, 130, 131–32, 187 (n. 131), 191 (n. 43); and line of succession, 44, 182 (nn. 10, 18); and government bunkers, 44–53, 68, 105, 182 (n. 15), 183–84 (n. 36), 184 (n. 53); Swiss, 60; Soviet, 60, 65, 187 (n. 123); Swedish, 60–61; and children, 138, 143–44, 145–56, 151–56, 207–8 (n. 2), 209 (nn. 56, 59), 210 (nn. 81, 87); after the crisis, 167–68, 169, 186–87 (n. 116), 195 (n. 159), 210 (n. 81)

Civil Defense Protest Committee, 149

Civil rights, 2, 8, 23–24, 70, 116, 162, 202 (n. 11)

Clark, Aurel, 77

Clark, Mark, 71

Clifton, Chester V., 106

Clinton, Bill, 112, 114

College students: studies of regarding feelings about nuclear war, 150; studies of regarding reactions to crisis, 155, 157–58

Commerce, U.S. Department of, xvi, 132

Committee for the Monroe Doctrine, 135

Communism: fear of, 3–10, 23, 24, 25, 115, 121, 140–43, 145

Congress, U.S.: members summoned by Kennedy, 16, 92; and civil defense, 28–29, 34, 59, 60, 75, 167; and news management probe, 107; and 1962 elections, 115–16, 122–27, 129–30, 132, 133, 163; and Kennedy record in, 116, 119

Conservatives, 23–24, 93, 116, 119, 121, 128, 133, 134, 135. *See also* Goldwater, Barry; Young Americans for Freedom

Cronkite, Walter, xvii, 95, 97

Cuba: government, xiii, xv, 12, 53, 97–98, 169; and Soviet Union, xiii, xv, 13, 115, 122–25; refugees, 12, 143; U.S. image of, 116, 117, 118, 119, 121, 124, 128, 135. *See also* Bay of Pigs

Curtis, Thomas B., 128–29

Dean, Robert D., 120

Defense, U.S. Department of: and U-2 flights over Cuba, xiii, xxi, 12, 13, 14, 115, 117, 119, 136; and military alerts, xiii, 53, 54, 169, 182 (n. 9); Strategic Air Command, xiv, xvi, 17, 53, 54, 169; and blockade, xv, xxii, 15, 16, 54–55; plans to attack Cuba, xix, xx, 56, 58, 59; and U-2 flights over Soviet Union, xxi, 56–57; nuclear arsenal, 14; and accidental war, 56–58; press restrictions, 98–99

Democratic Party, 33, 117, 118, 125, 127, 129, 132, 133, 134–37; divisions within, 23–24, 116, 121

Dillon, Douglas, 26, 115, 125

Dilworth, Richardson, 132

Disney, Walt, 142–43

Dobrynin, Anatoli, xviii, xix, xxi, 99, 101, 103

Dryfoos, Orvil, 92

Dulles, Allen, 12, 205 (n. 71)

Dulles, John Foster, 29

Educators: surveys of, 146–49

Eisenhower, Dwight D.: postpresidency of, xvii, 129–30; presidency of, 3, 5, 9, 11, 24, 29, 36, 38, 116, 131; and World War II, 33–34

Ellis, Frank, 61

Emergency News Service, 49, 184 (n. 39)

Emergency Planning, U.S. Office of (OEP), 42–43, 47, 48–49, 51, 52, 81, 82, 105, 168; National Resource Evaluation Center, 41

Escalona, Sibylle K., 149

Ex Comm, xix, 14, 15, 56, 91, 92, 125, 139,

164; pressures on, 20, 165; and Stevenson flap, 109–11; tapes of, 118, 119, 135,
136